Essays on English
and American Literature

By Leo Spitzer

EDITED BY ANNA HATCHER

PRINCETON, NEW JERSEY

PRINCETON UNIVERSITY PRESS

1962

Foreword

By Henri Peyre

"Great spirits now on earth are sojourning," exclaimed John Keats in an early sonnet in praise of three of his contemporaries. Great spirits are sojourning, or have only lately departed from our midst, in our own age. And not a few of those have arisen in the realms of linguistics, philology, criticism. With the same naïve bewilderment which contemporary scientists display, we might almost claim, as they do, that ninety percent of all the critics who ever lived are alive today. But numbers are of little moment in humanistic studies. Nobel or Pulitzer prizes are not bestowed on critics. Statues are but rarely erected to them. Their greatness can never be measured by quantitative standards, and is seldom granted unchallenged acceptance. Their chief bounty to their followers is in the zest, the stimulation, at times the exasperation, which they arouse in readers, and in the intensity of life with which even their works of circumstance are instinct.

Leo Spitzer was, along with E. R. Curtius, with E. Auerbach, with B. Croce, and with other eminent men still surviving like G. Lukacs and D. Alonso, among the truly great literary scholars of our age. America, which called him to the "paradise of exiles" which she offered to Europeans, gave him unstinted admiration. He taught at Johns Hopkins from 1936 on, published remarkable collections of essays at Vanni's in New York, at Smith College, at Princeton University Press, and scores of separate articles in learned journals. Still it may be regretted that Spitzer was not more often asked by university presses or by lecture foundations to compose comprehensive books, in which his passion for unity and structure in works of art would have expressed itself and the impatience of a ubiquitous conqueror of all the provinces of linguistic and literary knowledge might have been curbed.

Impressive volumes of Spitzer's essays appeared in Italy and Germany after his retirement from the Johns Hopkins University,

· v ·

and have been warmly received. Since his death at Forte dei Marmi, on September 16, 1960, there have been hopes for other publications. Collections of essays in English will doubtless now appear in Spitzer's adopted land, at which many of his most fruitful teachings were directed. The most pressing and the most timely need was to place at the disposal of scholars specializing in English (and American) letters a number of fugitive, but in truth of solid, rich, and permanently valuable pieces on literature in the English language. Professor Anna Granville Hatcher, the guardian of Spitzer's memory and of his tradition in Romance lexicography and philology, has put the learned world in her debt by this felicitous as well as pious initiative.

The literatures in the English language are the last to which Spitzer's attention came to be directed: he brought to his treatment of poets, from Marvell and Herrick to Keats and Yeats, of medieval songs and of Whitman's cosmic pantheism, a mature wisdom, a range and a breadth, and an acuteness in deciphering subtle texts which long years of interpretation of other literatures had developed. His early training in his native Vienna had been in the classics, then in Romance philology. He recalled, in one of the few autobiographical confessions he ever wrote, the humorous and moving first chapter of *Linguistics and Literary History* (Princeton University Press, 1948), how precise, how remote from the modern world and its contingencies, how obstinately unaware of recent literature and of politics, was then the study of philology. Austria at that time admired and envied the refined charms of Parisian life; but stern professors of philology were mostly intent upon endowing their disciples with the best tools for the analysis of linguistic phenomena. Generations of medieval people who had lived, loved, fought, prayed, sung, and traded were seen as if they had been chiefly concerned with transmitting philological forms and distorted phonetic changes from some hypothetical vulgar Latin idiom to one another.

Spitzer never was thus to sever language from literature, and either of them from life. He observed every detail of language, and of style, with a microscopic attention. It is even more engrossing to scrutinize those slight deviations from usage, those involuntary repetitions or recurrences, those stylistic idiosyncrasies of writers in a foreign language than in one's own. Scandinavians, Balts, Czechs, Dutchmen who by necessity or preference master several foreign idioms and make a point of analyzing stylistic phenomena with meticulous care have often proved the best students of Romance languages and of English. From a thorough examination of details which would remain unnoticed by the native speakers of French, Spanish, or English, Spitzer proceeded inductively to generalizations on the mental structure of the writer. A dazzling concatenation of inferences thus brought him to the discovery of secrets in the psychological, almost in the physiological, make-up of authors, which he then laid bare to eyes less piercing than his.

The method is less objective than it appears at first to be. Spitzer himself noted, in his essay on "Linguistics and Literary History" (page 23), that his "personal way had been from the observed detail to ever broadening units which rest, to an increasing degree, on speculation." There is some fallacy, even probably an inevitable element of trickery, in the *explication de textes*, just as there is in the experiments devised by Emile's tutor for Rousseau's ideal pupil. The texts selected must be significant, typical, subtle, rich, or else the subtlety of the explicator will be exercised in a void. The details from which Spitzer drew a whole array of original inductions were not seized in a purely haphazard fashion; his instinct, like that of a hunter, or of a photographer, or even that of a lover, slyly told him which prey would be most likely to yield. It is easy for the teacher demonstrating in a seminar the fertility of his ingenious method to pretend that he is merely eliciting, from some apparently indifferent detail in a text, untold riches. But of course the immense culture of Spitzer lay behind his attitude of an objective observer. René Wellek, in an article written after Spitzer's death which constitutes the fairest and the wisest evaluation of the great scholar's work (*Comparative Literature*, XII, 1960, pp. 310-334) courteously indicated how mistaken the average men among us would be if they thought they could emulate a giant to

whom the line of Oceanus in Keats's *Hyperion* readily applies:
"Knowledge enormous makes a god of me."

Like Socrates, Spitzer well knew which questions to ask, and
that pregnant answers come only to the questions which have
prompted them. He had not only a knowledge of half a dozen
languages and literatures so vast that it crushes any humbler
mortal; he also had mastered several ancillary disciplines, and
his sharp insight had enabled him to retain only the best of
Bergsonism, of Freudianism, of Hegel and Croce and Dilthey.
He never was the captive of any system, and he preserved to the
end, through glosses and footnotes and digressions, and admir-
ably clear style and a delight in living and in feeling which preserved him from pedantry. His most lasting love was for poetry,
and his devotion was to beauty and to grace. Quoting Goethe,
who knew better than any Frenchman that to be sensual is also
to be human (even all too human), he was amused when he
could gently upbraid an American scholar who found the theme
of Leda raped by the swan somewhat repulsive: "the graceful
body of a maiden encompassed by the harmonious lines of the
regal white bird" entranced him as it did Yeats in the poem
under discussion.

More pedestrian minds may balk at some of the assumptions
which underlie Spitzer's "criticism of beauties," as Chateaubriand had called the critical attitude which he wished to sub-
stitute for the earlier and carping "criticism of defects." He
readily took it for granted that "a great masterpiece is great in
all its parts." "Dans une grande âme tout est grand," also wrote
Pascal, or whoever composed the *Discours sur les Passions de
l'Amour.* Ingeniously, if not always convincingly, he endeavored
to prove it for passages in Rabelais or Racine which others had
judged to be defective; he might conceivably have done likewise, if novels had more often captured his attention, for digressions in Balzac, Tolstoy, Dostoevski, and Proust which some of
us would rather ascribe to those moments of relaxed tension or
of slumber that Horace himself acknowledged to exist in Homer.
We may even judge those weaknesses in great artists to be a
winning mark of their nonchalance, as they become sure enough

of their mastery to disregard the conventional demands for unity and structure.

Spitzer would not. He shared the passion for unity and organicity in literary works which animates, in our age of fragmentation of knowledge, the many monists among critics who want at all costs to reach the One behind the transitory Many. Born as he was thirteen years before the close of the nineteenth century, when a sense of mystery and respect for the unknowable were replacing the former positivistic faith and when intuition was being enthroned where pure intellect had once reigned, Spitzer never consented to give up searching for reasons; the real to him—that is to say, every detail present in a work of art—was rational, and susceptible to explanation, provided the interpreter succeeded in fashioning the right key. Some of us, probably lazier minds and less stubbornly determined to "take upon us the mystery of things, as if we were God's spies," in dying Lear's admonition, are resigned to see our knowledge hemmed in by ignorance. We do not claim to account for every strange whim of the inspiration of a genius. We would almost hail the irrationalist among critics who hopes to respect the irrationality of the work of art and, like the mystic, takes refuge in silence, or in beatific exclamations of rapture. Not so with Spitzer. He took issue with the American "new criticism," which occasionally became too cocksure in its resort to facile categories and in its terminology. In truth, however, he and its proponents differed but little. Nevertheless Spitzer was, if never "too proud to fight," still too proud to ally himself with any school.

His warnings against complacency and the gregarious acceptance of fads in our critical attitudes have been salutary. With all his subtlety, he never abdicated common sense. His method varied, as any critical method always must, with each talent, each kind of poetry to which he applied it. He well knew that the very best of methods, be it the *explication de textes*, easily degenerates into a set of recipes, mechanically and clumsily used by the followers of those who first invented it. In criticism as in educational reforms and as in politics, fifteen or twenty years are the usual maximum span of time after which the wear and tear brings out the faults and obnubilates the features which had at first dazzled us in their novelty. The exclusive stress laid by many an English-speaking critic upon imagery, as the best initiation into an author's secret chambers, rightly filled him with diffidence. He was just as impatient at the preposterous allegorical interpretations of masterpieces which seduce the ingenious spirits of an age brought up on Joyce and Kafka. *A Winter's Tale, Measure for Measure, Don Juan* are not made more profound because they are presented as a refined code for a philosophical message. Fielding, in *A Journey from this World to the Next*, already had Shakespeare protest, in Elysium, against his all too subtle decipherers: "I marvel nothing so much as that men will gird themselves at discovering obscure beauties in an author. Certes the greatest and most pregnant beauties are ever the plainest and most evidently striking. . . ." Fielding was perhaps too robust an optimist. But the crowning achievement of an immensely erudite and subtle mind is indeed to learn anew how to be satisfied with a simple and direct interpretation when it is adequate.

The essays which are collected here were scattered in a number of learned journals where they are not easily accessible. They are all important elucidations of specific texts in English literature, into which Spitzer, foreign-born and approaching those texts with fresh reactions and a wealth of rapprochements with ancient and other modern literatures, read profound meanings. The poems to which Spitzer applied his acumen were not chosen as particularly difficult. Like poetry, criticism should propose as its aim to "make familiar objects seem as if they were not familiar." Thus fairly simple Middle English poems, replaced in their European context, appear laden with new power and strangeness. Donne's "The Extasie," half mystical, half sensual (more so perhaps than Spitzer will allow, if a little less than French interpretations of the freedom left to the bodies, once the souls have departed from them for a higher communion), receives fresh light from an unexpected parallel with St. John of the Cross and from Isolde's "Liebestod" in Wagner's opera.

Herrick's playful jewel, "A sweet disorder in the dress," is interpreted as far transcending the seduction of some disorder in a woman's garments: it reaches the more universal plane of art, with the forces of wildness and those of civility struggling, as often they did in seventeenth-century poetics.

Marvell's gentle piece on the "Nymph complaining for the death of her Faun" is deftly analyzed by Spitzer as the metamorphosis of an ancient theme into a miraculously simple elegy in a baroque setting. Spitzer is no less at home in the English nineteenth century: audaciously, he affronted one of the most frequently elucidated, or obscured, of poems: Keats's "Ode on a Grecian Urn," overwhelming one of its recent interpreters, dazzling us with analogies drawn from other literatures, but, as always, bringing the reader back to an enhanced enjoyment of the poem itself, as a critic should do. The shorter commentary on Yeats's "Leda and the Swan" bringing in Saint Paul, Racine, the French Parnassians, likewise remains witty and lucid, and never crushes the poem under erudition. Edgar Allan Poe and Walt Whitman here represent American literature; both have long been familiar to Europeans. It took more boldness to approach American advertising as popular art, as Spitzer did in a lecture first delivered at Smith College in 1948. Most exiles or emigré scholars would shrug their shoulders with superior scorn at American advertising and its "attempts at esthetic appeal." Spitzer, on the contrary, stated outright that "to adopt a resentful or patronizing attitude toward our time is the worst way to understand it." From a poster, conspicuously displayed in drugstores some years ago, depicting snow-capped mountains and orange groves, he took the motto:

> "From the sunkist groves of California
> Fresh for you."

He then brilliantly analyzed all the evocative elements of poetry implicit in such a motto and read into and behind them a whole eudemonistic philosophy, with its promise of paradise to buyer and consumer. The Madison Avenue persuaders who hit upon his essay may well feel proud at being studied as gravely as lines of Shakespeare and Milton and Keats, and in no way found wanting.

Unlike most of the European-born scholars who came to America since 1930 and merely pursued over here what they had begun in their native land, but for a few occasional admonitions to the uncultured audiences of the New World, Spitzer undertook to observe, to analyze, and to appreciate the country which he had adopted. He deemed it a benefit falling to the lot of the emigrant scholar, as he stated in his preface to *Linguistics and Literary History*, that "his inner activity was . . . immensely enhanced and intensified" by his new surrounding. A second nature grew in him, which served "to make shine by contrast his first nature in the clearest light."

If Spitzer learned much from America and generously acknowledged it, he also served the study, not only of foreign letters, but also of English literature in this country. With all its remarkable achievement, American scholarship in the English field tends to remain a trifle provincial and self-centered. Departments of English often look upon themselves as private citadels on the university campus, communicating only within their haughty walls, suspicious of their colleagues in social sciences, in philosophy, even in other literatures, or of those who advocate a comparative approach. They require a perfunctory test in two foreign languages from their graduate students, but they only reluctantly open books in those languages themselves. Their haughty, or perhaps shy, isolation is probably responsible in part for some disaffection with the study of the literature of England, as offering too shrunken a "usable context," as Lionel Trilling deplored in a lucid article in *The Sewanee Review* (LXVI, 3, Summer 1958). Scholars in other European literatures are more readily invited by the very nature of their subject to stress contacts between the literatures of France, Germany, Russia, Spain with both philosophy and the fine arts. The broad approach of a universal man like Spitzer, whose knowledge admitted of no frontiers, who was unashamedly un-English in his approach, yet who threw ingenious or dazzling light on several texts of English literature, should prove enriching to the specialists of English and refreshing to the laymen.

In another respect also was Spitzer "un-English." He did not meekly agree with those who differed from him or who contradicted him. He was not placidly satisfied with agreeing to disagree and with eschewing arguing and demonstrating. Many of the essays presented in this book were polemical in their origin and remain polemical in their character. That is an old European tradition, with Renaissance humanists and with German scholars. Linguists and archaeologists have fallen heir to that tradition in America, literary critics but seldom. Ideas, however, if they are to be taken at all seriously, deserve fighting for, or about. Literary appreciation involves the whole of man: his intellect, his philosophical and religious beliefs, his sensibility, his dreams, his senses even, and his own way of envisaging life. It is not surprising that, like politics, it should in some people take on the appearance of an affair of the heart, in which one does not easily yield to a rival.

A novelist seldom starts his writer's career from mere observation of life; he usually is spurred to creation by the reading of other novels. A painter most often starts from other paintings rather than from the imitation of nature itself. Leo Spitzer often needed the springboard of another scholar's inadequate or unsatisfying critique in order to redress it, supplement what was first proposed, broaden the original framework, and then unfurl his own wings. At times, like many a polemicist, he was prone to read too much into what the previous scholar had said. As in the case of Milton's sonnet, "Methought I saw my late espoused saint," which he was led to interpret by the previous commentary of his distinguished Johns Hopkins colleague, George Boas, Spitzer prolonged the thought of George Boas, attributed to him what he might have thought and expressed in order to be all the more victoriously confuted by Spitzer.

Few of those whom Spitzer thus refuted or castigated, however, would resent thus serving as a pretext for a magnificent display of erudite profundity; borrowing the language of the fox in La Fontaine's fable, when he justifies the king of animals for devouring a few lambs, and occasionally their shepherd too, they might remark, when encountering the leonine figure of Spitzer in the Elysian fields:

> "vous nous fites, seigneur,
> En nous croquant, beaucoup d'honneur."

It is especially with his best friends and his closest colleagues that Leo Spitzer liked to engage in controversy: "both friendship and philological scholarship are dialectical in essence; friendship, which encourages the deepest interest in one's fellow scholars . . . must lead toward (friendly) disagreement." Thus Spitzer noted in his essay on Tennyson's "Tears, idle tears." Truth is what he loved above all else, and it was most safely pursued, for him, through the insights which the limitations of others provoked in him. Emerson used to contend that, next to good preaching, bad preaching was the most fruitful of all: it brought vigorous dissent. It is a solace for critics less universal than Spitzer to reflect that their inadequate attempts may have provoked one of their contemporaries to go further and deeper. The role of any critic should indeed be, not to solve any problems forever or for long, but to foment discussion and arouse keener intensity of life around the literary work under debate.

Acknowledgments

FOR their generous permission to republish those articles by Leo Spitzer, first published with them, that constitute the main material of this volume, thanks are hereby rendered to the publishers and editors of the following journals:

Archivum Linguisticum, Jackson, Son & Co., Ltd., Glasgow
Comparative Literature, University of Oregon Press, Eugene, Oregon
ELH, Johns Hopkins Press, Baltimore, Maryland
Hopkins Review, Johns Hopkins University, Baltimore, Maryland
MLN, Johns Hopkins Press, Baltimore, Maryland
Modern Language Quarterly, University of Washington Press, Seattle, Washington.
Modern Philology, University of Chicago Press, Chicago, Illinois
Studies in Philology, University of North Carolina Press, Chapel Hill, N.C.

To the President of Smith College special thanks are due for his generosity in relinquishing the copyright of *A Method of Interpreting Literature* (1949), of which two chapters are here reproduced.

Contents

Essays on English and American Literature

CHAPTER I

On Yeats's Poem "Leda and the Swan"*

A sudden blow: the great wings beating still
Above the staggering girl, her thighs caressed
By the dark webs, her nape caught in his bill,
He holds her helpless breast upon his breast.

How can those terrified vague fingers push
The feathered glory from her loosening thighs?
And how can body, laid in that white rush,
But feel the strange heart beating where it lies?

A shudder in the loins engenders there
The broken wall, the burning roof and tower
And Agamemnon dead.
                    Being so caught up,
So mastered by the brute blood of the air,
Did she put on his knowledge with his power
Before the indifferent beak could let her drop?

Mr. Hoyt Trowbridge's "Longinian analysis" of Yeats's poem (*MP*, li, 118-29), however subtle and far-reaching his observations may be, seems to me to suffer somewhat precisely from the goal which he has assigned to himself, that of proving that Longinus' categories of literary criticism, even though in need of supplementation or correction in detail if they are to fit the modern poet's approach, are still valid for the latter. In this manner Yeats's poem is made to exemplify Longinus' theories but fails to appear as an incomparable, unique poetic entity in itself. I think that, by the demonstration of the presence of the "five springheads" of the Longinian sublime, the poem tends

*From *Modern Philology*, 1954, li, 271-76.

to be converted into material for a Q.E.D. and, rather than a Longinian analysis of Yeats, to amount to a Yeatsian confirmation of Longinus. My experience with poetry would advise me to search in a particular great poem first for what is the most immediately striking, the most individual, the least "cataloguable"—rather than to dwell on those features which make it representative of a genus (however sublime the genus of the sublime may be) : I would search for the characteristic in each poem instead of offering laudatory statements which may apply to quite different poems as well.

Now what strikes me most in the poem "Leda and the Swan" is the rendering of the time-place sequence in the portentous event of the rape of Leda by the swan-god. Mr. Trowbridge has, it is true, dealt with several elements in the poem concerned with time (less with those rendering space) ; but by the "catalogue-construction" of his article he was forced to disperse them under different headings: thus under "figure" (= "departure from normal syntax") we are told about the effect of the "asyndeton" (I would rather call it "nominal sentence") in the opening words "A sudden blow" and about the actualizing present tense in the description of the rape, a tense that yields in the end to the past tense ("Did she put on his knowledge . . . ?"), which, in removing us from the event, concentrates on its meaning; under the heading "diction" we learn of the "bold metaphor" by which the conception of Helen is expressed in terms of what was caused by Helen ("The broken wall . . ."); and under "composition" an opinion of Arnold Stein, not entirely indorsed by Mr. Trowbridge, is reported, according to which the limpness of the last verse with its imperfect rhyme ("drop": "caught up") would correspond to the indifference and languor of the "post-orgastic situation." While all these observations may be not without value, they fail, scattered as they are in different paragraphs, to integrate into one coherent picture of a temporal-positional sequence. Nowhere does Mr. Trowbridge clearly state the basic situation as it offers itself to us *in the poem* and what develops *in the poem* from that basic situation. By treating the poem as an already constituted entity (as something already read), he deprives it not only of its pristine freshness (of the impression it makes the first time we read it) but also of its inner dynamics, which represents the truly poetic in it, of the *flüssige Band* (to use the Goethean expression) that holds the artistic entity together. I may be allowed, even at the risk of mentioning the obvious, to establish the temporal-situational sequence in "Leda and the Swan."

It is clear that the poem develops within a stretch of time that is marked by the temporal adverbs "still" in line 1 and "before" in line 14. The event of the rape which fills this stretch of time begins at the moment (or coincides with the moment) indicated by the first three words: "A sudden blow," with that sudden invasion that comes out of the nowhere of cosmic space, continues with the pervasive penetration of the bird-god into the "loosening" body of the girl, the moment of procreation ("A shudder in the loins engenders there . . ."), and ends with the "post-orgastic" weakening of the grip of the invader that "lets her drop." Thus the acme of strength appears in the direct brutal attack (whose unexpressed motivation we may supply by thinking of Leda's beauty) of the first moment; all the subsequent lines offer a comparative *decrescendo*[1] in bodily strength, while, conversely, the impact of the event grows more and more toward the end, at which time the event itself already belongs to the past (a circumstance that is marked by the preterite "Did she" in l. 14). This is one of the mysterious paradoxes of copulation and procreation (the theme of our

---

[1] To the critic versed in French Parnassian poetry, this end of a—truly Parnassian—sonnet of Yeats with a *decrescendo* in the historical narrative coupled with an increase in reflection must be a surprise. How would a Hérédia have treated the same subject? Surely, his last line in the sonnet would have been one of those "purple passages" in which the whole sonnet culminates and in which history is foreshadowed, either in its glorious or its fateful impact. Either he would have had Leda see in a vision the burning of Troy (as the Centaurs "see" *l'ombre herculéenne* or Antony "sees" in the eyes of Cleopatra his fleeing galleys), or Helen would have emerged triumphantly (as does Aphrodite Anadyomene, another creature born from the "blood of the air": "Radieuse, émergeant de l'écume embrasée / Dans le sang d'Ouranos fleurit Aphrodité").

poem) : the overpowering strength of a moment engenders events whose meaning will become clear only in their result in time (at no time can Leda become aware of this event—sex, while materializing its results by means of the body of woman, needs no mental collaboration on her part). By the sudden blow time has been arrested and history created. With this sudden blow, which itself has no antecedents, all subsequent events of history are given. The syntactically brusque beginning of the poem (the nominal sentence that spurns the empathetic potentialities of the verb) is the adequate rendering of an event offered without prehistory, itself creating history. Sex has ultimately no beginning, admits of no motivation. Yet, in spite of this truncation, we see in the temporal adverb of line 1, "the great wings beating *still*," a past *still* vibrating—but this is only the past of the raper, whose sudden blow must be due to an accumulation of passion. What happens in the poem has already begun before its beginning. Toward the end of the poem we realize even more the sovereign independence of the temporal rhythm pulsating in the raper : it proceeds and dies on its own momentum : the act of begetting will be only "a shudder in the loins" for the begetter, while the events he has created will follow their own track which will lead to the fall of Troy and the death of Agamemnon; and we are told of these dire events before the orgasm of the swan is spent. The temporal rhythm of the sexual act and that of the history engendered by it diverge (therefore the unharmonious "limping" rhyme "caught up"—"drop"). It is the metaphysical paradox of the physical act of sex that death and destruction may have been created even before this process of animal life is ended. The short time sequence of the act finds here its expression in the short form of the sonnet within whose limits it is contained, while the sweep of the historical consequences extends far beyond the framework of the sonnet.

But what of the rhythm of the victim? Her experience has no rhythm. Throughout the poem, from line 3 on, she is represented as "caught," she is still "caught up" in line 11 : the inconspicuous particle *up*, put into the relief of the rhyme, denotes brutal interception of time, the arrest of time, which is what the act of rape means for her to whose potential reaction the raper is indifferent.

Now we may pass from the temporal-rhythmical relationships suggested in our poem to the positional ones. For the rape amounts to a fixation of position as well as to an arrest of time: the swan is the vise in which the girl is "caught," by whose powerful body she is encompassed: his wings beat "above" her, her breast is pressed to his, her body is "laid in that white rush," the only movement granted her is that of the "loosening thighs," the movement of surrender. And, of course, the reader finds himself, too, drawn into the vise, helpless and numbed like the girl: we, too, feel the helplessness, the terror, the horror of closeness imposed (what more ghastly than to feel a "strange heart beating," to feel a heart that beats for one's self, but not in diapason with one's own?). Because what we really visualize in the picture unfolded in the poem is only the exposed parts of the entrapped body of Leda, our empathy inevitably goes toward her feelings immediately, directly, and only through her may we imagine also, delayed, the emotions of the passionate god: his heartbeat, the shudder of his loins in the act of begetting, the quasi-mechanical inevitability of the exhaustion which causes him to slacken his grip (one notices the nuance of inevitability in the verbal expression: "before the indifferent beak *could* let her drop"). The expressions "feathered glory" and "white rush"[2] must be admired, not only because of their denotation of sublime aspects of the swan-god, but because the transposition of terms (= glorious feathers, a rushing white thing) suggests the way in which Leda's first impressions have recorded themselves: central is the glory and the rush, the forces that overpower her (beauty, movement); marginal the feathers and the whiteness, the concrete elements. From the line "A shudder in the loins engenders there . . . ," direct access to Leda's feelings is denied us, for she seems reduced to a local indication: *there*. But what is the exact meaning of *there*? Its antecedent must be *body* in line 7. But what,

[2] They are called "metaphors" by Mr. Trowbridge. But, according to ancient terminology, I would rather consider them as "figures," examples, that is, of *hypallage:* e.g., *fulva leonis ira* instead of *fulvi leonis ira*.

in turn, is the meaning of *body*? Is it indefinite ("how can body . . . but feel . . . ?" = any human body, any human organism)? If so, the precise *there* would not be in order. Perhaps *body* is better understood as a mass-word referring to body as a substance, a substance subject to molding by a superhuman force (= flesh, human clay), as opposed to *heart* in the same line: it is Leda's body alone that "feels" the strange heart in its local position ("where it lies"). The adverb *there* would then mean "in this medium or substance" and derives its pathos from the opposition between the passive female body and the world-shaking events of history that will be begotten "there": "The broken wall, the burning roof and tower/And Agamemnon dead." The double miracle, temporal and spatial, that has taken place then and there mirrors itself in the wording of the line. Mr. Trowbridge rightly emphasizes the "leap of thought" which the "bold metaphors" require of the reader: by the omission of the missing link, the birth of Helen ("the effect is latent in its cause"), the reader must go directly from the rape of Leda to the Trojan War. But can we assume, as Mr. Trowbridge would seem to suggest, that the leap of thought imposed on us is devised by the poet in order to "fully support" his thought, as though the thought had arisen first in the poet's mind but had been in need of embellishment by "bold metaphors"?[3] May it not be rather that his thought itself arose

[3] Throughout his interpretation, Mr. Trowbridge speaks in terms of poetic art that makes crude reality beautiful. He thinks, indeed, that the subject matter of the poem in itself is "painful and even ugly." But from the purely aesthetic point of view, what could be more beautiful than the graceful body of a maiden encompassed by the harmonious lines of the regal white bird? How often have ancient sculptors not been inspired by this subject (does not Ovid also mention in his *Metamorphoses* an artist who "fecit olorinis Ledam recubare alis"?). Did not Goethe call Faust's dream of the rape of Leda (ii, 2) "die lieblichste von allen Szenen?"— Goethe, who allows his Homunculus to blame Mephistopheles for his "popish" insensitivity to the Greek beauty of that scene:

Du aus Norden,
Im Nebelalter jung geworden,
Im Wust von Rittertum und Pfäfferei,
Wo wäre da dein Auge frei!
Im Düstern bist du nur zuhause. . . .

not only immediately clothed with linguistic garment but (to change the metaphor) realized its fulness only through the words?[4] What is the thought? The mystery of copulation and procreation is that into a present moment a latent future inserts itself which one day shall be seen as a past that took root in that moment. Exactly so do the words of Yeats show the past (from the viewpoint of the future) already as a *fait accompli*, as existing in the moment in which its cause is engendered. No one can fail, of course, to grasp the correspondence (I prefer this term to "metaphor," which suggests a *quid pro quo*) of content and form offered by the construction of the participles (instead of verbal abstract nouns: "the broken wall" instead of "the breaking of the wall," etc.), whose epigrammatic concentration reflects the inevitability of Fate. But I maintain more: this construction, with its 2,000-year-old tradition in Latinity with which the poet must have been long acquainted, helped mold the thought itself. Moreover, it was precisely Roman historians or mythographers who preferred this construction (Livy: *duo consules interfecti terrebant*, "the murder of the two consuls"; Ovid: *in nova fert animus mutatas dicere formas*, "the changes of shape") which carries with it the ring of history. The same construction has been used with great effect by Racine, who often has his characters summarize past history in a series of *traits éclatants* (e.q. *Athalie* I, i):

> Faut-il, Abner, faut-il vous rappeler le cours
> Des prodiges fameux accomplis en nos jours,
> Des tyrans d'Israël les célèbres disgrâces,
> Et Dieu trouvé fidèle en toutes ses menaces;
> L'impie Achab détruit, et de son sang trempé
> Le champ que par le meurtre il avait usurpé?
> Près de ce champ fatal Jézabel immolée,
> Sous les pieds des chevaux cette reine foulée,
> Dans son sang inhumain les chiens desaltérés,
> Et de son corps hideux les membres déchirés;

---

[4] Valéry: "Les belles œuvres sont filles de leur forme, *qui naît avant elles.*"

Des prophètes menteurs la troupe confondue,
Et la flamme du ciel sur l'autel descendue;
Élie aux éléments parlant en souverain,
Les cieux par lui fermés et devenus d'airain,
Et la terre trois ans sans pluie et sans rosée,
Les morts se ranimant à la voix d'Élisée?
Reconnaissez, Abner, à ces traits éclatants,
Un Dieu tel aujourd'hui qu'il fut dans tous les temps.

Here, though on a vaster scale than in our poem, scenes, detached medallion-like from the flow of history and presented as if re-called (*rappeler*) by memory, are centered about concrete persons or places that were affected by startling historical events—an effect which the use of verbal abstractions would not have allowed ("the destruction of the impious Ahab" is less vivid a description than "the impious Ahab destroyed"). In our poem it is the poet himself who "remembers" the *traits éclatants* of history; it is he who sees them as immediate and objective consequences of the rape. Leda, as she feels the full bodily impact of the divine beast, is only a channel through which the forces of history pass, or a place ("there") in which they work. The objective visualization of history culminates in the predicative expression: "Agamemnon dead"—a Roman newspaper headline, as it were.

As for the phrase "Agamemnon dead," Mr. Trowbridge has failed to mention the breaking-up of the first tercet brought about by the segmentation of its last line, the second part of which, syntactically connected with the second tercet, has only a rhythmical relationship with the first:

... And Agamemnon dead.
                    Being so caught up. . . .

And yet this slight rhythmical bond is enough to make us sense an analogy of thought between the two events "Agamemnon dead" and "Leda caught up": parallel to the death of Agamemnon, the last link in a long cycle of historical events, there is suggested a metaphorical death of Leda (which will give birth to those very events) : her "being so caught up" is indeed equivalent to a momentary death, to suspended animation. That moment of stupor, of unconscious conception, could not be rendered better than by the second member of a sentence suspended in the air between the two stanzas. The words "dead" and "caught up" are, as it were, "semantic (if not phonetic) rhymes": they signify also the two horns of the paradox of potential and actual history.

In the last lines we are offered the essence of the tragedy of procreation by rape. Leda is able only to sense the physical power of the god concealed behind the beast, she cannot sense or share the true god's dark vision. An eternally tragic aspect of sex is the possibility of procreation as the result of ruthless carnality blind to the other, the lack of reciprocity and communication in the crucial moment of copulation. It is on that moment that Yeats cruelly focuses our attention: "Did she put on his knowledge with his power / Before the indifferent beak could let her drop?" And this irony of fact in sex is heightened by the ironical choice of the verb *to put on*: Yeats is reminding us (as Professor Anna Hatcher points out to me) of the triumphant passage in St. Paul's First Epistle to the Corinthians 5:51-54: "Behold, I shew you a mystery; We shall not all sleep, but we shall all be changed . . . for the trumpet shall sound and the dead shall be raised incorruptible, and we shall be changed. For this corruptible must *put on* incorruption, and this mortal must *put on* immortality. So when this corruptible shall have *put on* incorruption, and this mortal shall have *put on* immortality then shall be brought to pass the saying that is written, Death is swallowed up in victory. O Death, where is thy sting? O grave, where is thy victory?"[5]

But when Leda "dies" to the divine swan, her body conquered in the union, she cannot put on his immortality. With this one word "put on," rich in Christian connotations, there emerges the

[5] *Put on* must be understood in the biblical passage as in *to put on a garment:* the Latin text has *induere*, the Greek ἐγδύσασθαι, "The body receives an addition of qualities which it did not possess before. It is 'clothed upon' with immortality" (*The First Epistle to the Corinthians*, ed. J. J. Lies, Cambridge, 1910).

toto coelo difference between the pagan and the Christian climate. For sex here is a pagan thing, a rush of brute blood in the air that is peopled by demoniac gods. Jupiter represents that destructive overflow of vitality (or that overflow productive in destruction) which we recognize in demoniac characters such as Faust and Don Juan and which obeys only its own rules, is passionate or "indifferent" at its own time, and acts according to its own inner compulsions: the expression in the last line "before . . . *could* let her drop" underlines the demoniac compulsion to which the divine bird himself is subject. The act of sex, this physical result of the demoniac, denies the victim access to the mind, which, together with the body, constitutes the terrain of the demoniac.

This explanation is, of course, predicated on the necessity of giving a negative answer (or at least of feeling the answer fraught with doubt) to the question: "Did she put on . . . ?" In this last of a series of three questions asked in our poem (of which the first two are purely rhetorical), I see the apex of a line that develops from empathy to objectivity. The first question ("How can those terrified vague fingers push . . . ?") is entirely "empathetic": in what is called generally by the linguist *erlebte Rede* (*style indirect libre*), the author welds into his third-person narrative words or thoughts that one of his characters would have formulated in the first person (in our case, Leda would have asked herself: "how can my fingers push . . . ?—the rhetorical question is entirely hers). The second question ("and how can body. . . . But feel the strange heart beating?") comes from a sympathetic observer, who, however, no longer imagining the reaction of Leda, thinks in more generic terms—the rhetorical question is his own ("how can body . . . ," to be translated, not with Mr. Trowbridge "body . . . feels the strange heart beating," but "body must feel . . ." = "human flesh must feel . . ."). The third question is an entirely objective one asked by the poet, whose reflective mood has increased as the personal event of the rape recedes into history (note the preterite *did she*), and for the first time a question full of doubt, suggesting as an answer, in my opinion, no "beautiful, but unformulable, truth" but the tragic possibility that Leda in the moment of bodily union with the divine had no foreknowledge of the historical consequences of the rape. In my opinion, Yeats wishes to suggest a protest against the gods who let sex be the effect of power uncoupled with knowledge—an effect of their demoniac power.[6] But if this is the correct interpretation, why did Yeats choose the interrogatory form, which must needs weaken his protest? One may assume that the poet, being a mortal human himself, feels able only to ask a question about the commerce of man with the divine; but this question, which in such a context must suggest an "at least" (did she, after having been violated and before being cast aside, put on . . . ?), betrays to us his grave fear that it is possible for the gods to engender brutally, in the human flesh, with sovereign disregard for the human mind.[7]

[6] Mr. Trowbridge is, I believe, right in emphasizing, against other critics, that in this poem, contrary to other passages of Yeats, the episode of Leda and the Swan is not an annunciation of a new civilization.

[7] Note the use of the word "beak" in l. 14 (while in l. 2 "bill" had been used): it is the character of the bird of prey that is emphasized at the end of the poem—irrespective of the degree of strength with which he holds his prey.

CHAPTER II

■■

Explication de Texte Applied to
Walt Whitman's Poem "Out of the
Cradle Endlessly Rocking"*1

■■

I MAY STATE first that our poem treats the age-old theme of world harmony within which the bird is one voice, the sea another, and the poet the third. The classical and Christian ideas of world harmony have been treated by me in *Traditio* (II and III, 1944-1945) and it may be apposite for me to extract from this article a brief survey: Pythagoras and Plato had defined music as an art practiced not only by human musicians, but also by the cosmos. According to Plato's *Timaeus*, the music of the spheres is produced by Sirens each of whom, in her particular sphere, sings notes whose pitch is conditioned by the velocity of the revolution of her sphere. The totality of these notes produces that world harmony, or symphony inspired by loving rivalry, ἔρις καὶ φιλία, which is inaccessible to human ears, and which is willed by the demiurge, the world spirit. It was not difficult for the Christians to replace the pagan world spirit by the Christian God of Love and thus to associate the music of the spheres with

*From *Journal of English Literary History* (*ELH*), 1949, XVI, 229-49.
1 Since I have no thorough acquaintance with Walt Whitman's sources, I am forced to place him, not within the framework of his American *ambiente*, but somewhere in the cold space of world literature (as far as I know it), to treat the poem "Out of the Cradle Endlessly Rocking" as one among other poetic monuments belonging to the Western tradition, apart from the question of Whitman's familiarity or non-familiarity with these monuments. My ignorance, however, may in the end be redeemed to some degree: for I feel that the direct, concrete sources which may be established for a particular work of art are generally somewhat petty and trivial in comparison with the parallels to be found in international art, together with which the particular work combines in an eternal pattern. I have used Stovall's *Walt Whitman*, New York, 1934.

Christian *Caritas*. In Dante, the Pythagorean world harmony
will be sung, not by the Sirens of the *Timaeus* but by the pure
intelligences, the angels vying with each other in the different
revolving heavens through the physical and spiritual attraction
of that Divine Love "che muove il sole e le altre stelle." Already
Augustine had seen the world as a "magnum (musicum) carmen
creatoris et moderatoris." The theme that the music of nature
blends with human voices in praise of the Lord is first developed
in an exegetic text of Saint Ambrose, intended to interpret the
line of Genesis in which God is presented as satisfied with his
creation of the sea. In surging prose Ambrose offered a powerful
acoustic description of the harmony (*concentus* = συμφωνία) in
which are fused the song of the waves and the choirs of the
devout congregation in an island sanctuary: the voices of men,
women, children chanting psalms. "Quam dulcis sonus, quam
jucundus fragor ("refraction"), quam grata et consona resul-
tatio (= "harmonious echo") !" With Ambrose we find for the
first time in our occidental literatures the fusion of nature and
humanity into one *Stimmung*, into a unity of tone and atmosphere prompted by Christian feelings. It is this transcendental
unity which permits the single objects to lose their matter-of-
fact identity and to melt into the general atmosphere of piety;
whereas in the pantheism of the ancients, though the single
phenomenon may even change into another form (as in the
metamorphoses of Philomela or Echo), clear-cut forms still
continue to exist individually, not fused into an all-embracing
atmosphere.

After Ambrose we find birds presented in Latin medieval
poetry as psalmists of God, Nature's singers introduced into
the more sophisticated company of human singers. Among
these birds the nightingale figures predominantly. The classical
Philomela, the ravished, mutilated, sorrowing woman-become-
songbird (in accord with the ancient tendency to explain the
healing effect of music by tragic suffering overcome), becomes
in Christian poetry the singer, naturally endowed with divine
Grace, who sings to testify to Grace. In a tenth-century Latin
poem the nightingale sings at Eastertime, inviting all believers

to join with her in praise of the resurrected Christ. From now on medieval love songs reflecting the theological theme begin with a picture of Nature revived in spring, with the birds and the poet vying in grateful song (the *Natureingang* of the Minnesingers and troubadours). The word *refrain* (lit. "refraction"), which in Old French was applied to the twittering of birds as well as to the musical or verbal *refrain*, must be explained by the concept of the echo which is represented in the response of the birds to the music of the world. Similarly, the modern word *concert* (lit. "musical contest"), and the Elisabethan word *consort* ("concert") = *consortium* ("association"), are late derivatives from this same idea of peaceful strife, of musically harmonious emulation in the praise of God. The thirteenth-century Spanish poet Gonzalo de Berceo goes so far as to portray learned birds that serve as preachers of religious orthodoxy. Church fathers and prophets of the Old Testament, Augustine, Saint Gregory, and Isaiah, are presented as nightingales in an earthly paradise competing under the dictation of the Virgin Mary. A one-man concert is Saint Francis' famous canticle: "Altissimo onnipotente bon signore, / tue so le laude, la gloria e l'onore e onne benedizione." This minstrel of God, feeling that one human being alone would not be worthy of praising the Lord, brings into his poem all creatures which may testify with him to the greatness of the Creator: "Messer lu frate Sole" (the Lord my brother Sun), my brother the wind, my sister the water, my sister the earth—and my sister Death. According to legend, the last stanza was added by Saint Francis on the day of his death. The Saint does not mention his brother the bird, but we remember the painting of Giotto in which Francis is depicted as preaching to the birds.

In the Renaissance, the original classical concept of Pythagorean and Platonic World Harmony was revived by poets and scholars: Marsilio Ficino, Kepler (*Harmonices mundi*), and others. The Christian implications, however, which had come to be associated in the Middle Ages with that ancient theory were not disregarded by the Platonists, whether Catholic or Protestant. This we see in the *Musurgia* of the Jesuit Athanasius Kircher and in the writings of the Protestant Leibnitz. Thus when Shakespeare stresses the unmusical in Shylock or Cassius, he means that these characters are untouched by Christian grace. The Renaissance painter par excellence, Raphael, shows us Saint Cecilia, surrounded by such figures as Saint Augustine and Saint Mary Magdalen (the Christian theoretician of music and the representative of love rewarded by grace), in a moment of ecstasy when she, an earthly being, gifted for music, or endowed with grace, is privileged to hear the music of heaven. Dryden's "Song for St. Ceciilia's Day" and Milton's "At a Solemn Music" celebrate the reunion in heaven with God's music from which we earthly singers have been estranged through original sin.

> . . . disproportioned sin
> Jarr'd against nature's chime, and with harsh din
> Broke the fair *music that all creatures made*
> To their great Lord. . . .
> O may we soon again renew that song,
> And keep in tune with Heav'n till God ere long
> To his celestial consort us unite,
> To live with him, and sing in endless morn of light.

To die with the expectance of heavenly, Pythagorean-Christian music is sweet. Not only the sweetness of musical reunion with Christ, but the sweetness of a musical death for Christ is expressed by a seventeenth-century German mystic, Friedrich von Spee, who, in a language that has the simplicity of the folksong, gives a baroque twist to the classical motif of the tragic death of Philomela. He combines this motif with that of the Echo that we found in Ambrose, although the scenery here is not the all-embracing ocean, but a German forest. A nightingale exultantly sings out the name of Christ to which the echo responds with equal enthusiasm:

> Da recht, du fromme Nachtigal,
> Du jenem Schall nit weiche!
> Da recht, du treuer Widerschall,

Du stets dich ihr vergleiche,
Zur schönen Wett'
Nun beide trett,
Mein Jesum lasst erklingen. . . .

Then the "risings and fallings" of the two voices that descend in order to ascend to ever-higher pitch suddenly cease. The nightingale has died in the praise of *mein Jesum*,—a martyr of love and strife for God.

The English Romantics introduce into poetry their selves and their problems of disenchantment, caused by the waning of faith in the eighteenth century. Now the poet is isolated from the musical birds; no concert materializes. Shelley is startled to hear a lone nightingale "answering him with soothing song" when he sits "pale with grief beneath the tower." Or else he will address the skylark: "*Teach* us, Sprite or Bird, What sweet thoughts are thine. . . Teach me half the gladness / That thy brain must know." The bird is here a teacher as in medieval poetry, but not a teacher of a firmly established orthodoxy which is shared by bird and poet alike, nor a brother in the love of God. The teaching which the poet requests of the strange visitor ("sprite or bird") from another world is apparently concerned with the knowledge of ultimate things inaccessible to the poet. Keats, who apostrophizes the Nightingale ("Thou wert not born for death, immortal bird"), feels himself to be immediately thrown back "from thee to my sole self," and as the bird's voice fades away, the poet is left, unlike his medieval confrère, in "forlorn" uncertainty. Was this a vision or a dream?

The German pre-Romantics and Romantics do not express the feeling of basic isolation from nature. On the contrary, the Germans wished to recognize themselves in articulate nature. Along with the discovery of folk poetry and of Ossian there went the resurrection of those elemental spirits or sprites, those degraded demi-gods of antiquity who, in spite of the ban of the Church, had been able to survive in popular superstition and in whom were incarnated the irrational cosmic fears of man and the daemonic magic by which man may be seduced at any moment. Whereas Plato's Sirens sang their symphonic chorus in accord with a Pythagorean mathematical order, now the sirens of the folklore, the daemonic daughters of the *Erlkönig* in Herder and Goethe, sing to lure innocent children away from their parents. The mermaid by her singing and pleading attracts the fisherman toward the abyss (Goethe, *Der Fischer*: "Sie sang zu ihm, sie sprach zu ihm, da war's um ihn geschehn"), and Heine's *Loreley*, by dint of singing and combing her fair German hair, sends the boatsman down into the deep. Thus, as man, gradually dechristianized, realizes his own daemonic nature—we may remember Goethe's belief in his (and Napoleon's) *daimonion*—an ambiguous folkloristic religion of underworld Gods tends to replace the truly religious world of order and clarity that had produced the concept of musical world harmony. But though the orderly picture of the world has faded by the eighteenth century, the original desire of the individual to fuse somehow with nature has survived, particularly with the Germans, who always feel their own individuality to be somehow incomplete. This desire may assume two forms: the pantheistic and the religious. Werther, so much torn in his feelings, is never shaken in his craving for pantheistic union with nature; in fact, to integrate with the whole of nature is the purpose of his suicide. The religious variant is represented by Eichendorff. This Catholic poet is not a narcissistic intellectual mirroring himself in nature, but an unproblematic, gaily bird-like being, somewhat puerile perhaps, but living in unison with the aimless beauty of the world. No German poet has identified himself so thoroughly with the German forest and its denizens. He speaks in the first person in the name of the skylark which sings bathed in sunlight, feeling its breast bursting with song. His nightingale is called upon to announce the meaning of his poetic universe:

> . . . in der Einsamkeit verkünde
> was sie alle, alle meinen:
> dieses Rauschen in den Bäumen
> und der Mensch in dunkeln Träumen.

The rustling of the dusky leaves of the forest as well as the dark confused dreams of man carry the same message: the affirmation of the aimlessness of nature (human and non-human), whose inexplicability should be respected. It remained for the French Romantics, the seraphic Lamartine and the gigantic Victor Hugo, to celebrate pantheistic world harmony with their French articulateness, with the rhetorical grandiloquence and sonority of their voices. One was the flute, the other the organ. Victor Hugo's Satyr (*Le satyre*) dethrones the serene Gods of the Olympus and reveals himself with a stentorian voice as Pan, before whom Jove must abdicate. There is no doubt that Hugo saw himself as that animal-God, as the incarnation of a strange Gallo-Greek earthiness which owes more to Rabelais than to Theocritus. Never since the time of the early Christian hymns had one heard such powerful songs of world harmony nor since the time of Horace such strong affirmation of the rôle of the poet as *vates*, as Bard. In 1830 Victor Hugo writes:

> C'est que l'amour, la tombe, et la gloire, et la vie,
> L'onde qui fuit par l'onde incessamment suivie,
> Tout souffle, tout rayon, ou propice ou fatal,
> Fait reluire et vibrer mon âme de cristal,
> Mon âme aux mille voix, que le Dieu que j'adore
> Mit au centre de tout comme un écho sonore.

The poet himself is both the echo and the crystal placed in the center of the universe by a God whom he, so to speak, crowds out. Victor Hugo is the almighty sensorium that unites, reflects, and speaks for the whole of creation. Obviously the tiny voice of a bird would be superfluous in the concert of a thousand voices, or in the pandemonium set in motion by the Bard alone. For, unlike Saint Francis, Hugo believes that the poet may give voice to the world concert. Less optimistically and more modestly, de Musset saw in the poet the voice of suffering incarnate; he offers humanity his bleeding heart for food as the pelican does to her young. "Les plus désespérés sont les chants les plus beaux, / Et j'en sais d'immortels qui sont de purs sanglots." For Baudelaire the poet is the albatross, an exile from heaven plodding clumsily on this earth. Similarly for Matthew Arnold Philomela is a "wanderer from a Grecian shore" and her song is, as in Greek times, "eternal passion, eternal pain." The function of the Hugoian "sonorous world-echo" was taken over in the second half of the nineteenth century by the greatest sorcerer-artist of all times, the musician Richard Wagner. With him operatic art is used to express the will to love and death, which, according to Schopenhauerian philosophy, animates all of creation, man and nature alike. The opera which had been created in the Baroque period as a demonstration of the soothing power of music on all creatures—it is not chance that Orpheus, the tamer of animals and the conqueror of hell, was its original main protagonist—is called upon by Wagner to express the religion of the nineteenth century: pantheism, the voice of the forest in *Siegfried*, of fire in the *Walküre* and of the individual striving for dissolution in death in *Tristan und Isolde*. Wagner gave to his concept of world harmony an orchestration which interpreted the togetherness of voices in the world, each singing its own *unendliche Melodie*, in a novel density of design and compactness of texture which has overpowered millions of listeners on a scale never attained by any artist working with the medium of sound.

After this rapid and over-simplified survey it should have become clear that in the poem "Out of the Cradle" Whitman has offered a powerful original synthesis of motifs which have been elaborated through a period of 1500 years of Occidental poetry. The poems I have mentioned are not necessarily his immediate material sources; but I am convinced that his "bird or demon" is a descendant of Shelley's "Sprite bird," that the brother mocking-bird is one of Saint Francis' brother creatures, that his "feathered guests from Alabama" is a derivate from Arnold's "wanderer from a Grecian shore," that the conception of "a thousand singers, a thousand songs . . . a thousand echoes" all present in the poet is a re-elaboration of Victor Hugo's "âme aux mille voix" and "écho sonore." Be this as it may, the basic motifs in which the idea of world harmony has taken shape in Europe must be in our mind when we read

Whitman's poem, which becomes greater to the degree that it can be shown as ranking with, and sometimes excelling, the great parallel poems of world literature.

Our poem is organized in three parts: a *prooemium* (ll. 1-22), the tale of the bird (ll. 23-143), and the conclusion in which the influence of the bird on the "outsetting bard" is stated (l. 144 to the end). Parts one and three correspond to each other and occasionally offer parallel wording.

The proem, composed in the epic style of "arma virumque cano," not only defines the theme of the whole poem clearly but translates this definition into poetry. The proem consists of one long, "oceanic" sentence which symbolizes by its structure the poetic victory achieved by the poet: "Out of the Cradle . . . down . . . up . . . out . . . from . . . I, chanter of pains and joys, uniter of here and hereafter . . . A reminiscence sing." Out of the maze of the world, symbolized by those numerous parallel phrases, introduced by contrasting prepositions, which invite the inner eye of the reader to look in manifold directions, though *out of* and *from* predominate—out of the maze of the world emerges the powerful Ego, the "I" of the poet, who has extricated himself from the labyrinth (his victory being as it were sealed by the clipped last line "a reminiscence sing").

The longer the sentence, the longer the reader must wait for its subject, the more we sense the feeling of triumph once this subject is reached: the Ego of the poet that dominates the cosmos. It is well known that this is the basic attitude of Walt Whitman toward the world. "Walt Whitman am I, a kosmos, of mighty Manhattan the son! turbulent, fleshy, and sensual . . . ," he says in the "Song of Myself" (24). He felt himself to be a microcosm reflecting the macrocosm. He shares with Dante the conviction that the Here and the Hereafter collaborate toward his poetry, and as with Dante this attitude is not one of boastfulness. Dante felt impelled to include his own human self (with all his faults) because in his poem his Ego is necessary as a representative of Christendom on its voyage to the Beyond.[2]

[2] Cf. my "Note on the poetic and empirical 'I' in medieval authors" in *Traditio*, IV, 414.

Walt Whitman felt impelled to include in his poetry his own self (with all his faults) as the representative of American democracy undertaking this worldly voyage of exploration. "And I say to mankind, Be not curious about God . . . I see something of God each hour of the twenty-four, . . . In the faces of men and women I see God, and in my own face in the glass." "I am of old and young, of the foolish as much as the wise, one of the Nation of many nations . . . A Southerner soon as a Northerner . . . Of every hue and caste am I, of every rank and religion."[3] But in contrast to Dante, who knew of an eternal order in this world as in the Beyond, Whitman finds himself faced with an earthly reality whose increasing complexity made correspondingly more difficult his achievement of poetic mastery. Therefore Whitman must emphasize more his personal triumph. The complexity of the modern world finds its usual expression with Whitman in the endless catalogues, so rarely understood by commentators: in what I have called his "chaotic enumeration" ("La enumeración caótica en las literaturas modernas," Buenos Aires 1945), a device, much imitated after him by Rubén Darío, Claudel, and Werfel. This poetic device consists of lumping together things spiritual and physical, as the raw material of our rich, but unordered modern civilization which is made to resemble an oriental bazaar. In this poem it is only one specific situation whose material and spiritual ingredients Whitman enumerates:

[3] Whitman has expressed the necessity of his Ego for his poetry in the following prose lines of his "Backward glance o'er travel'd roads" : "I saw, from the time my enterprise and questionings positively shaped themselves (how best can I express my own distinctive era and surroundings, America, Democracy?) that the trunk and centre . . . must be an identical body and soul, a personality—which personality, after many considerations and ponderings, I deliberately settled should be myself—indeed could not be any other. . . . 'Leaves of Grass,' indeed . . . has mainly been . . . an attempt, from first to last, to put *a person*, a human being (myself in the latter half of the Nineteenth Century, in America) freely, fully and truly on record." Whitman could not realize that he was repeating Dante's procedure, that the poet of democracy must impersonate this sublime abstraction with the same consistency that made Dante impersonate the universal Christian quest for the Beyond. The sea must whisper its oracle "privately" to Whitman just as Beatrice in the Beyond calls Dante by his personal name.

the natural scene (Paumanok beach at night), the birds, the sea, the thousand responses of the heart of the boy-poet, and his "myriad thence-arous'd words"—they are all on one plane in this poem, no one subordinated to another, because this arrangement corresponds to Whitman's chaotic experience. Similarly the two temporal planes, the moment when the boy felt the "myriad words" aroused in him on Paumanok beach, and the other when the mature poet feels the rise of "the words such as now start the scene revisiting," are made to coincide because, at the time of the composition of the poem, they are felt as one chaotic but finally mastered experience: the boy who observed the birds now has become the poet. When defining his creative role here in the poem, Whitman does not indulge in chaotic enumeration of his qualities as he does in the passage from the "Song of Myself" in which he appears as a Protean demigod. Now he presents himself simply and succinctly as: "I, chanter of pains and joys, uniter of here and hereafter." Out of hydra-like anarchy he has created unity; and, as we see, he has gained not only an emotional, but an intellectual triumph; he represents himself as "taking all hints, but swiftly leaping beyond them" like a master philologian or medieval glossator (later he will insist on his role as cautious "translator of the birds' cry," lines 31 and 69). Whitman takes care to impress upon us the intellectual side of the synthesis he has achieved, a claim that is not unjustified and an aspect that should be stressed more in a poet in whose work generally only the sensuous and chaotic aspect is emphasized.

His "uniting" powers have been revealed to us in his first stanza, in fact in the first line of the poem which gives it its title. With its rocking rhythm, the line suggests the cradle of the infinite sea from which later, at the end of the poem, *death* will emerge. At this stage, however, death is already a part of the situation. It is present in the phrase "From a word stronger and more delicious than any," which the reader is not yet able to understand. Now we can visualize only the ocean, the main instrument in the concert of world harmony with which the song of the bird and the thousand responses of the poet fuse.

Whitman restores the Ambrosian fullness and the unity of *Stimmung* of the world concert of love, music, and ocean (but obviously without Ambrose's theism).[4] There will be no dainty *Vogelkonzert* in a German romantic nook, no dolorous dialogue between a soul estranged from nature and a bird-sprite in an English countryside; the American ocean, "the savage old mother," will provide the background and the undertone to the whole poem. In this Ambrosian concert of world harmony we may distinguish also the Hugoian voice of the poet consisting of a thousand voices; but the insistent repetitions "a thousand singers, a thousand echoes" give rather the effect of a struggle on the poet's part, a struggle with the infinite, than that of a complacent equation ("I am the universe!") such as we find in Hugo.

After the organ- and tuba-notes that resound in the proem, the tone changes entirely in the main part, which is devoted to the reminiscence proper, to the singing of the mocking-birds and the listening of the boy. Here we find a straightforward narrative interrupted by the lyrical songs or "arias" of the birds. Given the setting of nature within which the boy and the bird meet, the term *aria* (ll. 130, 139) with its operatic, theatrical connotation as well as the musicological term *trio* (l. 141) that immediately follows (applied to the ears, the tears, and the soul of the boy), may seem too *précieux*. In "Song of Myself," we recall, Whitman speaks of the tree-toad as "a *chef-d'œuvre* for the highest." But we must also remember that Whitman's world-embracing vision is able to contain in itself opposite aspects of the world at once together. In this vision the man-made or artificial has its genuine place near the product of nature and may even be only another aspect of the natural. The song of the mocking-bird, so naturally sweet, is an artifact of nature that teaches the human artist Whitman.

---

[4] But we should keep in mind that Whitman's pantheistic unification of the cosmos, as is true of all similar modern attempts, is informed by a pantheism that comes *after* Christianity, a pantheism-that-has-absorbed-Christianity. The Christian feeling for the unity of the world in God can never be lost in modern times, not even when God Himself is lost.

To return to our narrative, this offers us a development in time of the theme that had been compressed to one plane in the proem: the boy become poet. In such a development, we would expect, according to conventional syntax, to find the historical flow of events expressed by verbs. But to the contrary, this narrative section offers throughout an almost exclusively nominal style, that is, the coupling of nouns with adjectives or participles, without benefit of finite verbs or copulas. This is an impressionistic device known in French as *écriture artiste*, which was introduced by the Goncourts in their diary in the 1850's; for example, "Dans la rue. Tête de femme aux cheveux retroussés en arrière, dégageant le bossuage d'un front étroit, les sourcils remontés vers les tempes. . . ; un type physique curieux de l'énergie et de la volonté féminines" (*Journal des Goncourt*, 1856, 1, 134). This we call impressionistic because with the suppression of the verb the concatenation and development of happenings give way to the listing of unconnected ingredients, or, in pictorial terms, to touches of color irrespective of the units to which the colored objects belong. Accordingly, we find with Whitman: "Once Paumanok . . . two feathered guests . . . and their nest . . . and every day the he-bird to and fro . . . and every day . . . I . . . cautiously peering . . . ," a procedure that is brought to a high point of perfection in that masterpiece of the last stanza of the second part: "The aria sinking, all else continuing, the stars shining. . . . The boy ecstatic. . . . The love in the heart long pent. . . ." I see in these participles nervous notations of the moment which serve not to re-enact actions, but to perpetuate the momentary impressions which these have made on the boy when he was perceiving them. When the boy sensed that the melancholy song was subsiding, he jotted down in the book of memory the words: "Aria sinking," and we the readers may still perceive that first nervous reaction. The development of the boy is then given the style appropriate to a "reminiscence." The style here chosen is such as to impress upon us the fragmentary nature of the naked "reminiscence." Because of the non-finite form of the participles, single moments are forever arrested, but, owing to

the verbal nature of these forms, the moment is one of movement, of movement crystallized. Of course, such vivid rendering of a reminiscence is possible only in languages, such as
English or Spanish, that possess the progressive form, of which
the simple participle may represent the elliptical variant.[5]

Now, from line 139 on, while the initial rhythm of the stanza
seems to continue, there appear strange inversions such as "The
aria's meaning, the ears, the soul, swiftly depositing" (for "the
ears, the soul swiftly depositing the aria's meaning" and similarly in lines 140 and 141), inversions quite unusual in English, even
jarring upon the English *Sprachgefühl*. We must evidently suppose that the *extasis* (l. 136) of the boy is working in an
effort comparable to travail toward an intellectual achievement.
It is "the aria's *meaning*" that is now being found by him and
the jarring construction is the "impressionistic" rendering of
the difficulty with which this inner event is made to happen.
It has already been noted that the activities here reflected by
the sequence of participles and other modifiers are all of equal
weight. We have not yet stressed the extent to which the
"enumerative" procedure has been carried out in our stanza,
which indeed consists only of detached phrases of the type "the
... ... -ing (-ed)." The chaotic enumeration offered us here
is intended to show the collaboration of the whole world ("all
else," "the stars," "the winds," "the fierce old mother," "the

---

[5] One will notice that in the sentence quoted above from the *Journal des
Goncourt* the style of the diary is applied to a static picture, not to an
action in the making. "Dégageant le bossuage" stands in attributive relationship to "tête de femme" whereas *sinking* offers a predication about
the aria (in other words, *the aria sinking* contains a double beat). Moreover, the participles of the Goncourts are all grouped under one heading
"tête de femme" finally summed up as "un type physique. . . ," whereas in
Whitman's stanza we have a list of different actions, all of equal weight.
Accordingly, the Goncourt passage offers a tighter sentence structure.
This quality was evidently perceived by Lanson, who, in his *Art de la
prose*, p. 265, discussing this passage, remarks of the *Journal* in general:
"Ce Journal est très *écrit*; on n'y sent jamais l'abandon, la furie de la
notation improvisée." There is then a pose of diary-writing in the Goncourts. With Whitman, on the contrary, the sequence of nominal sentences
gives the effect of genuinely improvised notation, such as the boy himself
might actually have made at the moment in *his* "note-book," the book of
memory.

yellow half-moon," "the boy ecstatic," "the love," "the ears, the soul," "the strange tears," "the colloquy, the trio," and "the undertone of the sea") toward that unique event—the birth of a poet out of a child who has grasped the meaning of the world. The nervous, impressionistic enumeration is symbolic of the travail of this birth. On the other hand, the repetition in this whole stanza of the atonic rhyme *-ing*, an ending that had already appeared in the first line with the suggestion of *rocking*, evokes the all-embracing rhythm and permanent undertone or counterpoint of the sea, whether fiercely howling or softly rocking, as it comes to drown out the chamber-music, the *trio* of ears, soul, and tears in the boy. The rhyme in *-ing* is a *leitmotif* that orchestrates the arias of boy and bird and gives the poem a Wagnerian musical density of texture.

As for the songs of the birds, let us note first that Whitman has chosen to replace the hackneyed literary nightingale by a domestic bird of America, the mocking-bird, compared to which, Jefferson once declared, the European nightingale is a third-rate singer. The manner in which Whitman has "translated," to use his modest expression, the song of the mocking-bird into words deserves boundless admiration. I know of no other poem in which we find such a heart-rending impersonation of a bird by a poet, such a welding of bird's voice and human word, such an empathy for the joy and pain expressed by nature's singers. The European poets we have listed above have accurately defined or admiringly praised the musical tone of the bird-notes issuing from tiny throats, but no one attempted to choose just those human articulate words[6] which would correspond to birds' song if these creatures had possessed the faculty of speech (Eichendorff had the bird sing in the first person, but it sang conventional Romantic lines) : the simple, over and over repeated exclamations of a helpless being haunted by pain, which, while monotonously repeating the same *oh!* or giving in to the automatism that is characteristic of overwhelm-

---

[6] Onomatopoeas (for example *tweet-tweet*) such as occur in folk-poetry would be stylized phonetic approximations, neither human nor bird-like, of the inarticulate sounds of the birds.

ing emotion ("my love, my love"), call upon all elements to bring back the mate. Thus in one common purpose the whole creation is united by the bird in the manner of Saint Francis, but this time in a dirge that associates the creation ("Oh night"— "Low-hanging moon," "Land, land, land," "Oh rising stars," "Oh darkness") with the mourner, with his elemental body and his elemental desires: "Oh throat," . . . "Oh throbbing heart," . . . "Oh past," "Oh happy life," "O songs of joy."[7] The mournful bird shakes out "reckless despairing carols," songs of *world disharmony* in which love and death are felt as irreconcilable enemies ("carols of lonesome love"—"death's carols"). The long-drawn-out refrains of despair ("soothe soothe soothe," "land land land," "loved loved loved . . .") alternate with everyday speech whose minimum of expressivity becomes a maximum in a moment of tribulation that is beyond words ("so faint, I must be still, be still to listen, but not altogether still, for then she might not come immediately to me," or "O darkness, O in vain! O I am very sick and sorrowful"). The most dynamic American poet has here become the gentlest. We remember Musset's lines quoted above; Whitman's bird's song is a *pur sanglot*.

We may surmise that this lyric section (within a lyric poem) has been somewhat influenced by Matthew Arnold's "Forsaken Merman" ("Come dear children, let us away, down and always below. / Come dear children, come away down, call no more . . ."). But Arnold's merman is one of the last offsprings of that futile masquerade of elementary spirits revived by the Romantics, a pagan demon who is presented as *defeated* by Christianity instead of a figure dangerously seductive to Christians. But Whitman's mocking-bird, the spirit become human, who symbolizes all earthly loveliness subject to grief and death, will live forever. It is one of those historical miracles we cannot explain that in the age of machines and capitalism there should arise a poet who feels himself to be a brother to nature as naturally as did Saint Francis, but who at the same time was

[7] On this point, cf. Hermann Pongs, *Das Bild in der Dichtung*, I, 223 seq.

enough of an intellectual to know the uniqueness of his gift. To *him* the bird poured forth the "meanings which I of all men know, Yes my brother I know, the rest might not." This is again no boasting; this is the simple truth, a perspicacious self-definition of one who has a primeval genius of empathy for nature.

Now let us turn to the last part of the poem which begins with the words "demon *or* bird" (I, 144), an expression followed later (176) by my "dusky demon *and* brother." The Shelleyan ambiguity disappears here. This marks the end of the parabola that began with "the two feathered guests from Alabama" (26) and was continued sadly with "the solitary guest from Alabama" (51) and "the lone singer wonderful" (58). While the mood of the bird develops from careless rapture to "dusky" melancholy, a contrary change takes place in the sea. "The fierce old mother incessantly mourning" (133), the "savage old mother incessantly crying" (142) becomes the "old crone rocking the cradle,"[8] "hissing melodious," "laving me all over." The two opposite developments must be seen in connection. To the degree that the bird is crushed by fate, the sea develops its soothing qualities; to the degree that beauty fades away, wisdom becomes manifest. The sea represents the sweet wisdom of death. The forces of nature are thus ambivalent, Janus-like. Nature wills sorrow and joy, life and death, and it may be that death will become or foster life. "Out of the cradle endlessly rocking," that is (we understand it now), out of the cradle of *death*, the

[8] Professor Anderson has drawn my attention to the fact that the parenthetic mention of the "old crone" is not contained in the first versions of the poem. In fact, the whole inversely parallel development of the bird and the sea is missing in them: The "Shelleyan" expression "demon or bird!" occurs only from 1867 on, the 1860 edition having only "bird!" in the passage in question, although this is followed by two allusions to "(dusky) demon." Similarly the expression "dusky demon and brother" appears in final form only after several rewordings and owes its form to a meticulous carefulness on the part of that supposedly rather careless stylist Whitman, comparable indeed to that of the French classicist Malherbe, who changed his first draft: "Et ne pouvait Rosette être mieux que les roses qui ne vivent qu'un jour" into the exquisite lines: "Rose, elle a vécu ce que vivent les roses, L'espace d'un matin" (cf. my *Stilstudien*, II [1928], 18).

poet will sing life. By presenting, in the beginning, the sea only as a cradle gently rocking, there was suggested the idea of birth and life; but now, the gently rocking cradle is seen as the symbol of recurring death and re-birth. A poet is born by the death of the bird who is a brother and a demon. A brother because he teaches the boy love; a demon, because he "projects"[9] the poet, anticipates, and heralds him, stirs up in him those creative faculties which must partake of the frightening and of the daemonic. But while the bird was destined to teach the boy love ("death" being a reality the bird was not able to reconcile with love), the sea, wiser than the bird and the "aroused child's heart," has another message to bring to the boy: "Death, death, death, death, death" (173). This line is the counterpart of the mocking-bird's "loved loved loved loved loved!" and it is couched in the same exclamational style, as though it were the organic continuation thereof. The word *death* is "the word final, superior to all," "the key," "the clew" which awakes in the boy the thousand responses, songs, echoes, and the myriad words; and once he has discovered this *meaning* of life, which is death, he is no longer the boy of the beginning ("never again leave me to be the peaceful boy I was before"). He has become the poet, the "uniter[10] of here and hereafter," able to fuse the voices of the *musica mundana* into one symphony, and we the readers can now understand his words in their full depth. In the conclusion we recognize certain lines of the proem textually repeated but now clarified and deepened by

[9] This term must be understood in the light of what Christian theologians call "prefiguration" or "adumbration" (e.g. David, by his existence, announces or anticipates Christ, who will be the *final king*). The bird in its song of grief attempts to unite the whole universe and thereby anticipates the poet who, having absorbed the teaching of the sea (he is not land-bound like the bird), will be able *truly* to "unite" the cosmos in his poem.

[10] The "will to unite" in Whitman is reflected by his habit of leaping from the particular to a comprehensive *all* as in "the word of the sweetest songs, and all songs" or in a discarded version of our poem: "O how joys, dreads, convolutions, human shapes, and all shapes, spring as from graves around me!" One feels here the impatience of the "uniter."

the keyword; we understand at last the symphonic[11] value of "that strong and delicious word" alluded to in the proem. The liquid fusion suggested by the sea of death is symbolized by the fluid syntax of the last three stanzas; the relative constructions which we find in l. 165 "Whereto answering, the sea . . ." and l. 175 "Which I do not forget" weld the three stanzas together into one stream or chain which comprehends the question of the boy, the answer of the sea, and his choice of avocation, into one melody in which inspiration flows uninterruptedly from the watery element to the poet. The bird and the poet have been given their respective solos in the symphony. The bird's solo is the *aria* and the boy's the *trio* of ears, soul, and tears; the endless counterpoint and contrabasso of the sea has accompanied their detached musical pieces. Now all voices blend in an *unendliche Melodie*, an infinite melody, the unfixed form of nineteenth-century pantheism, with Wagnerian orchestration. "But fuse the song of my dusky demon and brother . . . with the thousand responsive songs, at random, my own songs . . . and with them the key, the word up from the waves." The last word in the poem, however, is the personal pronoun *me*. Though placed inconspicuously in an unstressed position in the short line "the sea whisper'd me," this personal word nevertheless represents a (modest) climax. It is to Whitman that has been

[11] It must be noted that the "symphonic fusion" in our poem was achieved by Whitman only in the process of time (cf. also note 7) : The title of the poem in the first versions, 1860 and 1867, was "A Word Out of the Sea"; the oracular word "Death!" appeared in two passages, repeated five times in each, and the climactic line: "the word final, superior to all" was preceded by a passage of six lines, in which was repeated several times the exclamation: "oh, a word!" The original versions show then the orchestra of the world concert dominated by the monody of the oracle; the fierce old mother "out of" whom "the word" was to come, was in the exalted position of the Delphian Pythia. It may be added that Whitman showed himself then also more conscious of the new "chaos" opening up before him as a consequence of his new awareness of his destination: "O a word! O what is my destination? (I fear it is henceforth chaos)." This line is deleted in the final draft because it would have jarred with the role of the "uniter" assumed by Whitman in the beginning, but its original presence confirms our view that the poet has felt it indeed to be his task to create cosmos out of chaos.

revealed the musical meaning of the world, the chord formed by Eros and Thanatos, the infinite cosmos created from infinite chaos, and, finally, his own microcosmic role in the creation. It is the knowledge of death that will make him the poet of life, of this world, *not* of the Hereafter. The promise in the beginning to sing of the Here and Hereafter can be said to have been fulfilled only if the Hereafter is understood as comprised in the Here.[12] We will note that no reference is made in Whitman's poem to the world harmony of the Christian Beyond in the manner of Milton. The fullness of life of which Whitman sings can come to an end only in the sealike, endlessly-rocking embrace of nothingness, an end that is sweet and sensuous ("delicious" is Whitman's epithet), and, indeed, he appears sensuously to enjoy the sound of the word *death* that he so often repeats. We may pause at this point to remember that in 1860, one year after our lyric was written, Whitman gives expression to the same feeling in the poem "Scented herbage of my breast":

> You [the leaves] make me think of death,
> Death is beautiful from you (what indeed is finally
>   beautiful except death and love?)
> Oh I think it is not for life I am chanting here
>   my chant of lovers,
> I think it must be for death . . .
> Death or life I am then indifferent, my soul
>   declines to prefer
> (I am not sure but the high soul of lovers welcomes
>   death most) . . .

The same feeling for the voluptuousness of death and the death-like quality of love we find not only in Wagner's *Tristan und Isolde* (1857), in which we hear the same words applied to the love-scene and to the death-scene, *unbewusst—höchste (Liebes-) Lust*. There is also the same motif in Baudelaire's *Invitation* of 1857, in which the "invitation" is the lure of death, described as voluptuous hashish and scented lotus. Perhaps

[12] Cf. the line in "Song of Myself" (48): "No array of terms can say how much I am at peace about God, and about death."

powerful personalities crave death as a liberation from the burden of their own individuality, and sensuous poets wish to have a sensuous death. Perhaps also the concurrence in one motif of three poets not in direct contact with each other means that their subtle sensitivity instinctively anticipated the death-germs implanted in a luxuriant, sensuous, worldly civilization of "Enrichissez-vous," of Victorianism, and the Second Empire. This was long before the *fin de siècle* generation of D'Annunzio, Barrès, Hofmannsthal, and Thomas Mann, when the theme of love-death, inherited from Baudelaire and Wagner, finally became the theme par excellence. But Whitman, unlike his two sickly European contemporary confrères, will remain for us not the poet of death (although the idea of death may have perturbed him more than once), but the unique poet of American *optimism* and love of life, who has been able, naturally and naïvely, to unite what in other contemporary poets tends to fall apart, the life of man and that of nature.[13]

A last question arises. To what sub-genre does our lyrical poem belong? It is obviously an *ode*, the genre made famous by Pindar, Horace, Milton, and Hölderlin, if the ode may be defined as a solemn, lengthy, lyric-epic poem that celebrates an event significant for the community, such as, with Pindar, the victory of a champion in the Olympic games. Ancient poems belonging to this very aristocratic genre are filled with erudite mythological allusions since the origin of the heroes must be traced back to gods or demigods. These odes are also written in a difficult language that cannot easily be sung, for they are replete with whimsical breaks and changes of rhythm and tone that reflect the fragmentary nature of the inspiration of the poet, carried away as he is by his divine enthusiasm or θεία μανία. Of course, as is true of all ancient poetry, the ode had no rhymes. In the period of the Renaissance this ancient genre was revived, but enjoyed only a precarious existence in modern literatures because the social set-up of Pindar's Greece was

---

[13] And in addition to all that—though this peculiarity is not represented in our poem—the vitality of the machine.

missing in our civilization, filled as it is with social resentment, and because the travesty involved in presenting contemporary figures as ancient heroes could only be sadly disappointing. The genre fared relatively better in Germanic than in Romance literatures because the Romance languages are not free enough in word-formation to offer coinages worthy of Pindar and because Romance needs the rhyme as a constitutive element of verse. Ronsard's Pindaric odes were signal failures. Whitman has acclimated the ode on American soil and democratized it. The lyric-epic texture, the solemn basic tone and the stylistic variation, the whimsical word-coinages and the chaotic fragmentariness are preserved. The latter feature has even found a modern justification in the complexity of the modern world. For the rhymeless Greek verse, Whitman by a bold intuition found an equivalent in the Bible verset, but he used this meter in order to express a creed diametrically opposed to that of the Bible. Theoretically, he could have borrowed expressions of his pantheistic beliefs from the mythology of the Greeks, but in reality he did away with *all* mythology, pagan as well as Christian. He replaces the pagan Pantheon by the deified eternal forces of nature to which any American of today may feel close. The Ocean is the old savage mother, not Neptune with the trident (a mother, a primeval chtonian goddess), and the bird is not Philomela, but the mocking-bird who is a demon of fertility (only in the phrase "feathered guests of Alabama" do we find a faint reminiscence of Homeric expression, the *epitheton constans*).[14] The Neo-Catholic poet Paul Claudel who, as recently as the last decades, gave the French for the first time a true ode and was able to do so only by a detour through America, by

[14] It may be noted that even this is no pure case of an *epitheton constans* since it does not reappear in later situations; on the contrary, as we have said, the gay epithet "feather'd guests from Alabama" will lead us to the melancholy "loneful singer wonderful." In the case of "the savage old mother incessantly crying" there is from the start no indication of "constancy" of attribution; "crying" is not an attribute, but a predicate. But that Whitman had the Homeric epithet in mind is shown by the line quoted above from "Song to Myself": "Walt Whitman . . . of mighty Manhattan the son" which is a travesty of the ancient type "Ajax the Telamonian son."

imitating Whitman (even the metric form of his free verse), found it necessary to discard Whitman's pantheistic naturalism and to replace it by the *merveilleux chrétien* which a hundred years ago Chateaubriand had introduced into French prose.[15] But it cannot be denied that Whitman's ode can reach a wider range of modern readers than can Claudel's orthodox Catholic *grande ode*. As for the solemn event significant for the community which the ode must by its nature celebrate—this we have in the consecration of Walt Whitman as a poet, the glorification, not of a Greek aristocratic athlete born of Gods, but of a nameless American boy, a solitary listener and singer on a little-known Long Island shore who, having met with nature and with his own heart, becomes the American national poet, the democratic and priestly *vates Americanus*.

[15] Cf. my interpretation of an ode by Paul Claudel in *Linguistics and Literary History* (Princeton, 1948, pp. 193 *seq.*). This ode, one of five intended "pour saluer le siècle nouveau," and reminiscent of Horace's *Carmen saeculare*, also glorifies the achievements of modern industry and in this manner replaces the *fin de siècle* pessimism of the poetic schools that preceded Claudel by a *siècle nouveau* optimism which harks back to Whitman.

CHAPTER III

....

"Tears, Idle Tears" Again*

....

IT SEEMS TO BE my lot to be drawn to criticism of the literary criticism of my best friends, not, I trust, because of some personal bent in me toward altercation, but rather because of an intense feeling on my part that both friendship and philological scholarship are dialectical in essence: friendship, which encourages the deepest interest in the achievement of one's fellow scholars, and philology, unswerving service to the Logos, the true meaning of works of literature—both must lead toward (friendly) disagreement: how can it not happen that to two persons who are one in their common purpose, but not in their particular nature, the true meaning that lies beyond personality will manifest itself *differently*? And it is my firm belief that critical discussion is the best way toward that *consensus omnium* which is the ultimate goal in philology as well as in any of the sciences.

This time I must disagree with Mr. Graham Hough's sensitive and thoughtful interpretation (*Hopkins Review*, Spring 1951) of Tennyson's poem "Tears, Idle Tears," insofar as he seems, in my opinion, to have failed to clarify sufficiently the nature of the element which Tennyson calls (l. 2) "some divine despair" and which contains the principle on which the structure of the whole poem rests. May the following discussion remind Mr. Hough of the many lively discussions we had together during his all-too-short stay at the Hopkins, discussions to which he brought all the charm of his personality, his boyish liveliness, the mature enthusiasm and the ever alert open-mindedness of a man who has seen as much of the world as he has read books.

As for the epithet "divine," Mr. Hough limits himself to para-

* From *Hopkins Review*, 1952, v, 4, 11-80.

phrasing this by "daemonic" (which term he defines as "some more than personal force, some more than private cause") and to pointing out a reflection of this daemonic element in the mention of the "underworld" in the second stanza. According to my own interpretation, "some divine despair" means quite literally "the despair of *some God*" (the Latinate use of the adjective instead of a noun in the genitive is paralleled by the phrase "the Aeolian harp" = the harp of Aeolus) : of a God as yet unnamed, but who will be clearly revealed (and named) in the end of the poem as the God of "Death-in-Life." Our philological interpretation must then, in contrast to the procedure of the poet, start with the definition of the nature and attitude of the deity which is atmospherically (*"some* divine despair") present in the poem from its very beginning. The particular god (or *Sondergott*, to use the classical scholar Usener's term) of Tennyson's making is neither Life nor Death, but Death-in-Life; surely not the Christian deity,[1] as Hough has felt; no more is he Thanatos or Pluto, the God of the underworld before whom man is doomed to appear after death, or even one of the aloof, serene Gods of Epicurus who dwell in the *intermundia,* unconcerned with man. The God Death-in-Life, who, like Christ, has his dwelling-place among the mortals, as his name indicates, while sharing the aloofness of the Epicurean Gods, is an impressive and sterile dark God wrapped in his own "despair" (his *intermundium* is life itself), "idle" as are the tears of the poet. With the invocation of the name of the God who had been "somehow" present, or latent, in the poem from the start, the poet's sad "thinking" has come to an end, but not, we must surmise, his despair and his idle tears. To find a name (or intellectual formula) for the source of our sorrows is not necessarily to free ourselves from their impact. The poem "Tears, Idle Tears," full of intellectual groping as it is, remains to its end an idle complaint—for the God Death-in-Life who in the end is revealed

---

[1] It is, however, striking that Tennyson's pagan god bears a name derived from a *topos* of the Christian sermon ("in the midst of life we are in death"). This Christian reminiscence serves only to underline his non-Christian nature.

as the personification of the *lacrimae rerum* will not be able to quench the tears.

And now that I have clarified the "particular theology" under-lying our poem—are our modern critics deaf to the claims of any God?—I would point out that our poem, from beginning to end, is conceived from the point of view both of the "remem-bering" poet and of the God "Death-in-Life" (for remembrance to our un-Proustian poet is just that: Death-in-Life). The latter aspect explains, for instance, the order in which the various melancholy pictures of life are enumerated in our poem: in stanza two the first example is that of the sail "that brings our friends up from the underworld": this is not only a poetic symbol for "submerged memory from which our friends and other fragments of the past can and do emerge" (Hough), but also the actual vista before the eyes of the God Death-in-Life; he must see both the memory of friendship and the death of friends (next line) only in terms of the to-and-fro movements of Charon's bark. For him friendship is ephemeral, tinged with the mourning of death; for Death-in-Life it is death that is the normal course of events. Again, consider the picture of birds as they awake to life in the morning through song, but who, as seen by our God, awake and sing at the moment when a human being dies. And, finally, this god will give precedence, among remembrances of love, to "remember'd kisses *after death*": "first love" will appear in the wake of kisses after death and of unhappy love (since, in the view of the dark god and of the melancholy poet, the former must share the mortality of the latter experiences). All the pictures we are offered in our poem—happy autumn fields, friendships, morning birds, first love—are full of brightness on the surface, but suffused with the deep dark shadows of mourning. It is death that is called upon here to interpret life.

The dual principle "Death-in-Life"[2] must needs be repre-

---

[2] The dualistic inspiration of our poem is also reflected in the lines of canto IV of "The Princess" into which Tennyson has inserted it:

46 so *sweet* a voice and vague, *fatal* to men
69 a *death's-head* at the *wine*

sented also in the structure of the poem; it is in this principle that the formal unity of the poem resides. (I find it strange that Mr. Hough, who judges Mr. Cleanth Brooks's treatment of "Tears, Idle Tears" in his book *The Well Wrought Urn* [1947] so severely [*disjecta membra* which Hough must put together again!], should not have welcomed the New Critic's emphasis on the structural aspect of the contradictory, or, as I would say, dualistic character of the epithets used by Tennyson in order to characterize the different remembered pictures: cf. particularly Brooks's statement, p. 194: "Tennyson cannot be content with *saying* that in memory the poet seems both dear *and* alive; he must dramatize[3] its life-in-death for us. . . . The dramatization demands that the antithetical aspects of memory be coalesced into one entity which . . . is a paradox, the assertion of the union of opposites.") Mr. Hough, rather than studying this clear-cut dualistic structure of the poem, would have recourse to a vague, for himself opaque,[4] sound

---

Compare also the terms used by Tennyson himself in the autobiographic note: "*The passion of the past*, the *abiding* of the *transient* was expressed in 'Tears Idle Tears.'"

The idea of personified Death-in-Life may have come to Tennyson by way of Coleridge's "Ancient Mariner," in which we find the opposite personification "Life-in-Death," the "spectre-Woman" mated with Death, "the Nightmare" with yellow lips, golden hair, and a skin "as white as leprosy," who dices with Death about the fate of the ship's crew and wins, as a result whereof the Ancient Mariner who has killed the Albatross must live on, like Cain, to endure a life worse than death. Coleridge's figure Life-in-Death is an elemental spirit related to the vague romantic world of folklore, Tennyson's Death-in-Life a near-classical deity.

[3] The word "dramatize" is perhaps better chosen than Brooks himself may have known (with him it means no more than "say dramatically, emphatically"): for in our short lyrical poem we have before us true dramatic development, with two protagonists of whom the first (the poet who sheds idle tears) becomes aware in the *dénouement* of the encompassing power of the second (the god wrapped in idle despair): the poet at the end of the poem comes to realize, in a manner reminiscent of ancient tragedy, that his personal act (of remembering) is nothing but a manifestation of an impersonal supernal power. (Brooks has taken cognizance only of the poet-protagonist, whom he calls "the weeper.")

[4] Let us, however, not forget his excellent remark about the end-sound of all the lines, either open vowels or consonants or groups of consonants that can be prolonged in reading (so that each line "trails away . . . into

symbolism he feels to be present in the poem and to replace the rhyme usual in modern poetry; but is it not true of all ancient-classic (and also of ultra-modern) poetry that the place of rhyme is generally taken by an inner architecture of the poem, involving the repetition of patterns or motifs, rhythmical, ideational, or verbal?

The dualistic structure of our poem is, in my opinion, twofold: first, as Brooks has seen, there is a dualism within the epithets chosen by the poet in his impotent revolt against remembered sensations:

> fresh but sad
> sad but strange
> dear, sweet, deep, but wild—

a dualism which, finding no final resolution in harmony, ends in a wild, "tumultuous" (Hough) discordance of despair which breaks out at the moment of the epiphany of the God (and of the realization by the poet of the principle that underlies remembrance of the past). The accumulated, contradictory, or disparate epithets (and here indeed sound symbolism is involved: all these simple, familiar, monosyllabic adjectives tend naturally to be prolonged and intensified in emotional speech)[5]

---

some infinite beyond"), with the exception of the penultimate line, whose end-word *"regret"* offers a "phonetic stop to this hitherto flowing emotion, heralding and isolating the final refrain." The "trailing away into the infinite" represents the still shapeless musing of the poet, while the "stop" manifests his clear realization of the disconcerting principle that informs our life. I feel here, as in the whole poem, a certain kinship of Tennyson with the Italian romantic-classical poet of melancholy, Leopardi.

[5] Such coupling of monosyllables which in spite of their shortness invite the imagination to wander is frequent in English: Penn Warren, *All the King's Men* (p. 57) writes: "It is life sniffing ether, and everything is sweet and sad and far away."

An American friend writes to me from France: "Chartres was so *deep* and dark and bright" "deep" was underlined in the original letter; similarly, Tennyson has exploited, by repetition, the phonetic dimension of the depth present in the English word "deep"). If my friend had spoken, not written, to me she would have used the emotional inversion and the ellipsis of the copula: *"Deep,* dark, bright — the cathedral of Chartres!" And this latter pattern is exactly the *spoken* prose basis of Tennyson's

leave us indeed in deep despair as to the irrevocably antithetic nature of the Janus-like God: no mortal can, by taking thought, exhaust the oceanic "depth" of the experience embodied in him.

But there is in existence, besides what I would call a horizontal dualistic structure, a second, a vertical dualism. The poet's "thinking of the days that are no more" takes the form of an exclamational pattern in which the refrain-words would serve again and again as subjects of elliptic sentences consisting mainly of emotionally ejaculated adjectives which describe the remembered bygone days:

> stanza 2: Fresh. . . .
> Sad. . . .
> So sad, so fresh, the days that are no more!
> (I shall supply each time the exclamation
> point evidently intended by the poet,
> but reserved for the last stanza—in
> which I shall use a double exclamation
> mark.)
> stanza 3: Ah, sad and strange . . .
> So sad, so strange the days that are no more!
> stanza 4: Dear. . . . .
> And sweet. . . . .
> . . . . deep. . .
> Deep . . . . . and wild. . . .
> . . . . the days that are no more!!⁶

---

poem, the contrasts remaining unresolved and emotionality being pressed into the simple, familiar English monosyllables. Only in English, with its long, semi-diphthongal vowels, is such an effect possible: German epithets of the type of *lieb, tief, schön* are rarer; and French monosyllabic adjectives cannot be prolonged at all in pronunciation: *frais, doux, cher, frais* cannot trail away into the infinite.

⁶ The construction in the last stanza should be the same as in the preceding ones: just as we must interpret, for example, in stanza 3, "so sad, so strange [are] the days that are no more" (the copula being omitted because of the exclamatory inversion of adjective and noun), so in the last stanza: "Deep. . . deep. . . deep. . . and wild. . . [are] the days that are no more." According to this hypothesis "O Death in Life" would be a vocative, interpolated by the poet, who now at last is able to address himself directly to that impassive deity who was present from the start because

ALFRED TENNYSON

From this syntactical-skeletal outline one cannot fail to grasp
the vertical, dualistic structure of our poem. The various epithets
are contrasted with the ever self-same subject representing the
harsh reality of "no more." A sensitive critic might perhaps
find the repetitiousness of this refrain cumbersome in its folkloristic or melodramatic manner, were it not, as Mr. Hough
takes pains to remind us, that the refrain has also a conceptual
function: that of having us draw over and over again the same
conclusion from the various pictures unfolded in the four stanzas;
it is as though human agitation met repeatedly with a disillusioned refrain ("vanitas vanitatum!" "mais où sont les neiges
d'antan?"), or rather as though the tumultuous waves of ejacu-
lations (the variation of adjectives bearing witness to the
groping of the "thinking" poet toward clarity) surged cease-
lessly against the dam of doom: "no more." Is this periodic
futile upsurge of life and emotion against the cold fact of death
not, in itself, a manifestation of the Janus Death-in-Life?

Thus our poem is traversed, lengthwise and breadthwise, by
structural antitheses or dualisms which form its "contextual-
formal" pattern: that of a certain mysterious harmony in disharmony, in accordance with an order of life which is far from
cosmic harmony: "the need for the beautiful mainly develops
when man is in disaccord with reality, lives in disharmony and
struggle, when he lives, that is, with greater intensity," wrote
Dostoevsky. Tennyson, living in intense disharmony with

only now he has found its name. But according to the punctuation used
by Tennyson which contradicts such an analysis, we would have to assume
a change of construction: it would be Death-in-Life that is identified with
the days that are no more, the latter being (1) dear, (2) deep, (3) wild,
(4) Death-in-Life. I suspect that the grammatical ambiguity is here inten-
tional and that the first as well as the second of my interpretations can
stand: it is the very nature of the *Sondergott* Death-in-Life that, although
one may invoke him (in the vocative) as a god who presides over the
flux of life, he *is* in reality identical with or immanent in that flux.
Mr. Brooks has asked himself the same grammatical question ("And
what is the status of the exclamation 'O Death in Life'? Is it merely a
tortured cry like: 'O God! the days that are no more'? or is it a loose ap-
positive: 'the days that are no more are a kind of death in life?'") —
without, however, finding any definite answer beyond the possibility of
poetic license.

reality, has created in the poem an artistic form which, while itself harmonious, bears the imprint of the basic disaccord in which he lived.

There is still another remark about the structure of our poem which needs to be made. For the sake of clarity I must here have recourse to a paraphrase of the poetic text, which procedure in Mr. Brooks's opinion is sheer "heresy." But since poetry creates, with material borrowed from our life (including our language) a new poetic world, it will sometimes be in order to use prosaic paraphrase (of course, not so as to reduce the poetic to our prosaic world) to appraise the distance from the workaday world which the poet has achieved in his creation. Tennyson has built our poem on the basis of a collection of pictures, all, as we have said, brought to a common denominator; we may suspect that spontaneous prosaic statements, not yet shaped into the unity of a poem, about the different "pictures" would have been of the type:

> (Remembered) birth of friendship is *fresh*
> (Remembered) loss of friends is *sad*
> (Remembered) death in spring is *sad and strange*
> Remembered kisses after death are *dear*
> (Remembered) vain hope of kisses is *sweet*
> (Remembered) first love is *deep and wild*.

(It does not matter that "remember'd" actually occurs only once in the text, in the last stanza, which draws the conclusion—it is to be supplied in all previous statements.) Now it is obvious that by this very subordination of all the pictures of remembered detail to the concept "the days that are no more," the epithets pertaining to each picture (fresh, sad, sad and strange, etc.) have all been applied to the superior concept (and the pictures of detail have been offered only as possible comparisons or examples: "fresh *as* birth of friendship, sad *as* loss of friendship," etc.: each image is extremely clear and precise, yet is only an instance or analogy of something more inclusive, as Mr. Hough writes). By an additive or cumulative, and very intellectual, procedure somewhat reminiscent of two devices of baroque

ALFRED TENNYSON

poetry (*versus rapportati*[7] and *Summationsschema*[8]), the concept "the days that are no more" has been made to appear all-inclusive since it has appropriated all the epithets predicated of the single pictures; the remembered past is at once fresh and sad and strange and dear and sweet and deep and wild. Thus the encroachment of Death or Life appears as a quantitatively as well as qualitatively predominant, mysterious, and inexhaustible factor of our existence.

Our discussion, like that of Cleanth Brooks, has insisted on the clarity of design of a poem otherwise famous for its somber irrationality: perhaps its very diaphaneity is apt to add to its melancholy beauty. Can there be anything more moving than the description of man's unhappy condition achieved with all the intellectual craftsmanship of which man is capable, than a thing of beauty made out of human despair, than the mournful triumph of art?[9]

It is instructive to compare the treatment of a similar theme in former centuries more bound by the tradition of the *topoi*: for instance a sonnet of Quevedo, the 17th century Spanish baroque poet, entitled "To show how all things warn us of death."

[7] Cf. Curtius, "Europäische Literatur und lateinisches Mittelalter" (p. 288): Milton "Aire, Water, Earth by Fowl, Fish Beast, was flown, was swam, was walkt."

[8] *Ibid.*, p. 289: the device known from the famous monologue of Segismundo in Calderon's "Life is a dream":

1st stanza: What crime have I committed by being born?
2nd stanza: Why are other creatures not punished in the same manner for being born?
3rd stanza: The bird is born to enjoy freedom.
4th stanza: The beast of prey is born to enjoy freedom.
5th stanza: The fish is born to enjoy freedom.
6th stanza: The brook is born to enjoy freedom.
7th stanza: What justification is there for man to be deprived of the divine gift enjoyed by brook, fish, beast of prey and bird?

[9] William Empson, in *The Kenyon Critics*, 1951, p. 134, writes: "It is naive . . . to imagine that in a 'pessimistic' poem . . . the despairing assertions are meant to be accepted quite flatly. The art-works which can be viewed as glorifying death-wishes cover a large field. . . . It seems to be a general rule, however, that if the effect is beautiful the lust of death is balanced by some impulse or interest which contradicts it."

Miré los *muros* de la patria mia,
si un tiempo fuertes, ya desmoronados,
de la carrera de la edad cansados,
por quien caduca ya su valentía.

Salíme al campo: vi que el sol bebia
los arroyos del hielo desatados,
y del monte quejosos los ganados
que con sombras hurtó su luz al dia.

Entré en mi casa: vi que, amancillada,
de anciana habitación era despojos;
mi báculo, más corvo y menos fuerte.

Vencida de la edad *sentí mi espada,*
y *no hallé cosa* en que poner los ojos
que no fuese *recuerdo de la muerte.*

This is a skeletal outline of the sonnet:

Stanza 1: I looked at the walls of my country, once
so strong, now weighted down by the years;

Stanza 2: I went out into the country-side and saw
that the sun had dried out the brooks and, by throwing
shadows, had darkened the daylight for the grazing
cattle;

Stanza 3: I went into my house and saw it de-
teriorated by age; my staff was bent and weak;

Stanza 4: I felt my sword conquered by age, and I
could not set my eyes on any object that would not be
a reminder of death.

One immediately sees that the baroque "sic transit gloria
mundi" motif (particularly apparent in the first stanza) is meant
as a Christian lesson to be learned by the reader ("recuerdo de
la muerte" = "memento mori") who should extract it from
the fact of aging (not from the manifestations of youth: love,
friendship); the poet who is speaking is an old man looking
back at his life and seeing in it pictures *reminiscent* of death
(not of Death-in-Life). The different pictures, expressed by
syntactical homologies (*Miré* "I looked"—*salí* "I went out"—
entré "I went in"—*sentí* "I felt"), as with Tennyson, add up

to one common denominator: "recuerdo de la muerte"; but with Quevedo the order of the universe is not yet shattered: we progress from public life to nature to the house to the self (which is seen as that of a public servant: with the sword). On the contrary, the theme of Tennyson is the existential despair of the single, lonely human individual—with the worm of death in the center of his life.

The source of Quevedo's sonnet is obviously Ovid's *Tristia*: its end corresponds textually to the line 1/11, 23, "quocumque aspexi nihil est nisi mortis imago" (wherever I look there is nothing but reminders of death), and the listing of dreary aspects of life is an ever-recurring *topos* in that ancient work. Ovid was, of course, pointing only to threats of death given with his personal situation as an exile in a barbarous country, with a sea voyage which came close to shipwreck, etc. (cf. the parallel wording 1/2, 23, "quocumque aspicio nihil est nisi pontus et aẽr" (wherever I look there is nothing but [choppy] sea and [stormy] wind). The baroque poet Quevedo took such statements of Ovid in an existential meaning, as referring to human life in general, and expressed thus his total disenchantment (*desengaño*) in a series of *imagines mortis*.

It may be suggested that Tennyson's disenchantment fed on the same literary source as Quevedo's: the pictures of death unfolded by the exile of Tomi in the first decade of our era. But while Ovid, on the brink of death, was still hoping for life (his basic pagan optimism told him: "if one god persecutes you another god brings you help" and "who can forbid *some deity* [*aliquod numen*] to protect us against the wrath of another god?" 1/2, 4 and 12), the disillusioned English romantic finds himself persecuted by *some divine despair*, by some desperate god who must refuse to protect man. The expression *some divine despair* is surely derived from the Ovidian *aliquod numen*—only Tennyson presents the *numen* not as helping man but as itself helpless.

Our comparison then has demonstrated the continuity of an Ovidian influence which inspired once a 17th century baroque poet of Spain, later one of 19th century Romantic England.

Nor is the theme of Death-in-Life dead in our own time. This idea, without the hypostasis of a transcendental god, but as an immanent principle of organic life, has been poetically paraphrased in the speech weighted down by doom of a somewhat Schopenhauerian Doctor in Hofmannsthal's "Das kleine Welttheater":

> Ich sehe einen solchen Lauf der Welt:
> Das Übel tritt einher aus allen Klüften;
> im Innern eines jeden Menschen hält
> es Haus und schwingt sich nieder aus den Lüften. . .
> Denn eingeboren ist ihr eignes Weh
> den Menschen: ja, indem ich es so nenne,
> verschleir ich schon die volle Zwillingsnäh',
> mit ders dem ein verwachsen ist, und trenne,
> was nur *ein* Ding: denn lebend sterben wir.
> Für Leib und Seele, wie ich sie erkenne,
> gilt dieses Wort, für Baum und Mensch und Tier. . .

> [This is the course of the world which I can detect:
> woe comes out of crevices,
> it sets house in every man's inside
> and descends on him from the air. . .
> For his own woe is inborn
> to man; nay, in calling it thus,
> I am veiling somewhat its full twin identity
> whereby it has coalesced with being, and I am
> serving what in reality is one: *for, living we die.*
> This dictum is valid for body and soul, as I see them,
> for tree and man and beast.]

Whereas Tennyson's procedure was that of re-creating a variety of carefully observed phenomena in order to extract therefrom the principle of Death-in-Life, Hofmannsthal's physician, a representative of the modern positivistic, scientific mind, begins by predicting the principle which he corroborates with his final factual enumeration of mortal beings.

Again, we may find our theme represented in a still more modern author, this time surely under the direct influence of

Tennyson, however strange such an influence may seem at first glance in the case of an author as fresh in inspiration and direct in expression as Hemingway, who, as it seems to me, has inserted in his novel *For Whom the Bell Tolls* a prose paraphrase of the Tennysonian poem. The action of this novel is located in contemporary Spain, that European country which is characterized by what Pedro Salinas has called "a culture of death"; and the period chosen is that of the Civil War, an event in which the American protagonist as participant was able to find the realization of his being by assuming a duty which entails his death: throughout the novel Robert Jordan is shown to us steadying and steeling himself against death. In a lengthy harangue which has the exuberance of a prose poem (and from which I am extracting a skeletal outline) the Gipsy woman Pilar, the representative of the spirit of Spain, enumerates the different occasions on which Robert Jordan may learn about the "smell of death":

(1) by staying below deck, with the portholes tightly closed on a ship that is pitching and rolling in a storm.

(2) by kissing the mouth of one of the old women who, early in the morning, at the Puente de Toledo in Madrid, come out of the slaughter house after having drunk the blood of the slaughtered beasts, the mouth of one of those old women with "pale sprouts in the death of their faces."

(3) by smelling in the city streets "a refuse pail with dead flowers in it."

(4) by smelling the sweepings of the brothels in the Calle de Salud: the "odor of love's labor lost mixed with soapy water and cigarette butts."

(5) by inhaling in the Botanical Garden an "abandoned gunny sack with the odor of the wet earth, the dead flowers, and the doings of that night": "in this sack will be contained the essence of it all, both the dead earth and the dead stalks of the flowers and their rotted blooms and the smell that is both the death and birth of man," "when thou inhalest deeply, thou wilt smell the odor of death-to-come as we know it."

Hemingway, this modern poet of metaphysical sensuousness, has chosen to center on sensations accessible to the nostrils, to the most drastically realistic, the olfactory sense (unlike Tennyson, the visual is here secondary, intended only to intensify the olfactory impressions). Moreover, with the exception of the first experience, the olfactory portents of death chosen by Hemingway are limited to a single background, the streets of Madrid, and to a single moment: morning, when indeed one should rather expect signs of awakening life. Morning soiled by the vestiges of the night—what symbol could be more expressive of Death-in-Life? Hemingway does not reminisce about a past become evanescent; he has us "smell" the remainders of last night's debauch: by choosing as culmination the smell of the earth after fornication at night he has suggested to us birth under the sway of death; birth of life is infected, according to him, with smell of death, just as with Tennyson the sight of life implies the sight of death.

If we consider the historical line which leads from Ovid to Quevedo to Tennyson to Hofmannsthal to Hemingway we must conclude that the sensation of fear of approaching death is rendered with greater dramatic forcefulness in our first and our last poetic text. Quevedo and Tennyson appear more reflective in comparison with Ovid and Hemingway, though of the first two Tennyson is more desperate than Quevedo. Surely our contemporary American is the most virile poet among the four enumerated, since he considers death-to-come as an experience which we must, like soldiers before battle, anticipate by steadying our nerves and training our senses—without the vain hopes of Ovid, or the Christian consolations implied by Quevedo, or the idle tears indulged in by Tennyson, or the scientifically detached hopelessness expressed by a character of Hofmannsthal.

CHAPTER IV

A Reinterpretation of "The Fall of the House of Usher"*

"When the mill of the poet starts grinding, do not attempt to stay it; for he who understands us will also know how to forgive us."—GOETHE

EDGAR ALLAN POE fares badly at the hands of contemporary critics, if we may judge from the treatment given "The Fall of the House of Usher" by such subtle commentators as Cleanth Brooks and Robert Penn Warren in their *Understanding Fiction* (New York, 1943). It may be worth while to re-analyze this little masterpiece and then to elucidate Poe's artistry still further by considering it from a comparatist viewpoint.

Let us first consider the strictures made by Messrs. Brooks and Warren against this "story of horror." "The Fall of the House of Usher," they hold, is "within limits, rather successful in inducing in the reader the sense of nightmare," but "horror for its own sake" cannot be aesthetically justified unless the horror, of true tragic impact (Macbeth, Lear), "engages our own interest." Poe's protagonist, Roderick Usher, fails to engage our imaginative sympathy; "the story lacks tragic quality, even pathos." Poe has narrowed the fate of his principal character to a "clinical case" which we the readers (and also the narrator) view from without. "Free will and rational decision" exist neither in the protagonist nor in the story. Roderick—it is his story alone, not that of his sister, the lady Madeline—does not struggle as he should against the doom embodied in his decaying house. Poe

---

* From *Comparative Literature*, 1952, IV, 351-63.

has "played up" the sense of gloom excessively, no doubt because of "his own morbid interest in the story."[1]

These are severe words from sensitive writers who in the same volume justly extol Faulkner and Kafka, often for proceeding in the same manner as Poe. We are asked to admire the logical and methodical behavior of the protagonist in Faulkner's story, "A Rose for Emily," as being worth both our interest and our pity, whereas Poe's portrayal of logic and method in madness should not win our interest for Roderick. Again, while Emily's crime of murder is explained by our critics as a consequence of her isolation from the world and her disregard for the limits between reality and imagination, Roderick's action is not to be explained in their eyes by similar motives—in fact, this possibility is specifically excluded.[2] And here it is striking to note the fact that, contrary to their usual practice, Brooks and Warren fail to analyze the developments in our story in their (pseudo-) logical concatenation, but are satisfied to offer us a general statement about Roderick's "vague terrors and superstitions," in which he indulges without "real choice."

We must then follow out in detail the carefully wrought concatenation of events which Poe has achieved in our story. I would contend that, far from being only the story of Roderick Usher, our story is, as the title indicates, that of "the House of Usher" (a "quaint equivocal appellation," as Poe tells us, because it embraces both the family and the mansion of the

[1] For critics who have always proclaimed the self-sufficiency of the literary work of art, this is a strange relapse into the "biographical fallacy"—premature recourse to the empirical biography of the writer *before* the literary work has been carefully analyzed.

[2] Our critics obviously appreciate, as would any American reader, the resistance to doom shown by Emily Grierson more than Roderick Usher's submissiveness to doom. But does their historical sense not tell them that Poe's attempt at exploration of the "attitude of doomedness" (or "le besoin de la fatalité," as Charles Dubos called it in Byron) was at the time a new step forward in the psychological study of hitherto neglected recesses and arcana of the human mind—an adventure, as D. H. Lawrence has said, "into vaults and cellars and horrible underground passages of the human soul" (quoted by Professor N. B. Fagin, *The Histrionic Mr. Poe*, Baltimore, 1949, p. 157)?

Ushers). Roderick and his sister Madeline, both of them un-
married and childless, are the last scions of the family. Although
Roderick is portrayed as the principal actor in the story and
Madeline as a shadow, glimpsed passing with "retreating steps"
only once before her death, Madeline is still a deuteragonist in her
own peculiar right, on the same level with her brother. The fact
that she is on stage only for a short time and has no lines to
speak (only "a low moaning cry" at the moment of death is
granted her) should not lead us to underrate her importance,
given her impact in the story and the interest which is aroused
precisely by her mysterious appearances.

Roderick and Madeline, twins chained to each other by incestuous love, suffering separately but dying together, represent
the male and the female principle in that decaying family whose
members, by the law of sterility and destruction which rules
them, must exterminate each other; Roderick has buried his
sister alive, but the revived Madeline will bury Roderick under
her falling body. The "fall" of the House of Usher involves not
only the physical fall of the mansion, but the physical and moral
fall of the two protagonists. The incestuous and sterile love of
the last of the Ushers makes them turn toward each other instead of mating, as is normal for man and woman, with blood
not their own. Within the mansion they never leave, they live in
an absolute vacuum.[3] In contrast to the gay comings and goings
depicted in the poem recited by Roderick ("The Haunted
Palace"), which reflects the former atmosphere of the mansion,
we are shown only an insignificant valet of "stealthy step" and

[3] Indeed it may be said that the invitation extended to the narrator by
Roderick (the "vivacious warmth" and the "perfect sincerity" of whose
greeting are stressed by the author) represents the last faint surge of
vitality in Roderick—the desire (hysterical as are all his impulses; he
writes the invitation in a "wildly importunate way") to fill his life with
some content in anticipation of the death of his sister. That Roderick had
wrestled before with the idea of death is shown by his reading habits.
Among the books of his choice are those centered somehow around the
concept of liberation (the *Ververt* and *Chartreuse* of Gresset, the *Journey
into the Blue Distance* of Tieck, *The City of the Sun* of Campanella),
including liberation in respect to sex (the *Belfagor* of Machiavelli, Pom-
ponius Mela's writings on the "Satyrs and Aegipans").

EDGAR ALLAN POE

a suspect, cunning, and perplexed family physician with a "sinister countenance" (it is quite logical that Roderick, after the
supposed death of his sister, should wish to keep her body as
long as possible in the mansion, away from the family burial
ground "exposed" to the outside world, away also from the
indiscreet questions of the inquisitive physician).

As to Madeline, although her physical weakness is great and
she is subject to catalepsy, she does resist the curse that is weighing down the family. "Hitherto she had steadily borne up against
the pressure of her malady"; and at the moment of death she
shows superhuman strength: "the rending of her coffin, and the
grating of the hinges of her prison, and her struggles within the
coppered archway of the vault" are compared by Roderick to
"the breaking of the hermit's door, and the death-cry of the
dragon, and the clangor of the shield"—the feats, that is, of the
doughty knight Ethelred in the romance of chivalry being read
to Roderick by the narrator. Surely "the lofty and enshrouded
figure of the lady Madeline of Usher," as she is presented to us
in an apotheosis of majesty in death, this female Ethelred returning, bloodstained, as a "conqueror" from *her* battle with the
dragon (a battle that broke the enchantment of death), is the
true male and last hero of the House of Usher, while her
brother has in the end become a figure of passivity whose body
is reduced to a trembling mass. If Roderick is the representative
of death-in-life and of the death wish, Madeline becomes in the
end the embodiment of life-in-death, of the will to live, indeed of
a last, powerful convulsion of that will in the dying race of the
Ushers.[4]

But what force moves Roderick to start the process of self-
destruction? Terms such as "clinical case," "vague terrors and
superstitions," may perhaps debar us from deeper psychological
insight. From the beginning Poe has made it clear that he will
deal in our story with the psychological consequences of fear.

[4] Madeline, in spite of her significant part in the plot, is seen by the
narrator and presented to the reader only as a picture, the picture of a
young woman dying at the acme of her beauty—a motif hallowed by the
tradition of Renaissance literature (Poliziano, Lorenzo il Magnifico,
Ronsard, Garcilaso).

When the visitor who is telling us the story receives his first glimpse of the decaying mansion, he turns, in order to divert his attention from the sinister sight, toward the tarn, only to see, with growing anguish, the dreary building reflected in its waters (a foreshadowing of the end of the story when these waters will close over the debris of the mansion)—and he writes the following significant words: "There can be no doubt that the consciousness of the rapid increase of my superstition . . . served mainly to *accelerate* the increase itself. Such, I have long known, *is the paradoxical law* of all sentiments having *terror* as a basis."[5] The psychological law formulated here by Poe (fear increased by consciousness of fear) is valid especially for the monomaniac Roderick, who, throughout the story, is conscious of his "folly." At the beginning he explains to the narrator: "I shall perish . . . I *must* perish in the deplorable folly . . . I have, indeed, no abhorrence of danger, except in its absolute effect—in terror . . . I feel that the period will sooner or later arrive when I must abandon life and reason together, in some struggle with the grim phantom, FEAR." And at the end he is described as "a victim to the terrors he had *anticipated.*" Fear is indeed a passion or a hysteria that accelerates and anticipates. What our story "teaches"—and I wonder why our critics disregarded the capitalized word FEAR which should have suggested to them a "lesson"—is that fear, by anticipating terrible events, has a way of bringing about prematurely those very events. And, since we

[5] Italics mine.—Our critics do not take up the question of the role of this visitor who is the narrator (except to deplore his lack of sympathy, understanding, and information in regard to Roderick, whom he seems to treat, according to our critics, as "a clinical case"). But his function is not that of interpreting Roderick to us, of making us "take him seriously as a real human being," but of serving to objectify the *fears* harbored by Roderick. When a person mainly rational and scientific in his approach to occult phenomena (note his remark about the "merely electrical phenomena" in which Roderick sees "appearances"), who is able to recount the events he has witnessed with such elaborate detail and such poise, is "contagiously infected" by the atmosphere of the mansion and by Roderick's "vague terrors," these terrors become thereby less vague and acquire objective reality. It was in order to make real, not Roderick himself, but Roderick's fears that Poe introduced the narrator into his story.

all are subject to fears, I do not understand how Poe's story should be lacking in general human interest.

Roderick fears the death of Madeline because this "would leave him (him, the hopeless and the frail) the last of the ancient race of the Ushers." The degeneracy of that race manifests itself in the overconsciousness of approaching extinction. And it is this fear that makes him see, in the figure immobilized by catalepsy, his sister dead—whom he then buries with hysterical haste. "Is she not hurrying to upbraid me for my haste?" he says when he hears her come back from the vault; fear has made him both anticipate and precipitate her death. There is no "vagueness" in Roderick's fears; they are clear-cut and precisely outlined in the text.

The narrator is no less careful to present from the beginning the peculiar state of Roderick's nervous agitation, which varies from indecision to energetic vivacity and concentration—a change, so the author tells us, like that from lethargy to most intense excitement in the opium eater. This manic-depressive state of his will culminates in his precipitate action. Similarly, Roderick's behavior before and after that action is motivated by what we would call today his schizoid nature; with him nerves and intellect act separately, though not unconnectedly. The crucial action is brought about by his intellect; but after he has buried Madeline alive he will be only a victim of his nerves. It is, however, his nerves that have from the beginning influenced his intellect. Suffering as he does from a "morbid acuteness of the senses" (why do our critics omit the important motto from Béranger: "Son cœur est un luth suspendu; Sitôt qu'on le touche il résonne"?), from a nervousness that does not tolerate accumulation of sensuous detail, he is necessarily driven (especially in his artistic productions) toward "pure abstractions," "distempered ideality," "nakedness of . . . design." And, since death represents the ultimate of abstraction, the zero degree of concrete reality, we are not astonished by the character of the picture he shows the narrator, a picture designed by an abstractionist *avant la lettre*, in which anticipation of death and nakedness of design converge: it shows the interior of an immensely long subterranean vault, without outlet, bathed in ghastly light. This is obviously the intellectual pattern that will materialize later in the burial of his sister in that donjon-keep which is "without means of admission for light" (until the moment when it will be invaded by the torches of the two men) and is situated "at great depth" and reached through a long, coppered archway.

The abstract pattern as it offered itself to the erratic mind of the amateur artist is acted out in reality by Roderick in a sudden move of concentrated energy.[6] But after the terrible deed has been accomplished, the morbidly acute nerves and senses take exclusive possession of the schizoid, polarized of course around the idea of death. When the storm rises, the portent of the fall of the mansion, it is his visual sense[7] that is stimulated: "there was a mad hilarity in his *eyes*"; he looks out toward the cloud formation which presages death. "And you have not *seen* it?" he asks the narrator, who answers: "You must not—you shall not *behold* this!"—"this" being "a faintly luminous and distinctly visible gaseous exhalation which hung about and enshrouded

[6] In the whole description of the mansion there is a pattern of "black-white" color arrangement (black, oaken, or ebony floors, dark draperies vs. the white enshrouded figure of lady Madeline which detaches itself from the somber background), and this contrast itself is in contrast with the gay, warm colors that once had made splendid our mansion: "in the greenest of our valleys"—"banners yellow, glorious, golden"—"all with pearl and ruby glowing." Black and white, the shades used more in drawing than in painting, are obviously related to the "abstractionism" of the protagonist—and perhaps to Poe's imagination itself, which was excellently characterized by a French critic in 1856 (quoted by Lemonnier, *Edgar Poe et la critique française*, 1928, p. 285) in terms of the *décor* we find in our story; Poe's imagination hovers "dans des régions vagues, où luttent sans cesse le rayon et l'obscurité. Un pas de plus vers la lumière et vous aurez le génie; vers les ténèbres et vous aurez la folie. Entre deux, c'est . . . un je ne sais quoi semblable à ces lampes que l'on porte avec soi dans les souterrains et les mines, et dont la lueur tremblotante dessine sur les parois de capricieuses arabesques . . ." Since Poe delights in describing the penumbra of the human mind in which light and darkness are capriciously mixed, we may perhaps assume that the pattern "black-white" prevailing in his *décors* is given by a more basic intellectual pattern.

[7] We notice that the "luminousness" of Roderick's eyes disappears after his horrible deed has been achieved: at the time, that is, when he is reduced to pure sentience (without power of ratiocination).

the mansion"—obviously an adumbration of the "enshrouded" figure of Madeline which we are to see later, and the signal to us that the House of Usher is giving up its soul. Later it is the auditory sense that predominates in Roderick; he is now able to detect every slightest sound accompanying Madeline's revival ("Said I not that my senses were acute?")—an event which occurs at the very moment the narrator is reading the Ethelred romance, so that the reading is accompanied by the sounds of Madeline's escape from the tomb which seem strangely to harmonize with the events of the romance. While Roderick hears only the sounds in the Ethelred romance that correspond to those caused by Madeline, these sounds themselves have another meaning in the story of Madeline. They spell her victory over the dragon of death, whereas Roderick is the embodiment of pure passive sentience; it is as if by the intensity of his feeling he had succeeded in conjuring up her presence and thus broken the spell of death, though in reality it is Madeline who has wrought her own liberation (it is she who has slain the dragon, whose fangs recede from its prey). A gust of wind opens the doors to disclose her majestic figure (note in the description of this scene the "as if") : "As if in the superhuman energy of his utterance there had been found the potency of a spell, the huge antique panels . . . drew slowly back, upon the instant, their ponderous and ebony jaws. It was the work of the rushing gust—but then without those doors there *did* stand the lofty and enshrouded figure of the lady Madeline of Usher."

We have already noted that at the end the house gives up its soul before its actual "fall"—as though it were a human being. Our commentators point out the continuous correspondences in the descriptions of Roderick and of the mansion: "The house itself gets a peculiar *atmosphere* . . . from its ability apparently to defy reality : to remain intact and yet to seem completely decayed in every detail. By the same token, Roderick has a wild vitality . . . which itself springs from the fact that he is sick unto death. Indeed, Roderick Usher is more than once in the story compared to the house, and by more subtle hints, by implications of descriptive detail, throughout the story, *the house is identified with its heir and owner* [italics mine]. For example, the house is twice described as having 'vacant eye-like windows'—the house, it is suggested, is like a man. Or, again, the mad song, which Roderick Usher sings with evident reference to himself, describes a man under the *allegory* . . . of a house." Such parallelisms[8] belong to the inner texture of the story. On the one hand, Roderick himself explains to the narrator the fact that "He was enchained by certain superstitious impressions in regard to the dwelling which he tenanted, and whence, for many years, he had never ventured forth . . . an influence which some peculiarities in the mere form and substance of his family mansion had, by dint of long sufferance . . . obtained over his spirit—an effect which the physique of the gray walls and turrets, and of the dim tarn into which they all looked down, had, at length, brought upon the *morale* of his existence." On the other hand, he expresses his belief in the "sentience," not only of all vegetable things, but also of "the gray stones of the home of his forefathers" (as well as of the fungi which covered them and of the decayed trees which stood around), and he sees evidence of this sentience in the influence they have had on the destinies of his family and himself. In Roderick Usher's world the differences between the human (animal), vegetable, and the mineral kingdoms are abolished. Plants and stones are sentient, human beings have a plant or animal quality (the influence of plant life on him seems to be reflected by his silken hair—"as, in its wild gossamer texture, it floated rather than fell about the face, I could not . . . connect its arabesque expression with any idea of simple humanity"), and Madeline's youthful body is buried by her brother among the stones of the vault. Life and tomb, death and fall, are one in that strange world. Obviously one cannot ask of

---

[8] One could add here the similar parallelism between, on the one hand, the description of the house as reminiscent of "the after-dream of the reveller upon opium" and of the vapor reeking up from the tarn as "leaden-hued" and, on the other, the characterization of Roderick's way of speaking as "that . . . hollow-sounding enunciation—that *leaden*, self-balanced, and perfectly modulated guttural utterance, which may be observed in . . . the irreclaimable *eater of opium*, during the periods of his most intense excitement."

Roderick any struggle against his *ambiente* or any choice of another, since he is part and parcel of this *ambiente*; since he *is* himself plant and stone (and, thinking only of stone and tomb, must bury his sister alive). It is precisely the doom of Roderick—this man with the receding chin "speaking . . . of a want of moral energy"—that he has been "eaten up by his *ambiente*" (an expression of Dostoevsky's: *sreda zaela ego*). He may crave momentarily for liberation (as is suggested by his symbolic gesture of opening the window to the storm and his "mad hilarity" at the approach of death); but none the less he knows that his life is sealed within the mansion and the attraction of the subterranean vault proves irresistible. Indeed, his proclivity for the subterranean seems to be shared by the house itself, which in the end will be buried underground (and which at the beginning had appeared reflected in the tarn as if doomed to fall therein).

The result of the interpenetration between the *ambiente* and the inhabitants of the house ("the perfect keeping of the character of the premises with the accredited character of the people") is what Poe calls "atmosphere" and describes in atmospheric terms. For us the term "atmosphere" in its metaphoric meaning is trivial, but from Poe's words we gather that he wishes the term to be understood not only metaphorically but in its proper physical sense[9] as well: "I had so worked upon my imagination [says the

---

[9] The dictionaries inform us that this term, coined in the Neo-Latin of 17th century physicists and applied to "the ring or orb of vapour or 'vaporous air' supposed to be exhaled from the body of a planet, and so to be a part of it, which the *air* itself was not considered to be," then extended to the portion of air supposed to be in the planet's sphere of influence, then to "the aeriform environment of the earth," was also used in the 18th century for the sphere within which the attractive force of the magnet or the electrifying force acts (what Faraday later called the "field"). The metaphorical sense, "surrounding mental or moral element, environment," is first attested in English in 1797-1803 ("an extensive atmosphere of consciousness"; cf. Scott, 1828: "He lives in a perfect atmosphere of strife, blood and quarrels"), and in German even earlier (1767 with Herder, "die Atmosphäre der Katheder"; cf. Schiller, 1797: [rhythm is] "die Atmosphäre für die poetische Schöpfung"). The German term *Dunstkreis*, which is the translation of "atmosphere," is used by Goethe in *Faust*, I 19, lines 2669-71, when Mephistopheles leaves Faust in Gretchen's room "to satiate himself with its [sensuous] atmosphere"

narrator] as *really* to believe that about the whole mansion and do-main there *hung an atmosphere* peculiar to themselves and their immediate vicinity: an atmosphere which had no affinity with the air of heaven, but which had reeked up from the decayed trees, and the gray wall, and the silent tarn; a *pestilent and mystic vapor*, dull, sluggish, *faintly discernible*, and leaden-hued." [italics mine] In Roderick's room the narrator feels that he *"breathed an atmosphere* of sorrow. An *air* of stern, deep, and irredeemable gloom *hung* over and pervaded all." Roderick him-self speaks of "the gradual yet certain *condensation* of an atmos-phere of their own about the waters and the walls" which have made him what he is. Conversely *"darkness*, as if an inherent positive quality, *poured forth* [from Roderick's mind] upon all objects of the moral and physical universe, in one unceasing *radiation of gloom*." The atmosphere, emanating from the total-ity of the objects and of the human being surrounded by them, is perceptible in terms of light and darkness; and this atmos-phere of "radiation of gloom" is what I have called the "soul" of the mansion, which gives itself up at the end in the form of "a faintly luminous and distinctly visible gaseous exhalation which hung about and enshrouded the mansion." We should also remember "the blood-red moon" shining through the zig-zag rift of the house, the light over Roderick's picture of the subterranean vault, the luminous quality of his eyes in the midst of the death pallor of his face, etc. Thus "atmosphere" is with Poe a sensuously (optically[10]) perceptible manifestation of the sum total of the physical, mental, and moral features of a particular environment and of the interaction of these features.

("Indessen könnt ihr ganz allein / An aller Hoffnung künft'ger Freuden / In ihrem Dunstkreis satt euch weiden").

[10] It may be remarked that, in the attestations given by Schulz-Basler for German *Atmosphäre*, it is rather the olfactory element that is stressed. The citations offered by the *NED* show already such a conventional use of our term that it is difficult to tell what was the original sensuous emphasis; the *NED* is not as explicit in this respect as one would wish it to be. Unless evidence to the contrary is discovered, I would surmise that Poe's concentration on the *visible* aspect of "atmosphere" is his peculiar contribution.

It is my conviction that we cannot understand the achievement of Poe unless we place his concept of "atmosphere" within the framework of ideas concerning *milieu* and *ambiance* which were being formulated at his time.) As I have shown in *Essays in Historical Semantics* (New York, 1948), the terms (*circumambient*) *air, ambient medium, milieu* (*ambiant*), *ambiance, ambiente, environment,* etc., are all reflections of an ultimately Greek concept, τό περιέχον, which represented either the air, or space, or the World Spirit in which a particular object or being was contained; and that precisely in the third decade of the 19th century, in consequence of the biological research of Geoffroy Saint-Hilaire on the action of the environment, the term *milieu* (*ambiant*) was applied to sociology by Comte and to fiction by Balzac, who liked to be considered a sociologist. The theory of the time was that the organic being must be explained by the environment just as the environment bears the imprint of this being. Balzac, who in 1842, in the preface to his *Comédie humaine,* used the term *milieu* in the sense in which Taine later developed it, wrote in *Le Père Goriot* (begun in 1834) his description of the owner of the Pension Vauquer: ". . . La face vieillotte . . . ses petites mains potelées, sa personne dodue comme un rat d'église . . . *sont en harmonie* avec cette salle où suinte le malheur, où s'est blottie la spéculation, et dont Mme Vauquer respire l'air chaudement fétide sans en être écœurée . . . toute sa personne *explique* la pension, comme la pension *implique* sa personne . . . l'embonpoint blafard de cette petite femme est *le produit de cette vie,* comme le typhus est la conséquence des exhalaisons d'un hôpital. Son jupon de laine tricotée . . . *résume* le salon, la salle à manger, le jardinet, *annonce* la cuisine et *fait pressentir les pensionnaires.*" [italics mine] The last sentence prepares us for the boarder who is to be the protagonist of the story, old Goriot, who is to be thought of as potentially present, with all his lack of dignity and his frustration, in the slovenly petticoat of Madame Vauquer. With 19th century determinism, mankind has developed far from the harmoniousness of Greek thought as expressed in the idea of τό περιέχον; man is now embedded in a milieu which may enclose him protectively like a shell, but may also represent his doom and weigh him down with its unshakable reality.

/ Placed against this background, "The Fall of the House of Usher" will appear to us as a poetic expression of sociological-deterministic ideas which were in the air in 1839, the date when Poe wrote this story. Indeed at one point Poe has Roderick summarize current environmental theory: ". . . an influence which some peculiarities in the mere form and substance of his family mansion had, by dint of long sufferance, he said, obtained over his spirit—an effect which the *physique* of the gray walls . . . had, at length, brought about upon the *morale* of his existence." From this scientific theory Poe distills the poetic effect—just as he does when exploiting, for artistic purposes, contemporary theories of hypnotism, phrenology, and "the sentience of things." Our story is determinism made poetic, "atmospheric."[11] To ask Roderick to "resist" his environment when his character is meant to be the poetic embodiment of determinism is not consonant with the historical understanding of the climate of the story written in 1839—the story reflects what has been correctly called "le réalisme des romantiques."

It is, of course, not by chance that Poe insists on "atmosphere" in his story; he is describing an environment, not realistically as did Balzac, but "atmospherically."[12] We are not offered

[11] In the theoretical appendix to *Understanding Fiction* our critics take up the term "atmosphere" to tell us, on the one hand, that "The Fall of the House of Usher" is an "atmosphere story" (as opposed to a plot, a character, a theme story), a story, that is, containing a considerable element of description, especially description intended to evoke a certain mood; on the other, that every story (not only Poe's "atmosphere story") possesses a certain atmosphere, which is the product of "the nature of the plot, of setting, of character delineation, of style and symbolism, of the very rhythms of the prose." But there is also the "atmosphere of an environment," exemplified in the description of the House of Usher (which description indeed produces a certain "mood") and defined by Poe in terms of the environmentalism of his time ("the perfect keeping of the character of the premises with the accredited character of the people").

[12] Professor Auerbach, commenting in his book *Mimesis* (p. 406) on the passage in *Le Père Goriot* discussed above, speaks of its "atmospheric realism" (that is, the realism with which the general *ambiente* of the Pension Vauquer is evoked). I have been using the term "atmospheric"

a description of the petticoat of the lady Madeline or of the thousand other details of the sort that serve to substantiate the heavy, oppressive, petty-bourgeois atmosphere of the Pension Vauquer, but only those details which are strictly connected with the main motif—the gossamer-like hair of Roderick, the blush on the cheek of the cataleptic Madeline, the vault and the archway, etc. It is as though the author, himself akin to his Roderick, had elaborated his story in terms of "abstract design" served by "acuity of senses";[13] in fashioning the environment of his story he has proceeded deductively,[14] starting from the concept of mad fear and giving it sensuous detail only

somewhat differently as meaning *"only* atmospheric" description, description rendering only the atmosphere.

[13] This is exactly what endeared him to Baudelaire: see Professor Peyre's *Connaissance de Baudelaire*, Paris, 1951, p. 111: "les deux hommes avaient en partage un curieux mélange de traits émotifs et de traits intellectuels, une sensualité capable de s'élancer vers les régions supérieures à l'air raréfié, et une puissance d'analyste et de logicien abstrait rare chez les poètes."

[14] This statement was corroborated by Poe himself (in 1842); see Fagin, *The Histrionic Mr. Poe*, p. 163: "A skillful literary artist has constructed a tale. If wise, he has not fashioned his thoughts to accommodate his incidents; but having conceived, with deliberate care, a certain unique or single *effect* to be wrought out, he then invents such incidents—he then combines such events as may best aid him in establishing this preconceived effect." I do not agree with the opinion expressed in Malcolm Cowley's otherwise excellent article (in *New Republic*, Nov. 5, 1945) that the idea of Poe just quoted should be paralleled with the American absorption with mechanical devices, as illustrated by the engineering achievements of his time; for we find the same emphasis on literary technique for the purpose of attaining a specific effect in the ancients, in Goethe, in Valéry. And it would seem paradoxical to condemn Poe (the arch-enemy of industrial progress), on the basis of the ambiguity contained in the word "technique," for his "engineering talent in poetry and fiction." A semantic fallacy is involved also in Professor Fagin's conception of the "histrionic" element in Poe. Fagin makes the passage quoted above, with its emphasis on skillfully contrived novelistic plots, on "effect," serve the quite gratuitous theory that Poe's genius is to be "explained" by a histrionic, effect-seeking talent which was not allowed to come to fruition on the stage proper in a man who wished to remain a "Mr. Poe": Poe has "somehow . . . missed his true vocation and destiny" (p. 2). Since fiction tends in general toward drama (as Henry James has taught us) and since the short story is the most dramatically concentrated form of fiction, it is not difficult for Mr. Fagin to represent the writing of a story in terms of an analogy with the production of a play, and to single out in Poe's stories the theatrical character of his

insofar as the senses are stimulated by this madness. And we may suspect that Poe indulged in the description of the monomania of fear precisely because this offered him patterns entirely intellectual, leading away from actual life and superimposing upon it another reality—that of madness. It is a remarkable feature of his romantic realism that Poe can accept environmentalism when it borders on irreality, whereas in Balzac the irreality of his monomaniacs grows out of earthy realism. With Balzac we see the solid ground on which the pyramid of his novels rests, with Poe only the peak of the pyramid which is bathed in the rarefied atmosphere of ratiocination. Our critics are wrong in reading Poe only "emotionally," not "conceptually."

If we compare both Balzac and Kafka with Poe, we find that the first two, while having an environmental realism in common which distinguishes their technique from Poe's atmospheric description, differ totally from each other in that Balzac's is an empirical (inductive) realism while Kafka's is a deductive realism (there is a deductive element also in Poe). Thus, environmentalism is portrayed (1) with empirical (factual) realism by Balzac, (2) with deductive realism by Kafka ("as-if realism"), and (3) with deductive irrealism by Poe ("only atmospheric" realism).

---

plots, settings, lighting effects (even "area-lighting"), stage props ("Max Reinhardtish at its lushest—and worst"), sound effects (in "The Fall of the House of Usher": "Melodrama? Grand Guignol stuff? Perhaps. But . . . how superbly staged!") synchronization, dénouements (similar to those of the Greek tragedy), character delineation, and the rest ("his stories are frequently dramatic productions in which Poe displays his craftsmanship as bard, playwright, stage-designer, electrician, actor, elocutionist, and above all, director"—p. 207). Apart from the fact that Mr. Fagin must confess that Poe as a playwright (in his *Politian*) was a total failure, and apart from the more general experience that any explanation of effect by defect, of genius by frustration, is a psychological error, the main fallacy in such reasoning is that, through the use of the metaphorical *word* "histrionic," the fundamental difference between the art of writing a dramatic story and the art of the stage is blurred. With the same reasoning the author of the *Commedia* could be represented as a frustrated producer. To take only the lighting effects (and God knows that Dante was a past master in those!), Fagin overlooks the essential difference between lighting effects *suggested by words* to the imagination of the reader and the material light actually released on a stage before our eyes.

If our critics fail to appreciate "The Fall of the House of Usher" while admiring Kafka's story "In the Penal Colony" (and probably Balzac's *Le Père Goriot*), the reason may be that with Poe's atmospheric environmentalism (which is realistic only insofar as he makes the atmosphere real) the details of the description are inspired, not by realistic observation of actual contemporary mansions, but by reminiscences of conventional *literary* patterns outmoded at his time (the haunted castle of Mrs. Radcliffe, etc.). It is surely not in his choice of such hackneyed stage props that Poe's inventiveness lies, but in the arrangement to which he subjects them in order to form patterns of intellectual design.

As for Kafka, though his story, "In the Penal Colony," is based on a deductive procedure similar to Poe's, he has chosen for the description of his entirely imaginative, even allegorical, environment what I would call an "as-if realism"; he offers such factual details of modern life that the reader, at least at the beginning of the story, believes himself to be in a realistic milieu. We seem to find ourselves with the French Foreign Legion on some remote island; and the description, by the enthusiastic officer, of the summary methods of jurisdiction practiced in the colony or of the executions by means of an elaborately devised machine produces at first an impression of factual accuracy (written in 1919, the story seems to anticipate Hitlerism). Only in the further course of the story do we realize the fantastic character of that jurisdiction and of that gruesome engine, both of which are contrived (deductively!) by the author only in order to symbolize the inevitable, if ununderstandable cruelty of any civilization.[15]

---

[15] The reader might find it more natural to compare the treatment of the castle motif in Poe and Kafka. And, indeed, the castle is in both somehow the embodiment of existential fear. With Poe, however, we see the castle (the mansion) dying of "its" fears, we are with him within the castle. In Kafka's *The Castle*, we are outside the castle, which seems very much alive, although the laws according to which it functions remain unknown to the protagonist, whose existential fear is motivated by his inability ever to find his place there (a symbol of the bewilderment of modern man faced with an institutionalized world which he cannot understand, but only fear).

■■

CHAPTER V

The "Ode on a Grecian Urn," or Content vs. Metagrammar*

*Auream quisquis mediocritatem
Diligit, tutus caret obsoleti
Sordibus tecti, caret invidenda
Sobrius aula.*
    —Horace, *Carmina*, 2, 10, 5

■■

PROFESSOR EARL R. WASSERMAN in his recent volume, *The Finer Tone* (1953), dedicates fifty pages to Keats's famous ode—a memorable example of painstaking research, of meditative searching into the meaning and form of an outstanding poem, of a never-abating will to understand every word and thought, of pertinent observations probably never made before, and of relevant questions asked. Mr. Wasserman's is a sturdy, hard-working, hard-thinking mind, undaunted by difficulties (even by those he himself may create), unwilling to rest before finding a solution which fully satisfies *him* (this severest of judges sits in judgment only upon himself—other scholarly opinions are not considered).

It is as though of the two alternatives proposed in the verses of Keats's *Endymion*,

> . . . There are seats unscalable
> But by a patient wing, a constant spell,
> Or by ethereal things that, unconfin'd,
> Can make a ladder of the eternal wind. . .

Mr. Wasserman had chosen the first as his motto: the patient wing, the constant spell. In addition there is noticeable in Mr. Wasserman a deep desire to transcend in his interpretation of

---

*From *Comparative Literature*, 1955, VII, 203-25.

poetry the academic drabness of the so-called historical school and to bridge the gap between the "new critics" and the "scholars" by adopting the by no means novel tenet of the former (that a poem is first not a historical document, but an organism in its own right which must be recreated by the critic) without abandoning the traditional methods of explanation (recourse to biography, to passages parallel to those of the poem under study drawn from other writings of the author or his contemporaries, etc.). To a European-born scholar, nurtured in a centuries-old tradition of both scholarly and aesthetic interpretation, especially in the classical and the French fields (who can only deplore the internecine war being waged within every department of English in this country between the "scholars" and the "critics"—as though a scholar in literature should not be conversant with both approaches), it is a source of great delight and relief that Mr. Wasserman, a scholar thoroughly trained in the history of ideas and in philological method, has developed far beyond his original background and has come to use devices of aesthetic criticism identifiable with those of the critics. Thus combining both approaches, he has surely succeeded in his purpose of showing that Keats is not a poet indulging in "luxurious sensuous experiences," but an artist of the word who in his poems "used both his head and his heart"—in other words, that intellectual structures exist behind the assumed warblings of that poetic nightingale.

If despite all these assets Mr. Wasserman has not always succeeded in carrying conviction in his interpretations, the fault seems to me to lie in a perhaps too eager acceptance of certain questionable habits of contemporary criticism—for instance, the tendency to make the poetic text appear more difficult, intricate, paradoxical than it truly is. This in turn involves on the part of the critic a verbal-metaphysical play that outmetaphysicizes the poem. What is fit for Donne may not always be fit for Keats, as Mr. Wasserman himself remarks, but does not always seem to remember. In general the critic should heed the witty advice of Croce, parodying the Nazis: "Mitsingen ist verboten." Furthermore, Mr. Wasserman makes extensive use

of poetic phrases, which for the poet were creations of inspired
moments, as technical terms, recurrent, ever-ready pegs on
which to hang more prosaic critical comment (e.g., "at heaven's
bourne," "sphery sessions"); he overemphasizes "imagery" to
the detriment of the subject matter and even the ideological
content of the poem; he appeals to certain sophisticated terms
such as "imagistic syntax" (or "metagrammar"), "mystic
oxymoron,"[1] etc., which perhaps contribute less to our descriptive techniques than they seem to promise.

Being no Keats scholar but only a practitioner of French
explication de texte, I may be allowed to offer my own relatively
simple explanation of the "Ode on a Grecian Urn" with the
hope that the difference of method and perhaps the traditional-
ism of my approach may not be without value (even if my interpretation should have been proposed by other scholars in
the past). In any case, I believe that *discussion* of a given theory
of a particular critic by fellow critics, detailed criticism of a
specific piece of work—a habit that in our days of anarchy,
spiritual isolation, and private language tends more and more
to disappear from our scholarly journals—can still give as
valuable results as in strictly linguistic matters. The *consensus
omnium* is as much an ideal for the explanation of poetry as it is
for etymological investigation. An essay written with the mental
energy of Mr. Wasserman not only invites but deserves the
careful weighing of its results by as many students in literature as possible.

I

Thou still unravish'd bride of quietness,
Thou foster-child of silence and slow time,
Sylvan historian, who canst thus express
A flowery tale more sweetly than our rhyme:

[1] Mr. Wasserman even coins a derivative from this classical term of
rhetoric: *oxymoronic*—a formation offending not only the classical
but also the American ear; in a sentence such as "[Pan's] is the
oxymoronic nature at heaven's bourne" the mixture of neologism and
solecism is painful. The Latin ear is again wounded by the coinage
coextential (p. 36); is this intended to be a portmanteau word (*coexist-
ent + coextensive*)?

What leaf-fring'd legend haunts about thy shape   5
   Of deities or mortals, or of both,
     In Tempe or the dales of Arcady?
What men or gods are these? What maidens loth?
   What mad pursuit? What struggle to escape?
     What pipes and timbrels? What wild ecstasy?   10

II

Heard melodies are sweet, but those unheard
   Are sweeter; therefore, ye soft pipes, play on;
Not to the sensual ear, but, more endear'd,
   Pipe to the spirit ditties of no tone:
Fair youth, beneath the trees, thou canst not leave   15
   Thy song, nor ever can those trees be bare;
     Bold Lover, never, never, canst thou kiss,
Though winning near the goal—yet, do not grieve;
   She cannot fade, though thou hast not thy bliss,
     For ever wilt thou love, and she be fair!   20

III

Ah happy, happy boughs! that cannot shed
   Your leaves, nor ever bid the Spring adieu;
And, happy melodist, unwearied,
   For ever piping songs for ever new;
More happy love! more happy, happy love!   25
   For ever warm and still to be enjoy'd,
     For ever panting, and for ever young;
All breathing human passion far above,
   That leaves a heart high-sorrowful and cloy'd,
     A burning forehead, and a parching tongue.   30

IV

Who are these coming to the sacrifice?
   To what green altar, O mysterious priest,
Lead'st thou that heifer lowing at the skies,
   And all her silken flanks with garlands drest?

What little town by river or sea shore,   35
  Or mountain-built with peaceful citadel,
    Is emptied of this folk, this pious morn?
And, little town, thy streets for evermore
  Will silent be; and not a soul to tell
    Why thou art desolate, can e'er return.   40

V

O Attic shape! Fair attitude! with brede
  Of marble men and maidens overwrought,
With forest branches and the trodden weed;
    Thou, silent form, dost tease us out of thought
As doth eternity: Cold Pastoral!   45
  When old age shall this generation waste,
    Thou shalt remain, in midst of other woe,
Than ours, a friend to man, to whom thou say'st,
  Beauty is truth, truth beauty,—that is all
    Ye know on earth, and all ye need to know.   50

Mr. Wasserman starts with the metaphysical framework of the poem as ostensibly reflected in the first line and with the "mystic oxymoron" or "mystic interfusion" supposedly contained in the description of the urn as a "still unravish'd bride": "Although the ode is a symbolic action in terms of an urn, its intrinsic theme is that region where earth and the ethereal, time and no-time become one. . . . 'Bride,' suggesting the first phase of the process of generation, has reference to the human and mutable, and consequently has the same paradoxical relation to 'unravish'd' that tomorrow has to midnight. . . .[2] Like the

---

[2] While opposed to what Mr. Wasserman calls rightly the "self-flagellating" habit of certain extremists among the critics of excluding by principle from *explication de texte* all elements outside of the poem, I believe that the timing of allusions to extraneous elements should be carefully devised. For instance, in the case of our ode, it would seem to me better critical strategy, instead of quoting from the start passages from other poems ("There is a budding morrow in midnight," "at heaven's bourne," etc.) or general ideas of Keats's, to reconstruct the poem for the reader by means of words and concepts borrowed as much as possible from the poem under study. The reader must be led to feel

humanity and/or[3] divinity of the figures, like the marriage-chastity of the urn and the virginity-ravishment of the maidens, the immortality of the urn and the temporality of the figures are delicately poised on each side of heaven's bourne, yearning towards that area of mystic interfusion. . . ."[4]

Instead of beginning as Mr. Wasserman does, I would first ask myself, in the down-to-earth, factual "French" manner: *What is the whole poem about,* in the simplest, most obvious terms? It is first of all a description of an urn—that is, it belongs to the genre, known to Occidental literature from Homer and Theocritus to the Parnassians and Rilke, of the *ekphrasis,* the poetic description of a pictorial or sculptural work of art, which description implies, in the words of Théophile Gautier, "une transposition d'art," the reproduction, through the medium of words, of sensuously perceptible *objets d'art* ("ut pictura poesis"). I feel that I am justified in beginning with such an obvious, "generic" statement by the title of the poem, "Ode on a Grecian Urn," which though located outside of the poem proper still belongs to it and contains the orientation intended for us by the poet, who, as is always the case, speaks in his title to his public as a critic.

Since, then, the ode is a verbal transposition of the sensuous appearance of a Greek urn, my next question must be: What exactly has Keats seen (or chosen to show us) depicted on the

---

the poem as self-explanatory and self-sufficient (for so it is meant in most cases by the poet), as unfolding itself organically before the reader without any commentator being needed. Help from outside introduced too early, and as if it were necessary, is apt to destroy the impression of the specific uniqueness and wholeness of the work of art. Only when the reader has fully understood the poem, helped perhaps more than he realizes by the invisible direction of the critic, may the latter come out from the wings and proclaim: "That is *not* all ye need to know. This poem must also be seen in connection with Keats's whole production and ideology."

[3] Why this legal-commercial device "at heaven's bourne"?

[4] Passages such as these, which present to us as already realized by the poet from the beginning what is generally only the final reward of long meditation, the *unio mystica,* provoke in the unprepared reader first a slight sense of vertigo, then a feeling of frustration at the premature solution of all problems, ostensibly reached so easily, so painlessly.

urn he is describing? The answer to this question will furnish us
with a firm contour, not only of the object of his description but of
this description itself, which may later allow us to distinguish the
symbolic or metaphysical inferences drawn by the poet from the
visual elements he has apperceived. In addition, this answer will
in our case point to several uncertainties of vision experienced by
the poet while deciphering his sensuous subject matter, uncertainties that may help us ultimately to discern *which particular message* Keats wishes us to see embodied in the urn and which to
exclude.

The poet describes an urn (obviously consecrated to the ashes
of a dead person) bearing in typically Greek fashion a circular
"leaf-fring'd" frieze (and it is, I submit, mainly for that reason
that the poem is circular or "perfectly symmetrical," as Mr.
Wasserman has said, in outward and inward form, thereby re-
producing symbolically the form of the *objet d'art* which is its
model).[5] The frieze represents inside of the fringe of leaves
three Greek "pastoral" scenes (just as the frieze of the cup described in Theocritus' first idyll represents three pastoral scenes
framed by a garland of ivy): (1) stanza I: the wild pursuit of
maidens by love-crazed beings; (2) stanzas II-III: the tender
wooing of a maiden by a youth; (3) stanza IV: the solemn ceremony of sacrifice enacted by a priest before a town community at
an altar. The circular form of the frieze makes it necessary for
the main elements of the first scene to reappear in stanza V
("with brede of marble men and maidens," "forest branches and
the trodden weed").

Our next question will be: What has Keats *failed* to discern
clearly on the frieze? In two passages he manifests indeed uncertainty, a wavering which becomes most conspicuous through
the repeated conjunction "or": (1) "What leaf-fring'd legend
. . . / Of deities *or* mortals *or* of both, / In Tempe *or* the dales

---

[5] Since already in antiquity the poetic *ekphrasis* was often devoted
to circular objects (shields, cups, etc.), it was tempting for poets to
imitate verbally this constructive principle in their *ekphraseis*. Mörike's
poem on an ancient lamp shows the same formal circularity motivated
by the form of the model as does Keats's ode on the urn; cf. my article
in *Trivium*, IX (1951), 134-47.

of Arcady? / What men *or* gods are these?" (stanza I); (2) "What little town by river *or* sea shore, / *Or* mountain-built with peaceful citadel . . . ?" (stanza IV)

In both cases, that is in scenes 1 and 3, as distinguished from scene 2 in which no such uncertainty is suggested, we have to do with identification of certain details which could not be discerned by the beholder of the urn. It cannot be chance that scenes 1 and 3 are also those in which the elements of the frieze enumerated are introduced by questions ("What?" repeated seven times in stanza I, "who?" "to what?" and "what" in stanza IV) whereas in scene 2 no such questions as to identity are asked. I infer that this uncertainty about identity, circularly repeated, is one of the main problems of the poem, and I further submit that this uncertainty is centered about *historical identity*. Keats simply does not know who precisely the Greek protagonists are in the scene of the pursuit and of the sacrifice; this question seems not to arise in scene 2 which, obviously because it deals with the eternal feeling of love, elicits no wish for specific historical identification. In other and very prosaic words, for scenes 1 and 3, but not for 2, Keats would be in need of a specialized archaeologist or historian of Greek civilization to explain to him the possible implied "factual" mythological or theological allusions.

In the light of these considerations, the first line of the poem, "Thou still unravish'd bride of quietness," becomes clear; not so in Mr. Wasserman's metaphysical or allegorical interpretation, which leaves the precise literal sense of the words "bride" and "unravish'd" in doubt: "Like the marriage-chastity of the urn and the virginity-chastity of the maidens, the immortality of the urn and the temporality of the figures are delicately poised on each side of heaven's bourne"; "'bride,' suggesting the first phase of the process of generation, has reference to the human and mutable, and consequently has the same paradoxical relation to 'unravish'd' that morrow has to midnight: the urn belongs to both becoming and immutability." I would interpret the words "still unravish'd bride of quietness" as an allusion to the quietness of the work of art represented by the urn which has not yet been violated by *archaeological or historical scholarship,* by rationalized explanation. We should believe then that the poet, having come upon a newly discovered Greek urn, describes its direct impact on himself before the professionals of history and philology have violated ("ravish'd") its secret, as they will infallibly do in course of time (*"still* unravish'd").

The first desire of the poet must then have been for the urn (that had so long been the "foster-child of silence and slow time") *now* to *speak* to him, to reveal to him the true history of which it must have been a witness. That is why the poet addresses the urn as "sylvan *historian*"; the term "historian" is in paradoxical contrast to "unravish'd bride of quietness," since the one must reveal, the other withhold. The urn, still unmolested by antiquarians, is itself a "historian"; yet this is a *"sylvan* historian" who expresses "a flowery tale more sweetly than our rhyme" in its "leaf-fring'd legend," not a professional historian who would furnish us with factual detail, with the who and what of man's past history. The urn's historical, "sylvan" account reveals to us history in the form of the never-changing beauty of nature, of forests, leaves, flowers, as Greek vases usually do.[6]

Thus the first stanza contains a series of unresolved paradoxical oppositions as the bewildered, restless, nearly anguished, and

[6] I am not sure whether Mr. Wasserman has not overcategorized "sylvan history" by playing it off against "pageant history" (to which Keats is known to have been adverse); while "pageant history" according to Wasserman "particularizes and hence confines deeds to the mortal world," "sylvan history seizes human passions and makes them 'almost ethereal by the power of the poet.' . . . Human history chronicles mutable becoming; but the urn is the essential historian and chronicles the essence of becoming. . . ." But Keats has created the term "sylvan historian" (not "sylvan history"!) only as a nonce word, valid only for the context of our ode, to be immediately forgotten, the perfect crystal of a snowflake which melts the moment after. One has here the uneasy feeling that an over-conscientious analyst has mapped out all the possible categories of history; in addition to the well-known genres of cultural history, social history, economic history, there now is created a new branch henceforth to be known as "sylvan history." And we must remember that the urn is called a historian by Keats only in the figure of speech called "lucus a non lucendo," since the failure of the work of art as a "historian" will be demonstrated in the poem itself (in stanza IV).

breathless seven questions of the poet show. His own quest at this stage for historical identity to be wrested from the silent urn still prevents him from taking in the whole beauty of the work of art, and he suggests, without any attempt at fusion, the manifold contradictions that anguish him at this first moment of contact with the ancient work of art: (1) "slow time"—*now*, the dramatic moment of the discovery of the urn and of its ultimate decipherment; (2) the urn's inviolate secret—the desire of the poet to learn it (his historical curiosity, which he may share with the professional historians); (3) history of which the urn is a witness—the beauty of eternal nature which is represented on the frieze; (4) the silence of the work of art—its expressive quality which "speaks" to the beholder; (5) the silence of the urn—the sound and fury suggested by the first scene depicted on the frieze.[7] It is these last two contrasts, the paradox of a speaking silence and of sounds rendered silently by the work of art, that will be expanded in stanza II:

> Heard melodies are sweet, but those unheard
> Are sweeter; therefore, ye soft pipes, play on;
> Not to the sensual ear, but, more endear'd,
> Pipe to the spirit ditties of no tone . . .

[7] One would expect the urn that holds the ashes of the dead to represent foremost the silence and quietness of *death*—but Keats in this truly Grecian (Pythagorean-Platonic) poem has carefully avoided any direct allusion to death that would bring the poem close to 18th-century poetry about graveyards. Keats's urn is from the beginning allowed to be only a Greek monument of beauty—conforming, that is, to that practice of the ancients, which Lessing in his treatise, *Wie die Alten den Tod gebildet*, had first formulated and which Goethe found consonant to his own philosophically meditative, while "thou canst not leave / Thy song" is and beauty. See the *Venetianische Epigramme* (1790), No. 1:

> Sarkophagen und Urnen verzierte der Heide mit Leben:
> Faunen tanzen umher . . .
> Cymbeln, Trommeln erklingen; wir sehen und hören den Marmor . . .
> So überwältiget Fülle den Tod; und die Asche da drinnen
> Scheint, im stillen Bezirk, noch sich des Lebens zu freun.

We may, incidentally, note Goethe's emphasis in this epigram on the audible quality of the animated scenes portrayed on the silent ancient monument of art.

I would say that Mr. Wasserman does not emphasize enough the strong contrast between *"wild* ecstacy" at the end of stanza I and *"soft* pipes" in stanza II, when he suggests (p. 29) that the theme of "ecstasy" forms a gradual transition between stanzas I and II: ". . . in the sense of 'the most exquisite passion,' the word ['ecstasy'] tends . . . to draw together the mortal and immortal symbols toward a point of fusion so that in the next stanza the poet may move into an empathy with them. . . . But in the sense of 'the passage of the soul out of the self' (ἐκ + ἱστάναι [read ἱστάναι] = to make stand outside) it describes the consummation of the symbols' empathic act [Question: Can the symbols themselves consummate an emphatic act?]. . . . The poet's own empathic advance is externalized, in part, by the contradiction of his attention as it moves from the total urn . . . to the frieze on the urn, to the intense activity in the frieze." In my opinion there is a total break after the first stanza; the wild chase and struggle sweeps past us, past the poet and us, making no bid for the latter's "empathy" (only perhaps for his attention) ; and the "ecstasy" here displayed, taking place only in the persons depicted, not in the poet and even less in the "symbols," is as ununderstandable as it is anguishing to the poet, who marks his reaction by the verbless staccato questions: "What maidens loth? What mad pursuit?" (the climate here is entirely "Dionysian"). In stanza II we have a new beginning. The poet is seeing another scene which has in common with the first only the presence of musical instruments; now there will be expressed soft feelings of love and the pipes will be played softly.

At this point Keats has realized that, just as it is impossible in this case actually to hear the sounds (wild or soft) of the instruments depicted on the frieze, so it may be true that the silent urn itself may contain, as it were, congealed sound, may *be* music and melody audible only to the "spirit." He has indeed remembered, most fittingly for the Grecian environment, the Pythagorean teachings about world harmony: "Heard melodies are sweet, but those unheard are sweeter"; that is, since we earthly beings with our gross ears are unable to hear the subtle harmony (based on numbers and proportions) of the music of the spheres, what we sense as silence may be nothing but that very celestial harmony. I feel entitled to bring this Greek concept (which after all is familiar to any cultured reader) to bear on our poem, since it is a *topos* with Keats, as I infer from four Keatsian passages quoted by Mr. Wasserman which reflect Pythagorean thought. The motto of Wasserman's book is taken from a letter of Keats's: "We shall enjoy ourselves here after by having what we called happiness on Earth repeated in *a finer tone* and so repeated." On p. 50 appear two passages from *Endymion*: "Silence was music from the holy spheres" and

> Aye, 'bove the withering old-lipp'd Fate
> A thousand Powers keep religious state,
> In water, fiery realm, and airy bourne;
> And, silent as a consecrated urn,
> Hold sphery sessions for a season due.
> Yet few of these far majesties, ah, few!
> Have bared their operations to this globe.[8]

[8] The unearthly Powers embodied in all elements except that of earth hold "sphery sessions"; they enact, that is, the concert of the harmony of the spheres which remains unheard by earthly ears—a speaking silence which may be compared to that of an urn consecrated to death (although Keats again avoids mentioning this concept, it is to death that the allusions to fate and "a season due" point). For us it is important to understand the close association in Keats's mind between the silent urn and the Pythagorean musical world harmony. Keats is not the first to have identified the silence of a historical monument, which by its transmundane melody overcomes death, with the music of the spheres. The 17th century Spanish baroque poet Quevedo heard melodious harmony in old books. Here are the quatrains of a sonnet addressed to his editor:

> "Retirado en la paz de estos desiertos
> con pocos, pero doctos libros juntos,
> vivo en conversación con los difuntos
> y escucho con mis ojos á los muertos;
>
> Sino siempre entendidos, siempre abiertos,
> o enmiendan ó secundan mis asuntos;
> y en músicos callados contrapuntos
> al sueño de la vida hablan despiertos."

Here then the silence of the "learned book" is a Pythagorean contrapuntal music of the spheres that "seconds" the thought of the poet; but the baroque poet does not fear to mention death; on the contrary he is convinced that the dead are "awake" and possessed of living truth, whereas life is a dream and an illusion. His Christian paradoxical thought

On p. 61 a line is quoted from "Bards of Passion and of Mirth"; the nightingale sings "divine melodious truth; / Philosophic numbers smooth." (Reference to a *topos* of Keats is at least as permissible as reference to parallel passages from Keats which are all informed by that *topos*.)

By the Pythagorean equation of silence and celestial harmony inaudible to man Keats is able to resolve the paradox of the silent but "speaking" urn and also to find the transition from things seen (with the eyes) to things heard (with the "spirit"). The sentence "Heard melodies are sweet . . ." is meditative and philosophical in content, and its syntax is that of quiet philosophical predication (a complete declarative sentence in opposition to the verbless, breathless question of stanza I and to the empathic exclamations which follow in stanza II). Only with the exclamation, "ye soft pipes, play on," does there begin the "emphatic act" of the poet, the identification of the poet with a picture seen on the frieze—an identification limited exclusively to scene 2 (the scene of sweet love which is expanded over two stanzas).

It is also true that with the exclamation "play *on*" another theme suggested in the beginning has come to the foreground— that of time. The urn perpetuates a particular transient moment of the past, the warm love of a youth for a beautiful maiden manifesting itself in song and the playing of pipes in the midst of nature, the moment before consummation, the troubadour moment of love, as it were. Love, song, tree have been, as Wasserman shows, withdrawn from the burden of time and have become "happy," i.e., happy in themselves, self-sufficient, timeless, as are all things beautiful (any German would remember Mörike's line: "aber das Schöne, selig scheint es in ihm selbst"[9]).

("life" = "a dream"), which is expressed in verbal paradoxes and metaphysical puns ("I *listen* with my eyes," "*awake* the dead speak," "the books *second* the thought of the poet"), is at variance with the Platonic paradox of Keats; with Quevedo this world appears shrouded in *desengaño*, with Keats as reflecting (in its works of art) the heavenly light of the Idea.

[9] Cf. Schiller's words, "In sich selbst ruht und wohnt die ganze Gestalt, eine völlig geschlossene Schöpfung . . . da ist keine Kraft, die mit Kräften

The empathic identification with what the poet sees on the urn reaches its climax[10] in stanza III, as is shown by the repetition of the word "happy" (six times) and "(for) ever" (five times)— a high point which can only be followed by painful disillusion when the thought of the non-artistic earthly reality of love assails the poet (end of stanza III).[11]

The description of the sacrificial scene in stanza IV offers us, as Mr. Wasserman has felt, a climate totally at variance with that of the second scene,[12] one of unassimilable mystery and

---

kämpfte, keine Blösse, wo die Zeitlichkeit einbrechen könnte," and other passages from Schiller quoted by Ilse A. Graham, "Zu Mörikes Gedicht 'Auf eine Lampe,'" *MLN*, LXVIII, 331.

[10] Mr. Wasserman believes (p. 37) that, "if the statement that beauty is truth is the total intention of the poem, then it is here [at the place of the climax in stanza III] that it belongs, and no where else. For this is what the poem has been saying up to this point." In my opinion the aphorism can come only after stanza IV, in which the poet has made the discovery of the impossibility of "historical empathy," coming then as relief and consolation.

[11] I find somewhat arbitrary Mr. Wasserman's suggestion (p. 30) that in the syntactical moods used in stanzas I-III there is to be found an increase in "empathy"; according to him the "least empathic" is the interrogative mood (in stanza I), the two next more empathic moods (which appear mingled in stanza II) are indicatives and imperatives, the climax of empathy being reached in the exclamatory sentences (stanza III). This is devoid of general validity for the language and of pertinence for our stanzas; surely the interrogative mood can be highly empathic in questions such as "Ah, did you once see Shelley plain / And did he stop and speak to you . . . ?" As to our stanza I, the questions are interrogative in form alone; they have in reality the emotional value of exclamations ("What wild ecstasy?" could be printed "What wild ecstasy!" Surely the exclamation as such does not "assure that the subject is engaging in the life of the predicative—has mingled—'and so become part of it'"). Furthermore, the indicative as such is neither empathic nor the contrary; "Heard melodies are sweet" is not empathic, but, as we have said, philosophically meditative, while "thou canst not leave / Thy song" is indeed empathic. Finally, exclamations such as "Ah, happy, happy boughs!" are empathic, but only thanks to the particular adjective "happy."

[12] It is regrettable that Mr. Wasserman's metaphysical terminology tends here as in other passages to blot out all concreteness even when he is proceeding in the right direction: "Keats now asks three questions. The first, like those of the first stanza, asks for identity: 'Who are these coming to the sacrifice?' But of course there can be no answer, *for at heaven's bourne there is only selflessness.* The next two questions

strangeness, of bleak desolation, of what I would call "the silence of history," without possibility of communication. The pattern of bewildered questions as to identity recurs, the questions becoming more troubled; and the poet's tentative filling in of the missing historical detail (in disjunctive questions of the type "what . . . or . . . ?") takes up much more space than in stanza I. Indeed, as Mr. Wasserman remarks, the "little town" with its lonely streets exists, not on the frieze, but only in the imagination of the poet; it owes its appearance only to the poet's inference from the scene on the frieze. If the whole population of the Greek *polis* attends the ceremony of the sacrifice, the town must have been left "emptied" and "desolate," and this (inferred) emptiness and desolation coalesces in the poet's mind with the same feeling generally produced in us by historical sites abandoned by man, ruined cities, excavations,[13] etc. At this moment the poet comes to feel the chasm of history implied in a monument of a dead civilization of which no survivors remain. Not even the artistic monument of the urn before him can bridge that abyss. However close he may have felt to the old civilization in scene 2 (both because of the high place sweet love enjoys in Keats's system of values and because this feeling transcends all

---

. . . ask for directions . . . these are spatial questions and can no more be answered than those of identity, *for heaven's bourne is essential space. The result of fellowship with essence is that we become* 'Full alchemiz'd, and free of space' " (p. 41). For me such statements as those in italics have the ring of pronouncements of a kind of phantasmic bureaucracy "at heaven's bourne," answering questions with the peremptory self-assurance evidently characteristic of celestial traffic cops. Again, what should one think of such allegorizations as: "The sacrificial altar towards which the procession goes is . . . *dedicated to heaven, a realm of pure spirit*: the immortal without the mortal, truth without beauty. And the town that the souls leave is *the town all souls leave in their human progress towards the heaven-altar*" (p. 42). No, the altar and the town are simply a nondescript Greek altar and a nondescript Greek town, and let us forget about "the realm of pure spirit" and the "heaven-altar" in order to concentrate on the one unchanging problem of the poem: What can a Greek urn teach us?

13 The association established here between the detail of the dead town and the feeling of the deathlike quality of history is symmetrically parallel to the association in stanzas I-II between the detail of the pipes and timbrels represented on the frieze and the poet's belief in the Pythagorean music of silence.

ages), scene 3 has shown him the failure of the urn as a "historian." The hermetic closedness, the incommunicative coldness of the religion of the ancient civilization which this scene purports to reveal to his eye becomes clear to his mind (and his capacity of empathy comes even less to fruition than in scene 1, which was only suspected to imply a strange mythology but did not portray strange religious rites as does scene 3). Even the sacrificial heifer "lowing at the skies" seems to revolt against the ceremony to which it must contribute and to interrupt the harmony of the spheres that prevailed before.

At this lowest point of "historical understanding"—lower than in scene 1, where the wild ecstasy of the Dionysian chase had at least succeeded in carrying the imagination of the poet with it, for all his failure to identify the participants—at this moment when the religion of a past civilization awakes no response in the poet and no historical message is audible, spiritual relief comes to him when, turning away from the detail of the three scenes, he looks at the beauty of the whole urn and of the whole frieze, "O Attic shape! Fair attitude!" the first vocative referring to the urn, the second to the persons represented on the frieze. The *archaeological* message of the urn is dead, its *aesthetic* message is alive "for ever" (indeed the desolate third scene was not devoid of its own beauty: "green altar," "all her silken flanks with garlands drest," "peaceful citadel," "pious morn"). Mr. Wasserman seems not to have felt the sudden rise of the poet's voice in happy exaltation, the powerful upsurge of feeling marked by that magic line, "O Attic shape! . . ," in which the urn, after having been as it were fragmented into various divisions under the microscopic scrutiny of the curious poet, now suddenly reassumes its unbroken flawless totality, rising again before his eyes, reborn as a perfect whole! And this vision of organic artistic beauty comes to the poet in the moment of his deepest depression as an enlightening consolation—in a formula of invocation directed as it were to a deity whose entity of "edle Einfalt und stille Grösse" he has clearly apperceived. One will notice that, while the poem opens as if Keats were not beginning but rather continuing a conversation with a "thou" to which

he attached descriptive epithets (such as "still unravish'd bride,"
"foster-child . . . ," "sylvan historian)," now the final definition
("O Attic shape . . .") amounts to an evocation of a presence,
of a *numen* (one will note the "O" of invocation, unique in the
poem) ; and here the "thou" follows the predication of being.
The beginning and the end of the poem thus form a chiastic
pattern which adds to its cyclic effect.

But even after the revelation of the aesthetic message of the
urn, the breath of mortality rising out of the sealed chambers of
history (what Goethe called the "Leichengeruch der Geschichte")
which chilled the poet's empathy does not entirely subside; for
he sees in the "silent form" of the urn *"marble* men and
maidens," a *"Cold* Pastoral," as cold and monotonous as the
idea of eternity (". . . dost tease us out of thought"). The phrase
"Cold Pastoral," corresponds to "sylvan historian" (of stanza I)
in reverse; the urn commemorates sylvan (i.e., pastoral) scenes
and, even though it occasionally perpetuates warm human love,
it is yet ultimately cold as history (or time or eternity). Thus the
work of art that survives death would breathe something of the
air of death. This idea—who of us gazing at the Venus de Milo
has not felt something of the presence of the majesty of death!—
is not expressed, although we may feel it latent under the actual
words of the poet. Systematically avoiding the word "death," he
prefers to cling to consoling Apollonian messages such as that of
the imperishable work of art as a "friend of man"—and, of
course, that expressed in the last two lines :

> Beauty is truth, truth beauty,—that is all
> Ye know on earth, and all ye need to know.

—a controversial passage which, I trust, will become clearer in
the light of the interpretation already suggested. Mr. Wasserman comments thus on these lines :

"Although the urn is able to reveal to man a oneness of beauty
and truth, it is not able to inform him that this is the sum total
of his knowledge on earth and that it is sufficient for his earthly
existence ('all ye need to know') ; for obviously he knows other

things on earth, such as the fact that in the world beauty is not truth, and this should be even more valuable within the world than the knowledge that the two are one at heaven's bourne. But more important, the symbolic action of the drama at no point justifies the urn's limiting its message; nowhere has the urn acted out the fact that man knows no more on earth than this identity of beauty and truth, and that this knowledge is sufficient.

"Now, it is significant that this is an ode *on* a Grecian urn. Had Keats meant *to*, he would have said so, as he did in the 'Ode to a Nightingale.' There the meaning of the poem arises out of the dramatic relations of the poet and the symbol; but *on* implies a commentary, and it is Keats who must make the commentary on the drama that he has been observing and experiencing within the urn. It is the poet, therefore, who speaks the words, 'that is all / Ye know on earth, and all ye need to know,' and he is addressing himself to man, the reader. Hence the shift of reference from 'thou' (urn) to 'ye' (man). I do not feel the objection frequently raised that if the last line and a half belong to the poet and are addressed to the reader, they are not dramatically prepared for. The poet has gradually been obtruding himself upon the reader's consciousness in the last two stanzas by withdrawing from his empathic experience and taking on identity. He has become distinctly present in the last stanza as a speaker addressing the urn, and proportionately the urn has shrunk from the center of dramatic interest; it is now but a short step for him to turn his address from urn to reader. Moreover, the reader has also been subtly introduced into the stanza, for the poet vividly marks his complete severance from the urn's essence by pluralizing himself ('tease us,' 'other woe / Than ours') and thus putting himself into a category wholly distinct from the urn; and by this act Keats has now involved the reader as a third member of the drama. Finally, when the reader has been filtered out of the plural 'us' and 'ours' by the reference to 'man' (48), the poet may now address to him his final observations on the drama.

"But the poet is no more justified than the urn would be in concluding that the sum of necessary earthly wisdom is the identity of beauty and truth. Certainly when he returned to the dimensional world in stanza IV he found the two to be antithetical, not identical. Something of the difficulty Keats encountered in trying to orient his meaning is to be seen in the three versions of the final lines that have manuscript or textual authority. Keats's manuscript and the transcripts made by his friends read,

Beauty is truth, truth beauty—that is all . . .

In the *Annals of the Fine Arts* for 1820, where the poem was first published, the line appears as

Beauty is Truth, Truth Beauty.—That is all . . .

And the 1820 volume of Keats's poems reads,

"Beauty is truth, truth beauty,"—that is all . . .

No one of these solves the problem, although each hints at the difficulty. Clearly each one strives to separate the aphorism from the following assertion by the poet; and at the same time each attempts to preserve a relation between the pronoun 'that' and *something* that has gone before. Then, since we have seen that the antecedent of 'that' cannot reasonably be the aphorism— since neither urn nor poet can be saying that all man knows and needs to know on earth is that beauty is truth—its antecedent must be the entire preceding sentence.

All that man knows on earth, and all he needs to know is that

When old age shall this generation waste,
    Thou [the urn] shalt remain, in midst of other woe
Than ours, a friend to man, to whom thou say'st,
    Beauty is truth, truth beauty.

Only this meaning can be consistent with the dramatic action of the poem, for it not only does not deny that in the world beauty is not truth, but also assimilates that fact into a greater verity. The sum of earthly wisdom is that in this world of pain and decay, where love cannot be forever warm and where even the highest pleasures necessarily leave a burning forehead and a parching tongue, art remains, immutable in its essence because that essence is captured in a 'Cold Pastoral.' . . . This art is forever available as 'a friend to man,' a power willing to admit man to its 'sphery sessions.' . . . The great end of poetry, Keats wrote, is 'that it should be a friend / To sooth the cares, and lift the thoughts of man,' for art . . . eases this burden by holding out to man the promise that somewhere—at heaven's bourne, where the woes of this world will be resolved—songs are forever new, love is forever young, human passion is 'human passion far above,' beauty is truth; that, although beauty is not truth in this world, what the imagination seizes as beauty must be truth—whether it existed before or not [pp. 58-61].

"Because the assertion that beauty is truth has the illusory appearance of being the most explicit and most meaningful statement in the 'Ode on a Grecian Urn,' nearly all examinations of the poem have concentrated on the concluding lines, only to discover that the apparently clear abstractions are an *ignis fatuus*, beckoning to a morass of quasi-philosophy. . . . The aphorism is all the more beguiling because it appears near the end of the poem, for its apparently climactic position has generally led to the assumption that it is the abstract summation of the poem, detachable from the first forty-eight lines and equal to them.

"But the ode is not an abstract statement or an excursion into philosophy. It is a poem about things: an urn, pipes, trees, lovers, a priest, a town; and poetic images have a grammar of their own that is contained in their dramatic actions . . . only a reading of the total imagistic grammar of the poem can unfold its intent, as the final lines alone cannot. Indeed, through such a total reading, the aphorism proves not to be a summation of the poem, nor even the high point of its intent, but only a subordinate functional part of the grammar of images [pp. 13-14]."

Believing as I do that the entire two last lines are intended as words spoken by the urn, I shall attempt to refute in detail the first passage quoted from Mr. Wasserman. The first argument (the urn cannot tell man that the identity of beauty and truth is the only knowledge needed on earth because "obviously [!] he knows other things on earth," etc.) is slightly reminiscent of the caustic comment I heard at the Hopkins in reference to our poem: "Beauty ain't truth and truth ain't beauty and you've got to know a helluva lot more than that on earth." Mr. Wasserman's argument seems to be an unnecessary endorsement, by a critic so deeply devoted to the spiritual, of that so-called "hard-boiled realism" or that radically unpoetic view of the world which takes for granted that poetry is "just illusion," an aberration from "normal" truth. This view of Paradise irretrievably lost in this world, questionable as a basis for understanding of poetry in general, is still less conducive to the particular understanding of a poet for whom Paradise was still close to our earth, and who, ordained in the Platonic faith,[14] could very well have postulated the absolute sufficiency "on earth" of his aesthetic religion. Keats in the 19th century believed that the beauty and truth of the transcendental idea is revealed "on earth" just as firmly as Du Bellay in the 16th had professed his faith in "l'Idée de la Beauté qu'en ce monde j'adore."

The second argument (the urn has not "acted out the fact that man knows no more on earth . . .") must fall if I am right in assuming that the urn has "acted out," on the one hand, the insufficiency of historical truth (in scenes 1 and 3 historical

---

[14] Mr. Wasserman has pertinently quoted, without identifying it with Platonism, a passage from a letter in which Keats defines the *summum bonum* Platonically: "What the imagination seizes as Beauty must be true—whether it existed or not." I may point out the similar identification of beauty and truth in Schiller's poem, "Die Künstler" (1789); cf. passages such as:

> "Nur durch das Morgenthor des Schönen
> Drangst du in der Erkenntnis Land. . .
> Was wir als Schönheit hier empfunden,
> Wird einst als Wahrheit uns entgegengehn. .
> Der freisten Mutter freie Söhne,
> Schwingt euch mit festem Angesicht
> Zum Strahlensitz der höchsten Schöne!
> Um andre Kronen buhlet nicht!
> Die Schwester, die euch hier verschwunden,
> Holt ihr im Schoos der Mutter ein;
> Was schöne Seelen schön empfunden,
> Muss trefflich und vollkommen sein."

identity was blurred, in scene 2 what was reached was only the metahistorical, and the whole frieze reproduces basically not history but nature), and on the other, the absolute self-sufficiency of the aesthetic message—the Platonic equation "beauty = truth" alone is precious knowledge, in contrast to historical erudition (or, perhaps, any kind of rational learning that tends to "ravish" the virginal secret of beauty). The questions as to historic identity, with their tone of bewilderment and anguish (in stanzas I and IV), in the final stanza give way to a polemic tone directed against the quest for historical knowledge—for such an exclusion is implied in the words "and this is *all* ye need to know."[15]

Mr. Wasserman's inference, from the correct observation that ours is an ode *on*, not *to* a Grecian urn, that it is the poet who must make the remark "that is all ye need to know . . ." is an obvious *non sequitur*. Note that in spite of writing *on* an urn the poet has all through the poem spoken *to* the urn ("thou") and that he may very well suggest his own conclusion by words lent to the urn. Indeed, agreeing with Mr. Brooks's interpretation, I think it in line with previous passages about the "silence" of the urn that the latter is finally allowed to *speak*, allowed, that is, to formulate the true message which according to Keats

[15] A similar anti-archaeological approach is to be found in "Kore," a less ambitious, short poem of Goethe's, written approximately at the same time (1819 or 1821) as Keats' ode (the virgin is Prosperpina, some ancient representations of whom Goethe had seen). By giving the poem the subtitle "Nicht gedeutet" (not explained) Goethe has chosen to proclaim, in contradiction to contemporary interpretations of ancient works of art such as Creuzer's and Welcker's, the right of the ancient work of art to "inviolateness." The first stanza of the poem scoffs at all attempts at factual identification by archaeologists:

> "Oh Mutter? Tochter? Schwester? Enkelin?
> Von Helios gezeugt? Von wer geboren?
> Wohin gewandert? Wo versteckt? Verloren?
> Gefunden?—Rätsel ist's dem Künstlersinn."

The factual "riddle" will then remain unsolved; what is all-important for the "artistic sense" is, as the second stanza proclaims, the "divine nature" of the Kore, that is the message of ever-self-transcending beauty embodied in Proserpina (and, supposedly, in her representations):

> "Die Gott-Natur enthüllt sich zum Gewinn:
> *Nach höchster Schönheit muss die Jungfrau streben,*
> Sizilien verleiht ihr Götterleben."

is embodied in it and of which he himself has finally became aware. The *ekphrasis*, the description of an *objet d'art* by the medium of the word, has here developed into an account of an *exemplary* experience felt by the poet confronted with an ancient work of art, an experience shown in the development of the poem, as Keats's purely aesthetic aspirations come to free themselves from all non-essential admixtures. It was Keats's achievement to have presented the "ode on" in the form of an "ode to," that is, in a manner that was consonant with the lofty emotion traditionally required for the genre of the ode and that would have satisfied even a Lessing—to have turned a lengthy enumeration of factual details, difficult to visualize, into one continuous, emotion-laden address to the urn[16] and into a dramatic search for the message contained therein.

As to Mr. Wasserman's contention that in the last stanzas the poet has gradually been obtruding himself upon the reader's consciousness and that proportionately the urn has shrunk from the center of interest—we have already said that the urn, far from having "shrunk," has been reborn and re-formed in the last stanza—how could the poet in that supreme moment have lost sight of it? Furthermore, the assumed "short step" by which the poet is supposed to turn his address "from urn to reader" is utterly impossible. It would surely be most awkward and didactic for the poet to end his conversation with the urn and then to turn to us and say: "and now I come to you, my fellow men, to tell you"—but with such a transition the shift suggested by Wasserman would be at least *possible*. Here, however, there has been no such transition, and a sudden "ye" following upon a series of "thou's" cannot belong to the same speaker; "ye" always needs an antecedent (the reference a few lines earlier to "man" serves in no way as preparation for such

[16] Only once, in the address to the "little town" which Keats has imagined only by inference, is the hymnic "thou" predication not limited to the urn and the things to be seen thereon. In this case the poet has allowed himself to range beyond the work of art into "history"—a sin of his imagination, as it were, which is symbolized by the misuse of "thou" and from which the poet will be called back by the whole form of the urn as it rises before his eye: "O Attic shape! . . ."

a shift) ; no substantive except a vocative can be the antecedent of a second-person pronoun.

Moreover, Wasserman assumes that in the last line and a half the poet is preaching a lesson to his fellowmen, whereas in reality Keats himself, who had "sinned" before against the work of art (by his historical curiosity), has only now learned the lesson (about its purely aesthetic message that endures whether the urn depicts "for ever" warm human love or a civilization from which "not a soul . . . can e'er return"). It must be the urn which formulates for Keats the lesson which he as well as mankind needs, and which both will be grateful to hear. The urn, which has in the last stanza grown in power of presence and has come to speak, must have the last word and this last word must be one of friendship and consolation for the community of man. Keats's own "numinous" experience with the urn had been a suprapersonal one and its exemplary value can be communicated to mankind only by the friendly *numen* itself to which he owes his experience and which, in a kind of reversed Ovidian metamorphosis, finds a human voice to speak warm human words from the marble of art and the silence of history. If the urn spoke only the short intellectual aphorism "Beauty is truth, truth beauty" without the personal address to humanity, as Mr. Wasserman suggests, it would not be humane. And how can one imagine that, having at the end endowed the urn of stone with speech, Keats should then undo the miracle he has wrought, interrupt (after five words!) the direct, suprapersonal flow of communication between work of art and mankind which he had helped create (through the delicate passage from "thou" to "us" of line 44 to "ours" and "man" of line 48), and take the limelight for himself just before the curtain falls, dismissing his audience with the complacent statement: "I the poet am telling you that what I have just said is all you need to know"? All of this would represent, in my opinion, an inadmissible lack of taste on Keats's part. In order to understand the final development of our poem the critic must have experienced religiously, even as Keats did, the numinous quality of the work of art.

There is also another reason for attributing the entire two last lines to the urn, a reason which suggests itself to anyone familiar with ancient art. A Greek urn generally bears an inscription or legend in epigrammatic form. As Paul Friedländer in his book, *Epigrammata* (Berkeley-Los Angeles, 1948), tells us: "The Greeks, while following the Orient in erecting and inscribing monuments, delighted in giving to a sepulchral inscription or a dedication to a god the meter and the style of Homer or of the elegiac or the iambic poets," the main form of inscriptional epigrams being the elegiac distych. These poetic inscriptions, the eloquent part of mute statues or tombstones, were supposed to address the passer-by:

> Tell them in Lacedaemon, passer-by,
> that here obedient to their law we lie.

> Stay, passenger, why goest thou by soe fast?

—and to be read by the latter, so that monument and traveler become engaged in a dialogue, "for ancient reading meant always reading aloud." To put it in the words of a Latin epitaph:

> quodque meam retinet vocem data littera saxo,
> voce tua vivet quisque leges titulos.
> (and since the letters on the stone contain my voice,
> they will come to life through the voice of you
> whoever shall read these lines.)

Up to the end of the ode it had been Keats alone who spoke to the urn, that is, thought aloud inquiring into its meaning. Why should he not have thought, in a poem that deals with the coming alive of an ancient work of art, of a dialogue between that work of art and its beholders, in which the urn would, in a Grecian miracle or metamorphosis, come to *speak* to them (in the form "ye" which includes the poet) *its inscription*, answering thereby the poet's quest for meaning as "a friend of man"—just as Greek sepulchral inscriptions would reward the passer-by, who after glancing at the monument (urn, stele, etc.) had reverently read the name of the deceased, with consoling words and friendly wishes ("but you farewell, o passer-by!" "godspeed, o stranger!"—Friedländer, no. 168) or even with moral admonishment ("gnome" or "paraenesis") meant for his lasting spiritual good. Note that the emphasis on the beauty of the sepulchral monument (which, in the intention of the artist and the sponsors, corresponds to the beauty of the person commemorated) is frequent in Greek inscriptions.

Thus the idea that the beauty of the work of art will survive that of the models which it portrays is given in the very Greek literary genre to which Keats conforms—combining with that idea the Platonic idea of the Idea which was his own poetic creed. And not only in content but also in form does Keats' final distych seem to be connected with the Greek genre of the sepulchral epigram;[17] his distych appears in the exact metrical form (the verse of five feet) in which Simonides' epitaph of the three hundred Spartans at Thermopylae is known in English; and the address to the passer-by ("ye") is found with Keats in the last of the two lines, that is, precisely in the part

---

[17] It must be borne in mind that, in addition to true sepulchral inscriptions, the Greek developed the literary genre of pseudo-inscriptions, destined for the reader, in which the work of art would be described. Hellmuth Rosenfeld, who in his book, *Das deutsche Bildgedicht*, Leipzig, 1935, is mainly concerned with the survival of that genre in German poetry, distinguishes the following ancient types of the "Bildgedicht," that "aesthetically challenging hybrid form in which the work of art in its repose, and poetry that consists in movement, are brought to perfect union"; it may consist in (1) an objective address to the reader by the person who has donated the work of art as an *ex-voto*; (2) a fictional device by which the work of art itself is supposed to speak, to introduce itself, or to answer questions of the reader; (3) the further development in which the poet takes over the part of the reader in the dialogue with the work of art (the dialogue may become then a monologue of the poet); (4) finally, the variant in which the poet (who points at the work of art: "behold . . . behold . . . !") describes it for an ideal spectator or re-enacts, as if personally moved, the scene represented in the work of art as dramatic action. Rosenfeld calls this type, in reminiscence of the Homeric scene, "teichoscopic." It seems obvious that Keats's ode contains the elements (2), (3), and (4), arranged in such a way that (2) (the answer of the work of art) and (3) (the address of an ideal spectator) grow organically out of (4) (the "teichoscopic" presentation of the urn). I may add that I have found in Rosenfeld's collection of German "Bildgedichte" no parallel to the "aesthetic apperception developed in time" which is so characteristic of Keats's ode.

of the distych that corresponds to the Greek pentameter in which the good wishes for the traveler are usually expressed. We must take into consideration the basic *topos* quality of the "ye" of the inscription and of the dialogue between monument and traveler inherent in an inscribed Greek urn; while in Greek inscriptions questions as to historical identity are asked and answered, Keats, who has asked the urn questions of a historical nature, receives an answer, in the Greek form of the historical epigram, but containing a message of non-historical (aesthetic) content. While the ancient sepulchral epigram was dedicated to the commemoration of a particular dead person, the epigram of Keats's making contains a general message addressed to the living exclusively. Contrary to Mr. Wasserman's assertion, it is the poet who in the last stanza of our ode has "shrunk" from the picture and it is the urn that will "for ever" converse with the passers-by—all readers of Keats's ode ought to become passers-by, pausing before the immortal urn and listening to its consoling message.[18]

[18] Now that we have seen the correspondence between the final lines of the ode and the Greek practice of inscribing sepulchral monuments, we may go further and ask ourselves whether even earlier in this poem there may not be another such parallel. The repeated "questions as to historical identity" in stanzas I and IV, which appear fraught with so much personal emotion on the part of the poet, may have their antecedents in similar questions inscribed on Greek monuments and ostensibly addressed by the passer-by to the monument. Cf. Friedländer's description of a column surmounted by a Sphinx and bearing the inscription: "O Sphinx, dog of Hades, whom do you watch over as you sit on guard over the dead?" This is followed by the name of the particular dead person, as answer. But Keats's questions, addressed as they are to the Sphinx of History, admit of no answer from History. The dialogue inherent in the sepulchral inscription was made explicit by the Neo-Latin poet Pontanus, who in his *Tumuli* (1518), often imitated by the French poets of the Pléiade, had a *Viator* repeatedly ask questions (as to historical identity) which were answered by the *Genius* or the *umbra* of the deceased. In Remy Belleau's *Bergeries* (1572) we find prose descriptions of sumptuous Renaissance tombstones followed by epitaphs in verse form which read like poetic answers to the silent inquiry of the beholder. I do not, of course, claim that Keats had actually seen or studied any of the particular Greek inscriptions mentioned above (or their Renaissance derivations); but the poem was evidently written by one who had been immersed in that particular atmosphere that any museum of classic art creates.

To return to more philological questions, the three different punctuations in the next to last line do not serve, as our critic concedes, to clarify the precise reference of the demonstrative pronoun *that*. They only show, I believe, the hesitations of the poet in regard to the relationship of the aphorism to the rest of the legend. He was uncertain whether or not to present the intellectual epigram as a self-sufficing unit. It is most outspokenly a self-sufficing unit in the version of the volume of 1820; *"Beauty is truth, truth beauty,"—that is all* . . . ; while in the version of the manuscript, generally and, as I believe, correctly reproduced in our current editions; *Beauty is truth, truth beauty,— that is all* . . . [without quotation-marks], the flow of speech within the distych is least interrupted and the sharp intellectualism of the—anti-intellectual—maxim is allowed to be counteracted by the tone of the heart with which the work of art shows— by the pronoun "ye"—its concern for "man."

As to Mr. Wasserman's own proposed solution, that the antecedent of the pronoun *that* is the entire preceding sentence:

> When old age shall this generation waste,
> Thou shalt remain, in midst of other woe
> Than ours, a friend to man, to whom thou say'st,
> Beauty is truth, truth beauty . . .

—by which interpretation it is possible for Wasserman to hold that it is not the urn but the poet who states the sufficiency for man of the knowledge about the identity of beauty and truth "at heaven's bourne"—against this hypothesis I would contend first that, for *that* to refer to the whole sentence from "When old age" to "truth beauty," the content of this sentence is not sufficiently general to be called "all ye know on earth" (the *particular* experience made by the poet with *this* particular urn would then be termed to be *"all* ye know on earth"); second, the idea that for Keats "beauty is truth, truth beauty" *at heaven's bourne* is known to Mr. Wasserman from his wide readings of Keats, but is obviously unexpressed in our poem; if on the one hand readers of the poem are told that the fact that the urn will "for ever" remain to them as a friend is the only knowledge they need *on earth,* and on the other hand the urn proclaims "Beauty is truth . . . ," how could the readers deduce that the aphorism "Beauty is truth . . ." is only valid *at heaven's bourne*? Such "help from without" provided by the critic destroys the poetic organism.[19]

If on the contrary one accepts my interpretation that historical learning is the one thing that is excluded from what "ye need to know" and that the aesthetic experience with the urn has led the poet to express (through the final distych) his Platonic religion of art, I believe that the unity of the poem remains intact and that the final lines are indeed the quite naturally developed abstract formulation of the actual experience of the work of art by the poet dramatically portrayed in this ode of *ekphrasis.*

As to the second passage extracted above from Mr. Wasserman's comments, I will limit myself to saying that I am unable to recognize the cogency, at least for romantic poetry, of any "imagistic grammar" (or metagrammar or syntax). The use of these metaphors for a sequence of images is obviously meant to imply a rigor traditionally associated with those grammatical terms; for any particular statement in a given language "grammar" requires the use of certain forms, a use generally and automatically followed by all the practitioners of the language:

> La grammaire qui sait régenter jusqu'aux rois
> Et les fait, la main haute, obéir à ses lois . . .

Surely the coiners of the terms "imagistic grammar (or syntax)" did not intend to convey to us the idea that the images of a given poem have been prescribed to the poet (by poetry or taste?) in the same way as the mood, indicative or subjunctive, in a given sentence is dictated by the rules of the grammar of his language. Since Wasserman speaks of the "imagistic grammar *of a particular poem,*" he must mean nothing more ambitious than "coherent or consistent evolution of the images within the economy of the particular poem." Now I think that "imagery" (a technical term non-existent in other languages) has always been

[19] See note 2 above.

somewhat overrated by English literary critics, who delight overmuch in that sensuous element which for them makes a poem a poem (an attitude for which there are historical reasons—see E. L. Stahl's article on Coleridge's theory of poetry in *Weltliteratur, Festgabe für Fritz Strich*, Bern, 1952); and Wasserman's idea of the "imagistic grammar" goes even further in this direction in proclaiming implicitly an autonomy of the images—his claim being that only out of the "total imagistic grammar of the poem" could one deduce content (or "intent"). According to Wasserman, the aphorism "Beauty is truth . . ." cannot be the culmination of the poem because its imagery has supposedly not "acted out" the final maxim. But how is the critic entitled to disregard the intellectual thread of thought marked by the sequence of phrases (even if in part imagistic), "sylvan historian," "O Attic shape!," "silent form" "Cold Pastoral," which culminates in the aphorism "Beauty is truth . . ."? I would rather hold that no imagistic sequence could be established as valid unless it is confirmed by the final aphorism.

No mythologema in the world such as "imagistic grammar" will convince us that in European poetry prior to symbolism and surrealism images have a life of their own, untutored by ideas. It is indeed because of the idea of the poem ("the aesthetic, not historic message of the work of art") that Keats offered to our view the three different scenes (or sets of images) on the frieze in which his historical and his aesthetic sense were not equally satisfied (reaching equilibrium only in scene 2, not in scenes 1 and 3)—whether these three scenes once existed on a Greek vase he actually happened to see or whether he himself invented (or modified) the three scenes so as to suit his general thesis about the work of art. Thus, in my opinion, the critics, after having indicated the material detail and the clear contours of the sculpture described in our poem, should have established its firm ideological architecture (the particular step or nuance it represents among poems dealing with art, or philosophies of art) before analyzing the (in our poem surely subordinate) imagery. The images of our poem do not have the power to reduce the final aphorism to a subordinate position;

on the contrary, the final aphorism, which stands out so clearly for any unbiassed reader and must necessarily be connected with ideas previously suggested in the poem, cannot but reduce the images to subordinate position—to the position of embodying the idea.[20] It is ironical that Mr. Wasserman, a disciple of the author of *The Great Chain of Being*, when explaining a rather simple poem of ideas should abandon his vantage point, history of ideas (which includes the history of ancient ideas).[21]

To establish an imagistic metagrammar which would ignore the all-controlling "intellectual grammar" of a poem would be to set in motion a dangerous "sorcerer's apprentice." Let us have, in our explanations of the classical poems of English literature, less of imagistic magic or alchemy that smells of the lamp, and more of that open air of crystalline lucidity around the work of art—as this is present in Keats's ode, in which thought and image have become naturally one because image has not encroached on thought, because thought has found its appropriate embodiment. The beautiful line "O Attic shape! Fair attitude! . . ." is in itself the perfect incarnation of image serving thought.

[20] In other words: the images of our poem are not of an associative nature (as are for instance those of Rimbaud's "Bateau ivre") ; only if they were could the predominantly imagistic approach be justified.

[21] It is paradoxical to see at work in Mr. Wasserman two tendencies which would seem to be mutually exclusive: on the one hand an all-too-eager metaphysical allegorization, on the other subservience to imagistic metagrammar; in both cases there is in evidence an excess of the *meta*, an estrangement from that *aurea mediocritas* which avoids the extremes of literary criticism. (But these "excesses" stem, of course, from one virtue for which no praise is adequate—Wasserman's passionate desire *fully* to understand the poem.)

CHAPTER VI

●●●

Marvell's "Nymph Complaining for the Death of Her Fawn": Sources versus Meaning*

●●●

IN THE considerable literature in which attempts have recently been made to define the meaning of Marvell's poem there may be distinguished three schools of thought: one that takes literally the love of the nymph for her fawn (Legouis in his book on Marvell published thirty years ago; T. S. Eliot in his essay on Marvell; Lecomte[1]); a second that proposes an allegorical ex-

* From *Modern Language Quarterly*, 1958, XIX, 231-43.

[1] The bibliography of this discussion may be found in the two articles by LeComte and Miss Williamson in *MP*, L (1952) and LI (1954), to which there must be added the article by E. H. Emerson and Legouis' rejoinder in *Études Anglaises*, VIII (1955), 107-12.

Needless to say, I share the outspokenly "French" horror of Legouis ("un esprit français . . . n'arrive pas à se débarrasser d'un excès de logique quand il étudie la poésie anglaise") when faced with the lack of logic implied by the assumption of allegorical explanations that explain only parts of the literary work—a procedure, now current in America, obviously based on the gratuitous belief that an allegorical explanation is in itself of higher quality than a non-allegorical one (whereas the true touchstone of any explanation is whether or not it actually "explains" convincingly and completely), a belief that in turn may represent an excessive reaction of over-compensation for traditional American qualities which have come to be felt in certain quarters as too pedestrian: good sense, matter-of-factness, realism. As for Marvell, the various ambiguities which Emerson, enthusiastically followed by some American critics, found in our poet can generally be discarded, after a close analysis, in favor of one explanation that alone fits the context. In other words, Marvell, like Góngora for whom Dámaso Alonso has found the key of understanding, is "difficult, but clear." Those poets ask from the reader the effort to make his way through the maze of ambiguities toward the unique true explanation. The critic who stops at pointing out several possible meanings has stopped halfway on the road that Marvell expected him to travel. To superimpose contemporary anarchy of meanings on Marvell's poetry is a blatant anachronism.

planation (the fawn is Christ [Bradbrook and Thomas] or the
stricken Anglican church [Douglas Bush, E. H. Emerson]);
a third that attempts to reconcile these two views by admitting
"religious overtones" without claiming that the "ground bass"
is religious (Karina Williamson and, it seems to me, Legouis
in his latest utterance: "la perte de son faon par une jeune
âme *religieuse*"; italics mine).

In this discussion critics have analyzed mainly the vocabulary
and the imagery of the poem according to its historic or stylistic
provenance, with the blind faith that the origin of the images
or motifs must decide implicitly the meaning of the poem. If Le-
Comte is able to prove the pagan origin of expressions such as
"nymph," "Diana's shrine," or of the central motif of the grief
for a pet that has been killed (in Ovid, Virgil,[2] etc.), he believes
that no religious meaning is implied in the poem. If, on the contrary, Miss Williamson has located the origin of the motifs
"fawn" or "feeding among lilies" in the Song of Songs,[3] she
is convinced that the meaning of the poem includes religious
overtones.

It has been for a long time my conviction that what I would
call "imagistic positivism" (the exaggerated reliance of contemporary critics on imagery to the detriment of other elements
of poetry) is likely to preclude the understanding of a poem
such as Marvell's in which structure, thought, psychology, must
play parts at least equal to imagery. In the case of our poem,
it strikes me as strange that none of the critics has analyzed
this from beginning to end as a structured whole whose parts
correspond to the phases of the psychological development of

[2] But why does he not mention also the ancient and Renaissance tradition of epitaphs for pets (Catullus, Martial, Navagero, Du Bellay,
Ronsard, etc.)?

[3] It may be noted, however, that the comparison in the Song of Songs
of the beloved with a roe or hart is not identical with Marvell's presentation of a deer as a lover: in the first case a human being is represented
with the freshness, unpurposiveness, and mystery of nature; in the second,
an animal in nature with the potentialities of feeling of human beings.
Surely the first is a more sensuous, the second a more spiritual approach
—and the second is the procedure of our metaphysical poet, who is following, as we shall see later, a medieval tradition.

the Nymph. This is the more indicated since T. S. Eliot has remarked that "the suggestiveness of the poem" is "the aura
around a bright clear center" (Marvell takes a "slight affair,
the feeling of a girl for her pet,"[4] and gives it a connection with
that "inexhaustible and terrible nebula of emotion which surrounds all our exact and practical passions"), which remark is
echoed by Miss Williamson: "The experience manifested in the
poem is felt to belong to the total of human experience."

But none of these critics tells us what exactly and actually
the "nebula of emotion" or the "total experience" of the Nymph
who has lost her fawn is, although that nebula of total experience seems to me clearly, if discreetly, indicated in the poem.
Whenever the critics think that a "slight affair" is treated with
enormous seriousness of tone, either the poem cannot be good
(but all critics are agreed as to the excellence of our poem), or
there must be a flaw in their understanding. In a good poem
form cannot go its own way, apart from content. Obviously,
then, the poem is not about a "slight affair"—how could it
possibly be if the end of the Nymph is that of Niobe?[5]

The protagonist of our poem is, indeed, not the fawn, but
the Nymph, who dies together with the fawn, and it is quite
incomprehensible why the critics have shown no curiosity as
to the reason why a young girl whose pet has died should herself have chosen death. To explain this reason, my analysis will
consist in simply repeating elements expressed in the poem as
well as in pointing out some elements that are only slightly, but
clearly, suggested in it. The delicate art of the poet has so willed
it that, in the inner monologue of the Nymph that is the poem,
the description of her pet reflects on her own character in indirect characterization, the increasing idealization of the fawn

---

[4] How does this assertion fit another, to be found later on in the article
on Marvell, emphasizing the "precise taste" of Marvell's which finds for
him the proper degree of seriousness for every subject which he treats?

[5] The presence of this ancient motif has been mentioned only in passing
by LeComte. Indeed, at the end of his article, when he comes to formulate
pointedly the role of Marvell's Nymph, he says that if she should be
given a name, it should be "Silvia rather than Pietà"—he should rather
have contrasted with the Pietà the ancient equivalent of a mourning
mother.

allowing inferences about the maiden who so idealizes it. It is the task of the commentator—a commentator who should be less a "professional" of literary criticism than a simple reader who asks relevant human questions[6]—to bring out clearly the deep tragedy of the Nymph. We are, indeed, given an indirect description of her feelings while the animal is dying (ll. 1-92), after its death (ll. 93-110), and before the death of the Nymph, when she is planning the consecration by a monument to her own as well as to the fawn's memory (ll. 111-22).

The poem starts with the address of the Nymph to the fatally wounded fawn in which she reveals her, as it were, modern attitude of revulsion against the wanton slaying of a harmless animal. That this is a passage significant for the history of ideas (or feelings) has been duly noted by Legouis, who devotes one and one-half pages to the rise and growth of this feeling as expressed in English literature. But I would point out two other, more personal, attitudes of the Nymph that are expressed in the first verse paragraph (ll. 1-24), both indicative of a feeling that her life has come to an end with the death of the fawn: that of evangelical forgiveness for the murderers of the pet—she does not "wish them ill," but prays for them, weeping (ll. 7-12)—and that of readiness to offer her own life as a sacrifice to the God of revenge (ll. 18-24). That this is indeed the meaning of these lines may perhaps be contested. Legouis translates (italics mine):

> Quand bien même ils laveraient leurs mains criminelles
> *dans ce sang chaud qui se sépare*
> *de ton cœur et dont la vue perce le mien,*
> ils ne pourraient se purifier: leur souillure
> est empreinte sur eux d'une pourpre trop éclatante.
> Il n'y a pas au monde *un autre animal*
> semblable qu'ils puissent offrir pour racheter leur péché.

---

[6] We have indeed come to the point where the quiet de-humanized professional of literary criticism considers it his duty to deal with "imagery" and similar specialized, technical, or philological questions, to the exclusion of the human element which is at the bottom of all poetry and consequently should inform philology, the humanistic science.

But if "this warm life-blood" were that of the fawn "which doth part/From thine" (understood as "thy heart," with "heart" taken from the following "wound me to the heart"), this anticipative ellipsis would seem rather difficult. More important, however, how should we understand that the criminals who killed the fawn would think, in order to become guiltless, of washing their bloody hands in the blood of their victim (would Lady Macbeth wash off her guilt in King Duncan's blood)? And how would the lines 23-24, which obviously allude to a sacrificial offering (a *deodand*), connect with the preceding lines, especially if "such another" meant an animal, as Legouis has it: in the preceding lines there was to be found only an allusion to criminals who wish to wash off their guilt.

Thus I am led to believe that in "this warm life-blood" the pronoun "this" represents the first person ("my") and means the warm blood of the Nymph who would wish to redeem (a new Iphigenia, as LeComte has seen) the spilt blood of the fawn, though to no avail for its murderers whose "stain" is irremovable.[7] With this explanation the lines "There is not such another in / The World to offer for their Sin" connect excellently with the thought of the preceding passage: "no other *being* (including me) could atone for that unique fawn." What strikes us here is that at the moment of the fawn's death the Nymph is already considering her own death, a death of expiation which she, however, seems to reject at this time because of her unworthiness. Thus this first part of the poem must be interpreted not only in the light of the history of ideas, but as a story of an extraordinary human being, the Nymph.

What this story has been we learn from the second paragraph (ll. 25-36): it is the story of her love for Sylvio, who betrayed her. We notice that between Sylvio and the troopers there exists a certain analogy (the vocatives *inconstant Sylvio—ungentle men*, underline this parallelism): both acted wantonly, cruelly,

[7] "This warm life-blood, which doth part / From thine" must then mean "which now departs [must depart] from thy life-blood"; "and wound me to the Heart" belongs rather together with "Though they should wash their guilty hands" (if they should wash . . . and wound me . . . , that is, kill me).

regardless of the "smart" of the girl; both killed, the one her young loving heart, the others the young object of her later love. Sylvio's frivolity appears in the words with which he accompanies his gifts, the fawn and the silver chain: "look how your Huntsman here / Hath taught a Faun to hunt his *Dear*"— words that made a deep impression on her at the time, but which gained an even stronger significance after Sylvio's breach of faith, as is indicated by the elaborate manner in which she reports these words:

> One morning (I remember well)
> . . . nay and I know
> What he said then; I'm sure I do.
> Said He. . . .

These simple words and this simple syntax carry a sense of convincingness and sincerity. What is more, the repetitious phrasing seems to imply that the maiden, even now, must make an effort not to wince at the hurting quality which those words still contain. She realizes, of course, in retrospect, that Sylvio spoke as a "huntsman" who saw the fawn in the light of his huntsmanship (as an animal trained to "hunt his *Dear*," to pursue her, frolic around her) and that she herself was for Sylvio the huntsman nothing but a quarry or a plaything.

Thus in his words, she now realizes, fate had spoken. What should we think of the puns in this passage (*dear—deer, heart—hart*)? They seem practically superfluous, but they are probably intended to characterize the ambiguous atmosphere of "huntsman's frivolity" which is proper to Sylvio's adventures.[8] The

---

[8] The puns may be considered within the framework of the other examples of metaphysical wit to be found in our poem and also within the framework of other puns to be found in the poetry of Marvell and Marvell's contemporaries. But, believing as I do that any stylistic device is an empty form which may be filled by most diverse contents, I should prefer to treat each manifestation of wit, puns, etc., *in situ*, in the precise situation in which it appears. It is the juncture of a particular *significandum* and *significatum* that gives precise meaning to any stylistic device (as well as to any linguistic utterance). Consequently, I feel entitled to treat the puns of the passage just mentioned separately from the other examples of wit which we shall find in our poem.

sober significance of lines 25-36 is that the early experience of the Nymph who suffered from her lover's faithlessness must be seen together with the love which will develop between her and the fawn: the one conditions the other. There is also an indication of a parallelism in the Nymph's and the animal's fate: both fall prey to wanton, cruel men. Although the Nymph's feelings for Sylvio are worded in a simple, untragic manner ("smart" is the only word that allows us to measure her grief), we may assume that a deep wound has existed in her since the time of Sylvio's betrayal.

There apparently followed upon the adventure with Sylvio, as the third paragraph suggests (ll. 37-46), a respite from grief, respite from deep feeling, in which the playful animal helped the Nymph to forget. The fawn first meant to her relaxation, a "content" in "idleness": the sportive nimbleness of the fawn invited her to the "game" of racing, of "hunting." But with the lines "it seem'd to bless / Its self in me" a new note is sounded. The happiness enjoyed by the animal in her company, within her atmosphere, could not be depicted more graphically than by the surprising reflexive use of the English verb "to bless" that I may translate by the Italian *bearsi* (which has a relation to *beato, beatitudine*, similar to that between *to bless oneself* and *bliss*). The fawn "called itself blessed," "found its delight, happiness, bliss in her."

Strangely enough, Miss Williamson has failed to list this extraordinary use of the verb "to bless" among the expressions with "religious overtones." It is first attested in 1611 in the biblical passage (Jeremiah 4:2) : "the nations shall bless themselves in him" [sc. God]. The pivotal line "it seem'd to bless / Its self in me" with its solemn (as if religious) ring marks the first sign of true love[9] that came to the Nymph and asked from her

---

[9] It must be noted that in the episode which, according to LeComte, constitutes the model of our poem, Virgil's *Aeneid*, VII, 475ff. (Sylvio's stag wounded by Ascanius; cf. also the story of Cyparissus in Ovid's *Metamorphoses*, X, 106ff., which is an imitation of the Virgilian passage), we find as the only active person the mistress who tames her stag and takes loving care of him (". . . soror omni Silvia cura / mollibus intexens ornabat cornua sertis / pectebatque ferum puroque in fonte lavabat"; cf. in Ovid:

the response of love. The wording of the next lines, again very
simple and truly convincing, "How could I less / Than love
it? / O I cannot be / Unkind," sounds apologetic: the Nymph
herself feels the momentum of the totally unexpected, sudden
inner development. The Nymph, who had experienced incon-
stancy and frivolity in love, has now received a new revelation,
that of pure, unsolicited, gratuitously, unselfishly offered, abiding love that developed imperceptibly, gradually, out of gaiety
and playfulness (the even flow of the lines in question mirrors
this development).

But, as the next paragraph (ll. 47-54) shows, the Nymph,
even at the moment of the fawn's death, is still not quite prepared to believe that the revelation of true love that was im-
parted to her was final: "Had it liv'd long" might the fawn
not have developed into another Sylvio? (We infer from the
lingering comparison and from the lingering doubt even at
this moment how deeply wounded by her first experience the
Nymph still is.) But no, she is now assured that the fawn's
love "was far more than the love of false and cruel men"
("cruel" being a word used by her now when she is able to
compare Sylvio and the fawn).

The next three paragraphs (ll. 55-92), the last of which ends
with the words "Had it liv'd long . . ." that gives the answer to the
question voiced there, are inspired by an ever-growing sureness about the significance of her love. In these paragraphs
Sylvio is finally forgotten, yet some of the Nymph's statements
suggest to the reader the contrast between then and now:

> It is a wond'rous thing, how fleet
> 'Twas on those little silver feet.
> With what a pretty skipping grace,
> It oft would challenge me the Race:

"tu [Cyparissus] pabula cervum / ad nova, tu liquidi ducebas fontis ad
. . . undam, / tu modo texebas varios per cornua flores. . .") . With Marvell
it is the fawn who has the active part: it is he, already trained by Sylvio,
who by his loving behavior makes his mistress love him. And, of course,
there can be no question in Virgil or Ovid of the animal becoming
superior to its mistress.

And when 't had left me far away,
'Twould stay, and run again, and stay.
For it was nimbler much than Hinds;
And trod, as on the four Winds.

We may contrast the fawn's "silver feet" with the "silver chain" given by Sylvio: now there is no need for a chain, since the fawn, more faithful than Sylvio, though it leaves the maiden temporarily, always returns to her, leaves her playfully to return faithfully.

The commentators who point out that lines 67-69 may be inspired by Pliny, and the expression "trod, as on the four Winds" by the Psalmist, have missed the main point: the contrast between the nimbleness given to the animal by nature and its unfailing conscientious returnings to its mistress (note the repeated *stay* in Marvell's wording and the repeated *fuga* in Pliny: with the latter, the stag runs—stays—runs; with the former it stays—runs—stays). When we read lines such as "It oft would challenge me the Race," we realize—and perhaps the Nymph realized it too at that point of her "Complaint"—that the fickle hunter's definition of the fawn has unexpectedly come true, only in another sense than was meant by him: the fawn has been trained to "hunt Sylvio's *Dear*," to hunt her "constantly."

The reader will note the lavish use of metaphysical wit in these paragraphs which are intended to extol the fawn's virtues and its beauty, qualities that become more and more of a supernatural kind as they transcend the Nymph's own virtues and beauty. The description proceeds by a comparison (or identification) of these virtues and beauties with those of other objects and beings in which they are traditionally embodied in undefiled purity. The fawn was nourished with milk and sugar by the fingers of the maiden—it became more white and sweet than this food (it acquires, in addition, sweet fragrance[10]) and its feet

---

[10] For Miss Williamson this is an echo of the Song of Songs: "his lips like sweet lilies, dropping sweet myrrh . . . his mouth is most sweet." But I find in the epitaph of the French Renaissance poet Du Bellay on the dog Peloton (in *Divers jeux rustiques*) the lines:

more soft and white than her (or any lady's) hand; it lies in a
bed of lilies and feeds on roses (so that its mouth will seem to
bleed)—had it lived longer, it could have become "Lilies without, Roses within."

This sequence of images which climaxes in this last "witty"
identification may have its origin in the Song of Songs, but its
function here is the metamorphosis of the animal into a paragon of virtues that are not found combined even in a human
being: the coolness of virginal chastity and the flame of ardent
love (the rose being the symbol of the latter—witness the fawn's
rose-kiss that seems to come from a bleeding heart). Wit, which
here, as always with Marvell, has a functional role, suggests
the possibility of a miracle: the possibility of moral or spiritual
qualities becoming sensuously perceptible as though they were
objects in outward nature in a καλοκἀγαθία of their own. A
miracle is after all nothing but the substantiation of the supernatural.[11]

Here I may permit myself a digression about metaphysical

> Peloton ne mangeoit pas
> de la chair à son repas:
> ses viandes plus prisees,
> c'estoient miettes brisees,
> que celui qui le paissoit
> de ses doigts ammollissoit:
> *aussi sa bouche estoit pleine*
> *toujours d'une douce haleine.*

[11] On the contrary, "poetic miracles" performed by a Marino have, it
seems to me, no supernatural connotations: with him the transformation
is from one sensuous object to another, more perfect in its sensuous
beauty. To choose an example, parallel to Marvell, in which a comparison
between animal and human body is involved:

> Mentre Lidia premea
> dentro rustica coppa
> a la lanuta la feconda poppa,
> i' stava a rimirar doppio candore,
> di natura e d'amore;
> nè distinguer sapea
> il bianco umor da le sue mani intatte,
> ch'altro non discernea che latte in latte.

Thanks to the alchemy of *amore*, the white hand of the beloved becomes
milk (milk that encompasses milk)—an entirely sensuous miracle.

wit in general. In T. S. Eliot's statements on this subject (espoused by Miss Williamson) one feels a certain embarrassment, as though he, who appreciates so highly 17th century wit, had not reached a description quite satisfactory to himself, when, after having set wit (but not entirely) apart from "erudition" and "cynicism," he writes the final sentence: "It involves, probably [!], a recognition, implicit in the expression of every experience, of the other experiences which are possible" (and this is basically the same idea as that, quoted above, on the "slight affair," supposedly treated in our poem, to which the poet would have added that "inexhaustible and terrible nebula of emotion" that surrounds all our "exact and practical passions").

But such a description of wit seems to me far too general: would the metaphysical poet add any other experience to the one he is treating?[12] Marvell envisages a metamorphosis of the fawn into lilies and roses, a very precise change related to its way of living, not some vague connection with, or nebula of, "other experiences." His metamorphosis seems to me based on a public belief in miracles whereby a supernatural development may not only become physically perceptible in beautiful forms, but may live a physical life of its own according to a precise pattern of psychological analogy. The fawn who lies in a bed of lilies and feeds on roses (that is, is pure as the lily and embodies, like the rose, the flame of love) may become lilies and roses

---

[12] Probably Eliot's description was prompted by the lines of Cowley on wit which he quotes:

> In a true piece of Wit all things must be
> Yet all things there agree . . .
> Or as the primitive forms of all
> (If we compare great things with small)
> Which, without discord or confusion, lie
> In that strange mirror of the Deity.

It seems to me that Father Ong was better inspired when, quoting the same lines of Cowley, he considered as a secondary result of a poetry that moves on higher and lower planes at the same time, what he calls the "omnivorousness" which enables wit poetry "to devour all sorts of experience in one gulp," "to digest all experience, raw if necessary, and make something of it."

because organic beings may, in a sort of mythological metabolism, become what they eat.

This is, of course, a miracle of the poet's making, but one that goes back historically[13] to medieval religious beliefs, according to which the spirituality of saints and martyrs acted in similar analogy on the physical world. Metaphysical wit has here simply laicized, and preserved in poetry, the substantiation of the supernatural current in hagiographic legend. To give but one example, borrowed from Curtius' *European Literature and the Latin Middle Ages* (appendix on "comic spirit in hagiography") : St. Lawrence, when grilled over the flames, is reported by St. Ambrose to have said to his torturers: "arsum est, versa et manduca" (my body is cooked, turn it to the other side and eat it)—the underlying idea being that the saint's supernatural fortitude was able to triumph over physical pain to the point that he could accept, in its most extreme form, the transformation of his flesh into meat to which, then, all the normal culinary procedures (the mechanics of cooking) and pleasures (the eating—which here becomes anthropophagy) may be applied, while his mind remains miraculously intact (able to formulate the physical miracle).

[13] This historical succession has been proved by Father W. J. Ong, S.J., in his classical article, "Wit and Mystery: A Revaluation in Medieval Latin Hymnody" (*Speculum*, xxii [1947], 310 ff.), who attests wit (including puns, paradoxes, etc.) in the hymns of Prudentius, Thomas Aquinas, Adam of St. Victor, used as a device to express certain paradoxical mysteries inherent in the Christian dogma (for example, the Tri-une Godhead). One facet of the same procedure is what I am treating here: wit expressing miracles, the miracle being different from the mystery in that the former constitutes a temporary interruption of the so-called laws of nature while the religious mystery is above those laws or underlying them.

The historical fact, stated by Eliot, that poetry of wit is absent from 18th and 19th century poetry may be explained in the same manner as the disappearance of allegory in those same centuries. At that time belief in the concrete reality of abstract qualities of perfection had become lost while previous centuries had retained from earlier medieval thought the capacity of thinking, at least poetically, of shapes into which perfection is able to materialize. In allegorical poetry, abstractions assume a body; in poetry of wit, abstract qualities concretize themselves in objects. With a renascence in the 20th century of abstract thought, as a reaction against the overcrowding material world, poetry of wit has been reinstated.

The comic spirit in hagiography is probably at the bottom of metaphysical wit. Just as, according to Bergson, all comic effect is a result of mechanization of the organic, in the process of living flesh becoming meat we are faced with a mechanization of a spiritual force—whose comic effect is, of course, different from other comic writing, surrounded as it is, at least for the believer, with awe. Some of this quasi-religious comic spirit or awesome wit (poetry being, as is so often the case, the re-enactment in secularized form of ancestral beliefs) is also present in Marvell's suggestion that the animal lying among lilies and feeding on roses may become all lilies and roses. Here the poetic miracle has inherited from the truly religious miracle its paradoxical logic, its psycho-physical analogy, and the mechanization of the spiritual (there is no "cynicism" involved in such a transfer).

The extension of the originally religious wit to secular subject matter[14] may have been encouraged by certain genres of pagan poetry that were revived in modern poetry, for instance, by the Ovidian metamorphosis: for the change of the fawn into lilies and roses is nothing but an Ovidian imagination. With Ovid such a metamorphosis would fancifully explain, according to a mythical, that is pre-scientific, science of analogy, the birth of an object or being in nature by means of a legendary event that once befell a human being (the cypress was originally the youth Cyparissus, the laurel was originally the nymph Daphne), the underlying idea being one of pantheism which "sees a nymph behind every tree." Certain analogies obtain between the form of the object in nature and the human situation that gave birth to it. With Ovid the change of forms is from the human to the non-

---

[14] What is called in English "metaphysical wit" is called in French *préciosité*, although the realization of this identity has not yet found its way into orthodox French literary history. The usual definition given for *précieux* passages: "une métaphore poussée jusqu'au bout" (*il en rougit, le traître*, said of a dagger; *brûlé de plus de feux que je n'en allumai*, said of a lover) would seem to suggest a futile automatic game, while in reality the "metaphor pushed to its extreme" originates in France as elsewhere in religious poetry (La Cépède, D'Aubigné, etc.) and has, even in its better-known secular variety, inherited something of that "miraculous psycho-physical parallelism" that is characteristic of the belief in the efficacy of spiritual forces. In that poetic world there exists a blushing of shame that may become indistinguishable from blood, a love whose flame is more consuming than actual fires multiplied.

human, the latter being anthropomorphized. When the Christian spirit moves the medieval and the Renaissance poets, their metamorphosis will emphasize the superhuman that is present in the physical: we will remember the medieval tradition (not lost in the Renaissance) of *Ovide moralisé* which will give to the pagan metamorphosis Christian religious or moral overtones (cf. the *Roman de la Dame à la Lycorne* mentioned below in note 15).

Thus Marvell's wit in our poem is located at the point of confluence of two powerful literary currents, Ovidian and Christian —no wonder that modern classifications of our poem, now as pagan, now as Christian, do violence to one-half of its inspiration since it participates in both currents. We shall find, in harmony with that Protean quality, inherited from Ovid, of poetry of wit, or its "omnivorousness," as Father Ong calls its ability "to attract into its orbit experiences on most various levels provided that they are brought together with a higher meaning"—we shall find in our poem several other examples of wit, of psychophysical analogy and change of forms, particularly in the scenes of the death and the afterlife of the fawn.

The death of the fawn (ll. 93-100) is surrounded by an atmosphere of beauty and virtue combined in a miracle. It is the death of a "saint" who, in spite of his "calm," is accessible to human emotions to the point of shedding tears, tears of farewell to love (as it appears from the comparison with the tears of the "brotherless *Heliades*"). And the tears will become beautiful substances: wit will compare them, in their fragrance and visual beauty, with "gumme," "frankincense," and "amber" (the last of which, suggested by Ovid's metamorphosis of the sisters of Phaëthon, has probably given the impulse to the series of analogies).[15] It is the acme of metaphysical wit that the liquid

---

[15] The coupling of Christian with pagan elements, which I mentioned above as characteristic of our poem, is reflected by the outspoken reference to a metamorphosis of Ovid (the Heliades) following immediately after the expression "holy frankincense" which points to Christian church service.

The lack of nuances in the poetic sensibility of those critics who decide for an "either-or" in our poem may be explained in part by their unfamiliarity with medieval lay poetry that combines the worldly and the

substances into which the tears of the fawn have been changed can themselves be presented anthropomorphically: "So weeps the wounded Balsome." In the world of poetic identification of opposites the road between human being and thing may be traveled in both directions. The final identification of the flowing tears with solid amber suggested to the poet a further "substantification" of the tears of the animal, their congealing into "two crystals" (each representing one eye of the fawn), a jewel, as it were, a thing of beauty that will forever preserve the essence of the transient moment of the fawn's death, a pagan relic to be offered in a golden vial (which should also contain the Nymph's tears, that are less "crystallized" and "overflow" its brim) to Diana's shrine. It is only at this moment and by this gesture that our realization that the destiny of the fawn and of its mistress is one and the same becomes final. Both being too sublime for this world of wantonness and cruelty, both victims of their own purity, they belong together forever like their tears that will be preserved in the shrine of chastity.

---

unworldly to a degree unbelievable for us moderns; for instance, in the 14th century French *Roman de la Dame à la Lycorne et du Chevalier au Lyon*, we find the story of the love of a noble lady, who is a paragon of virtue and grace, for a courageous and virtuous knight. This story is replete with romantic adventures à la Chrétien de Troyes of one of whose heroes the knight riding on a lion is reminiscent—while the *dame à la lycorne* rides the unicorn which equals her in virtue (ed. Gennrich, ll. 183 ff.):

> ... par ce qu'est [la dame] de tout biens affinee
> *Jhesu Christ* volt, que li fust destinee
> *Unne merveille*, que chi vus conterai:
> C'est d'une bieste, que *Diex* donna l'otrai,
> Et tel franchise e si tres grant purté
> Il li donna, qu'ele avoit en vilté
> Tous vilains visces ...
> Pour ce donna a la dame tel don
> *Li Diex d'Amours*, que tous temps aroit non:
> La dame blanche qui la Lycorne garde
> Qui onc nul teps de mal faire ne tarde. ...

Here then, in a medieval secular, if moralizing, love story, it is Christ and Amor who give to the perfect lady the animal that, in bestiaries and tapestries alike, was thought to embody Christ. The evidently present "religious overtones" do not guarantee the presence of a religious poem.

In the whole description of her relationship with the living
animal the Nymph has kept herself in the background, minimiz-
ing the depth of her feeling and indeed comparing herself disad-
vantageously with the animal (she "blushed" at its whiteness).
Even in death the white fawn will transcend her: for while her
own final destiny is not mentioned, she is assured that he will
dwell in Elysium with the other white animals that embody
purity. The animal that has "stayed" with her (faithfully) is
asked not to "run too fast" toward Elysium (l. 109)—a graceful
conceit: even in death the deer will preserve its natural fleetness.
And even in the monument to be erected after her death the
figure of the fawn will be of "alabaster" that never can be "as
white as thee," but whiter than the "marble" that will perpetuate her own figure. While the relationship between mistress and
animal will be expressed by the position of the fawn's image at
her feet (just as on medieval tombstones traditionally faithful
dogs lie at the feet of their masters), the mistress will remain
forever the human mourner rather than the traditional owner.
The Nymph will become a Niobe,[16] endowed, if not with the
boastfulness, with the disconsolate feelings of that "unhappy"
mother. Her evolution, which began with simple delight and
enjoyment of a graceful young being, after having reached the
depth of true love, ends in the grief of a bereaved mother. Her
tears (that overflow all boundaries) will petrify into the statue
that weeps, that is "engraved" by her tears: the two aspects of
grief, the feeling of numbness and of dissolution, are brought
together in the image of the stone-that-weeps.[17]

[16] Niobe was killed by the arrows of the two children of Leto whom
she had offended, Apollo and Diana—we may surmise that it was Diana
who killed Marvell's Nymph out of pity for her fate.
[17] We witness here the paradoxical coupling of two opposite attitudes
as before when "cold virginity" and "ardent love" were found combined
in the fawn. Already in Ovid, *Metamorphoses*, vi, 303 ff., we find:

> deriguitque malis . . .
> . . . intra quoque viscera saxum est:
> Flet tamen . . .
> . . . et lacrimas etiam nunc marmora manant.

But the "witty" idea of the statue being "sculptured" by the Nymph's
tears belongs, of course, to Marvell.

This tragic story could be called in modern (Freudian) terms one of frustration overcome by sublimation[18]—and as such it would verge on comedy, replacement of love for a person by love for an animal (the stock situation in which old spinsters are involved) coming dangerously close to the grim caricature of Flaubert's *Un cœur simple*. But Marvell has placed this story of disillusionment within a baroque setting of sad beauty,[19] a metamorphosis of ancient tradition being overlaid by the feeling for the transiency of things earthly. The *lacrimae rerum* are made to crystallize into things of beauty that commemorate tragedy (the statue, the crystals in the golden vial), just as in another, typically baroque and conceptual, poem of Marvell's, disillusionment becomes beauty, tears become jewels:

> What in the world most fair appears,
> Yea, even Laughter, turns to tears;
> And all the Jewels which we prize
> Melt in these pendants of the Eyes.

We understand now the particular tone of our "Complaint" in which the protagonist tells her story in an "inner monologue" of rather simple, direct words which contrast with the sophisticated examples of metaphysical wit.[20] This stylistic contrast reflects

[18] In Gottfried of Strassburg's medieval romance *Tristan und Isold* we have perhaps a story reminiscent of that of Marvell, though leading to a quite different conclusion. With Gottfried, the absent Tristram, thinking faithfully of Isold and reflecting how he could relieve her loneliness, sends her the graceful dog, Petitcreü, a dog possessed of miraculous qualities, about whose neck is hung on a chain a bell with a tone so sweet that all who hear it forget their grief. But Isold, unwilling to forget her grief while Tristram is unable to forget his own, finally decides to tear the marvelous bell from the chain of the dog—which thereby loses immediately its miraculous power. By parallel wording the poet emphasizes the exemplary behavior of these two faithful lovers who refuse consolation: Tristram "who has given up his joy and his life to grief . . .", Isold "the faithful, constant one who has given up her life to longing and to Tristram."

[19] Another baroque combination of sadness and beauty consists in presentation of the beauty of the world as undermined by transiency (the motif of "sic transit gloria mundi").

[20] To that rather modern technique belong those temporal elements in the spoken complaint that mark the passing of time ("The wanton

the inner contrast between sadness and beauty: the sadness of disillusionment is reflected convincingly by the simple speech, not unknown to Marvell, while the miraculous metamorphosis into sensuous beauty finds its expression in the mirages of wit.[21]

Troopers . . . / *Have shot* my Fawn"; "Oh help! o help! *I see* it faint"; "Now my Sweet Fawn *is vanish'd*", "for *I / Will but bespeak* thy Grave"). It may very well be that the second passage just quoted reflects the *auxilium vocat* of Silvia in the *Aeneid*, but Marvell has fitted it into the, as it were, temporal economy of the "Complaint."

[21] After having handed in this article to the *MLQ*, I read a study of our poem by D. C. Allen, published in *ELH*, xxiii (June 1956). I am pleased to note that he considers the fawn a *surrogatus amoris*, but he fails to follow through in detail the development of the motif in the poem and rather concentrates on the history of the *topoi* that went into its composition (without mentioning, however, the—for me essential—parallel of Niobe).

CHAPTER VII

....

Understanding Milton*

....

I REGRET that I must write this article which is directed polemically against my distinguished colleague in philosophy at The Johns Hopkins University, George Boas, a man whose elegance of thought, whose independence of mind, urbanity, wit, and cultivation I have learned deeply to appreciate—but "amicus Plato, magis amica veritas." And my article will be directed against a certain trend in philosophical esthetics, a speculative branch of the humanities before which I, as a practical philologist, have always stood in awe—but "amica philosophia, magis amica philologia." For I must write this article because I feel that Professor Boas' trend of thought threatens to shake the basis, not only of my personal *religio philologi*, but of all philological endeavor. If Boas is right in his assertions—then philology has no right to existence. I am conscious of the pitfall involved in this situation: everyone who writes about his faith is apt to assume an air of hypocritical naïveté or self-righteous saintliness while the iconoclast has sincerity, penetrating intelligence, and wit on his side. But I hope I may overcome this danger by close reasoning.

Whereas all philology rests on the assumption that all men on earth are basically alike and that the modern commentator is enabled, by his training and studiousness, to approximate and, perhaps, restore, the original "meaning" of a work of art composed at another time and place, Professor Boas' thesis, expressed in an article entitled "The Problem of Meaning in the Arts" (in "Meaning and Interpretation," Univ. of Cal. Pub. in Philosophy XXV [1950], 301-25), is that meaning in art is "problematical": the idea that there must be in existence a meaning in the work of art in the form either of a message to the

* From *Hopkins Review*, 1951, IV, 4, 16-27.

reader (or beholder) or of a deliberate intention on the part of the artist is simply not tenable, he tells us—and the actual development of our contemporary "unintelligible" art would seem to favor such a thesis. Especially is it true of poetry, he continues, that "there exist experiences which escape language": given the "ineffableness of the unique" and man's incapacity of "expressing any specific quality whatsoever," the result must be that the precise meaning of a poem cannot be brought home to the reader. Before proceeding to show us that in the last forty years the singular experiences of man have increased to a degree unheard of before and that consequently the arts expressing these experiences must become more and more inaccessible to the average public, Boas opens up before us a historical diptych: that of Shakespeare and Milton. While Shakespeare's sonnets are generally understandable and owe this advantage to his lack of personal expression, Milton is, evidently, thought by Boas to be on the way toward modernity in that he strives to communicate more personal experiences, assimilable only by the—relatively rare—readers who, in addition to knowing his biography, would have had experiences similar to his:

"Let us imagine that we are artists and that the focus of such experience is . . . a natural occurrence: falling in love, climbing a mountain, frustration, conflict, what you will. One does not simply fall in love; one falls in love with a given woman at a given time in given circumstances in spite of given obstacles. One climbs a specific mountain, is frustrated in satisfying a definite desire, is in conflict with a particular person or group or natural force, within specific restrictions. Did any poet ever write a poem on being in love with anyone whomsoever? Such a piece of literature would be a treatise on erotogenesis, certainly of great scientific interest, but by its very nature of but limited individual relevance. The love sonnets of Shakespeare come about as close to this as any poems which I have been able to find, plucking the same strings as had been plucked by countless Italian poets before him. His loneliness, his longing, his delight are expressed in the most general terms, made vivid only by his similies and metaphors and music. To this very day, in spite of the scratching and digging of pedants—and whose verses have been studied more than Shakespeare's?—we do not know whom he was addressing, nor what kind of person it was, nor even whether it was a man or a woman or both. The Lauras, Corinnas, Sylvias, Lesbias of such poems have become tags which help us to find the verses which we want in an index. They have but that minimum of personality which we can reconstruct from the poems addressed to them. They are cruel, taunting, faithless, cold, fickle, but such adjectives are but the faintest adumbration of a soul. This is why, one imagines, such poems are called universal in their appeal, eternal in their themes. They approach the generality of mathematics as a limit and hence can be understood by all who read.

"How great a contrast one finds in such a sonnet as Milton's on his dead wife, brought to him like Alcestis from the grave! But it should be observed that this poem would be as opaque as wood, did we not know something of Milton's biography. Were we ignorant of his blindness, how could we possibly understand the terminal couplet?

> But O as to embrace me she enclin'd
> I wak'd, she fled, and day brought back my night.

Should the time come when Milton's biography would be lost, then doubtless some critic would arise to point out that to Milton dreams were more real than waking life, and we should wonder at his remarkable ability to recall and write down the details of what he dreamt. But we have not reached that condition of ignorance and consequently we utilize what we know of the poet's biography to help us interpret what he saw and felt when he dreamed of Katherine Woodcock. And when we go further and learn that he never actually saw this woman, having married her after his blindness came upon him, the poem takes on still another color, for we now see and possibly feel the greater pathos of the blind man's reaching after his dead wife in a dream. But unless we are blind ourselves, unless we have suffered a similar loss, unless we have striven to justify the ways of God to man, dictating the expression of our thoughts and emotions to rather indifferent daughters, how can we say that we have completely understood the meaning of those fourteen lines? We can symbolize it only as a blind-man's-experience-of-dreaming-of-his-dead-wife-whom-he-had-never-seen, and few of us can pretend to having shared in so singular an adventure."

I must question the starting point of Boas' reasoning: "this poem[1] would be as opaque as wood, did we not know something of Milton's biography." For the case, postulated by Boas, in which Milton's sonnet would have come to a posterity ignorant of the facts of his life, one of two possibilities would obtain: either our poem would have survived alone, or the whole collection of poems in which it is included would have been preserved.

Let us consider the first possibility. It is true that the poem "Methought . . . ," thus isolated, would not allow us to infer therefrom the fact of its author's blindness. But would it therefore be to us "opaque as wood"? Surely the poem as it stands offers immediately a quite satisfactory and coherent meaning: one as self-evident as is that to be found in the poem of the Italian 15th century poet Giovanni Pontano "Pontanus uxorem Ariadnam in somnis adloquitur" (which, I suggest, might not have been unknown to Milton) :

[1] For the convenience of the reader, I shall place here the text of the poem:

> Methought I saw my late espoused Saint
>   Brought to me like *Alcestis* from the grave,
>   Whom *Joves* great Son to her glad Husband gave,
>   Rescu'd from death by force though pale and faint.
> Mine as whom washt from spot of child-bed taint,
>   Purification in the old Law did save,
>   And such, as yet once more I trust to have
>   Full sight of her in Heaven without restraint,
> Came vested all in white, pure as her mind:
>   Her face was vail'd, yet to my fancied sight,
>   Love, sweetness, goodness, in her person shin'd
> So clear, as in no face with more delight.
>   But O as to embrace me she enclin'd
>   I wak'd, she fled, and day brought back my night.

Nocte quidem, coniunx, tecum vagor et tua mecum
  umbra venit; sic nox luxque diesque mihi est.
Luce autem sine te tenebris obversor et ipse
  me sine sum; sic lux nox tenebraeque mihi est.
O valeant luces, lateat sol; sic mihi, coniunx,
  vives, sic moriar vivus et ipse tibi . . .[2]

I submit that Pontano's experience "sic lux nox . . . mihi est" is
basically Milton's: for the bereaved husband, the nocturnal
vision of his wife alone can replace the life of day enjoyed by his
fellowmen. The same paradoxical inversion of day and night on
the part of one bereaved is also found in Petrarch (whom Pontano in turn may have remembered): ed. Chiorboli, no.
CCLXXXII:

Alma felice, che sovente torni
  A consolar le mie notti dolenti
  Con gli occhi tuoi, che Morte non à spenti,
  Ma sovra 'l mortal modo fatti adorni,

Quanto gradisco che' miei tristi giorni
  A rallegrar de tua vista consenti!
  Cosí comincio a ritrovar presenti
  Le tue bellezze a' suoi usati soggiorni.[3]

[2] Pontanus Addresses His Wife Ariadne in a Dream
At night, o wife, with thee I wander and
thy shade accompanies me; thus dark night for me is light and
  day;
But in day-light without thee I am wrapped in darkness
and I myself am without myself; thus the day is for me night and
  darkness.
O farewell, light, let the sun be hidden; thus wilt thou
be alive for me, o wife, and I will die, while yet alive, for thee.

 [3] O blessed soul who often returnest
  to console my painful nights
  with those eyes that Death has not extinguished,
  eyes become splendid beyond the mortal way,
  I do thank thee that thou hast deigned
  to cheer with the sight of thee my sad days!
  Thus I begin once more to see present before me
  thy charms at their accustomed place.

Here we find in line 2 a *notti* which would seem to be contradicted by the *giorni* of line 5; but as Castelvetro (and later commentators, cf. the note of Chiorboli)[4] proposes: "P.[etrarch] is speaking of his days which, deprived as they are of the sight of Laura, are for him perpetual nights."

Milton then, in my opinion, has written a poem perfectly understandable without the hypothesis of blindness, indeed one repeating a poetic pattern familiar to other poets of the Renaissance (enjoying unimpaired vision!),[5] but to this he has added a new element, a poignant and perspicacious observation absent from the more intellectualistic poems of his predecessors and truly revelatory of his insight into the nature of dreams: the gentle and loving movement, on the part of the wife of the dream, of coming closer to her husband, bending down to him to embrace him, means the destruction of the sweetest of dreams. It is as though the world of dreams did not permit the bodily contact (suggested by the dream itself) of the quick and the dead. And the poet must sharply and painfully perceive the forbidding rigor of the barriers between the dream world and that of reality in which he must live on in irremediable loneliness; moreover, given the suggested parallel between his dead wife and Beatrice[6] who in the beyond became the embodiment of Charity and Virtue

[4] Chiorboli, it is true, thinks that *notti* refers to true nights (the appearances of Laura at night) and that *giorni* means "my days, my life." But it is not impossible that Pontano gave the poem the same interpretation as Castelvetro.

[5] With Milton himself, we find this pattern applied to the description of (the end of) Adam's vision (*Par. Lost*, VIII, 478): "She disappear'd, *and left me dark,* I wak'd."

[6] Milton's conception of his dead wife is indeed more Dantean than Petrarchian: in the last stanza of the sonnet on Laura quoted above, the poet seeks to see his deceased Beloved as a human person, as the person she was on this earth:

> Sol un riposo trovo in molti affanni,
> Che, quando torni, *te* conosco, e' ntendo
> A l'andar, a la voce, al volto, a' panni.

> One solace I find in my many tribulations:
> That when thou dost return I know thee and I sense that
>   thou art thee
> By thy step, by thy voice, by thy face, by thy rainment.

("my late espoused Saint"; "purification"; "love, sweetness, goodness"), these barriers serve to separate the world of the Ideal and this sublunar world where he must dwell—until the day when he may have "full sight" of his Beatrice, without veils, "in Heaven without restraint." In our poem Milton presents himself as a Christian Platonist who experiences the harrowing realization that, for all his craving for reunion with the Ideal, in this life there exists no intermediary realm between Earth and Heaven. This was evidently a truth which Milton ratified in his waking hours and if he portrays in the poem his hopes and disillusionment, it is in order to proclaim the harsh necessity for dreams to recede before reality—quite the reverse of the interpretation proposed by Boas (as the only alternative for a reader ignorant of Milton's blindness): "that to Milton dreams were more real than waking life."[7] Milton has evoked the dream in order to insist on its inevitable ending: the return to sober, disillusioned waking life—this is the attitude of what Milton's Spanish contemporaries would have called *desengaño*.[8]

Thus the sonnet "Methought" stands as a perfectly meaningful artistic unit even for a reader who may know nothing of

[7] As to the continuation of Boas' sentence "[if we had no biography of Milton] we should wonder at his remarkable ability to write down the details of what he dreamt": Dante had the same ability which he explains to us with the graphic metaphor of "copying" from the "book of memory"—and even men less poetic than Dante are able to note the details of a dream vividly dreamt!

[8] Something similar has been felt and expressed by Mr. Fitzroy Pyle in an article to be quoted later, only his feeling is blurred by the idea that what separates Milton from his wife is blindness: ". . . when he imagines that she bends down to kiss him *and so to reveal her face*, his fancy cannot cheat so well as one might wish, and he is tolled back from her to his sole self. That we are reminded of the conclusion of Keats' *Ode* is not fortuitous, for both poems are examples of willing surrender to but partially directed idealizations of fancy; yet it is typical of Milton's habitual certitude of mind that even in the dream state he will not *endow the visionary figure with a face supplied by guess-work*." The two passages I have put in italics should be replaced, in my opinion, by *and so to be one with him as husband and wife are one on earth* and *blur the frontiers between this and the other world*. But it is true that at the end of both this poem of Milton's and of Keats' *Ode to the Nightingale* a motif of *desengaño* is present.

Milton's blindness, as would be the case according to our first alternative (this poem alone surviving). According to our second alternative, however (the poem handed down together with the whole collection of Milton's poems to a posterity still ignorant of the "biography" of the poet, as is Boas' supposition), it is doubtful whether a reader could remain ignorant of the fact of Milton's blindness, given the position of our poem in the collection: it appears in our editions after the sonnets "When I consider how my light is spent" and "To Mr. Cyriac Skinner. Upon his blindness." Since we may suppose that the poet has expected us to read his poems in the order in which he has printed them, this must mean that he wished his reader to know that he was blind —and the last line of the sonnet "Methought" was intended to contain a second meaning, superimposed on the first (the first being the meaning, so to speak, of the poem as an isolated unit, the second that of the poem within the collection): the "night" is not only "the night of my days without her," but also "the night of blindness" (the night of the blindness which is actually Milton's).

Thus, in awakening from a vision in which he had enjoyed both the light of the shining presence of his "Saint" and the light of his own "fancied sight," he falls into darkness piled on darkness—a revelation which comes to us in the last word of the poem as shock upon shock. And the impact of this shock comes, in my opinion, only from the fact that we have not been prepared for the poem to take this turn by any previous allusion (only when reading the last word "night" is the reader reminded of Milton's blindness of which he had read in two previous sonnets). For I do not believe, as do other commentators, that allusions to blindness are contained in line 10: "her face was vail'd" or in line 8: "without restraint." As to the veiled face of the wife in the dream, did not—a fact known to all commentators—Euripides present Alcestis (to whom indeed Milton alludes in the first stanza) as veiled when returning from the netherworld to an Admetus who was surely not blind?[9] Whether

[9] We could have to do here also with a reminiscence of Dante's second Canzone in the Vita Nuova, where the dead Beatrice appears clad in a veil—as a sign of humility.

or not Milton was influenced by this detail in Euripides we cannot know. In any case, the veil surely has a positive function in our sonnet: that of foreshadowing, while withholding, the perfect heavenly bliss that is to come in the eternal future: now, on this earth, Milton sees his wife purified from any earthly stain, as the embodiment of virtue and charity, but veiled because his inner eyes, his "fancied sight" (not his physical [blind] eyes) are still unable fully to apperceive a Saint; then, in heaven, he will have "full sight" of her (as opposed to the veiled appearance) "without restraint" (without limitation of time—forever, not only one moment as in the dream—by no means "without the restraint of blindness") ; "for now we see through a glass darkly; but then face to face; now I know in part, but then shall I know even as also I am known" (I Cor. 13:12).[10] No commentator, as far as I know, has seen the tripartite *crescendo* arrangement in our sonnet, reminiscent of the poem "At a solemn Musick":

I. The ancient pagan tradition represented by Alcestis: Alcestis comes back from the Tartarus "pale and faint" (the souls are shadows in Virgil's *Aeneid*)

II. the ancient Jewish tradition ("the old Law") represented by the physical (ritualistic) purification of woman:
"mine" (my wife, as opposed to Alcestis) returns purified from the flaw of womanhood as such ("childbed taint")

[10] In the lines "And such, as yet *once more* I trust to have/Full sight of her in Heaven without restraint," the *once more* suggests to Professor Parker (cf. note 13) that "full sight" had, once before, been vouchsafed Milton (ergo, the figure must represent Mary Powell) ; if, for our part, we interpret "full sight" in a spiritual sense, must not this suggest (the impossible conclusion) that Milton had, already on this earth, enjoyed that consummation which, however, can be realized only in Heaven? The fact is that it is impossible, in any interpretation, to see in *once more* an opposition to "once before," else, "once more . . . in Heaven" is nonsense. We evidently must assume a slightly illogical use of *once more*, or rather, a telescoping of two coordinated statements: "I hope to see her once more"—and "then, in Heaven, with full sight, without restraint."

· 124 ·

III. the Christian tradition represented by the physical and
moral purity of the Saints and the hope tendered to
man of rebirth and reunion with the latter:
the Christian wife returns "pure as her mind," "love,
sweetness, goodness in her person shin'd so clear, as
in no face with more delight"

Thus, in a continuous rising movement, extending up to line 12,
we were allowed to glimpse ever brighter and clearer light and
bliss (from legend to the religion of Law to the religion of
Charity)—only to be precipitated, in the last two lines, back into
the abyss of the darkness of earthly life. This is truly a baroque
poem of *desengaño* with its violent contrasts of light and darkness, of heavenly dream and crushing reality.

Looking back now to the beginning of the sonnet, we realize
the harsh contrast between the world of the Greek myth and the
Christian world[11] of Milton; while with Euripides Jove's son
Heracles possessed the "force" to wrest Alcestis from the grave,
Milton is powerless to incorporate into his life the dream of the
Ideal. *But O . . .*—with these two short, but heart-rending words
the announcement of his disillusionment is prepared to be completed in the final line: "I awak'd, she fled, and day brought
back my night," whose rhythm is, paradoxically, reminiscent of
Caesar's triumphant "veni vidi vici." For Milton there can be
no triumph of the ancient heroic sort! In Euripides' tragedy the
hero is Heracles, the conqueror of death, not Alcestis,[12] who,

[11] We may note that in the triptych Greece-Judaism-Christianity the
second "panel" is the most subdued of the two: not only are Judaism
and Christianity woven into one (Judeo-Christian) pattern by the pronoun *mine* ("*my* wife") so neatly opposed to Alcestis, but also the Jewish
intermezzo is reduced to two lines (in comparison with the whole
quatrain given to the Greek scene).

[12] We will remember that Alcestis with Euripides returns from the
Tartarus veiled, does not speak a single word, and has, so to speak, no
longer any personality after her forces were spent in the sacrifice of
her departure from this world where one is allowed to "see the light of
the sun."—It remained for the Italian poet Alfieri to change Alcestis
outright into a Christian saint whose return to earth, after her sacrificial
death, is made to foreshadow the bliss of heaven. Cf. Lilo Ebel, "Die
italienische Kultur und der Geist der Tragödie" (Freiburg i. B. 1948),
117.

though revived, must be forever a "pale and faint" shadow; in Milton's vision, however, the Christian *Beatrix* from the beyond plays an active role—even though her gentle gesture cannot quite reach him: while showing himself reduced to helplessness in contrast with Heracles, Milton has glorified the intercessory attitude of the Christian woman, which, owing to the cruel separation existing between the two worlds, is not allowed to come to fruition.

In view of this grandiose picture of man between two separated worlds how irrelevant[13] would be the personal detail that Milton was blind at the time of his second marriage and hence had never seen his wife! Such a subject could theoretically have appealed to Milton only if he had approached it from a symbolical viewpoint: he perhaps would have insisted on the limitation of our physical senses concomitant with the power of the human imagination which may grasp the superhuman aspects of a human being, of the "human face divine" (*Par. Lost*, III, 44)— but this would be a quite different poem and it is indeed one Milton has not written. We are forced by evidence outside of our given poem (but found within the collection of Milton's

[13] I owe to a student of mine, Mr. Karl Denner, knowledge of the discussion engaged between Messrs. W. R. Parker and Fitzroy Pyle in *Review of English Studies*, XXI (1945), 235 and XXV (1949), 57, about the identity of the "late espoused Saint" in our poem, Parker opting for Mary Powell, Pyle for—the traditionally accepted—Katherine Woodcock. While I believe biographical evidence to be overwhelmingly in favor of the latter identification (*late espoused Saint* must mean "recently married"), both writers (perhaps Mr. Pyle less than Mr. Parker) treat the poem only in view of their extra-poetic program of identification, not as a self-contained organism. Thus the detail of "purification from child-bed taint" is interpreted in view of the question, whether it applies better to Katherine Woodcock or to Mary Powell in the light of the "threescore and five days of purification" prescribed by Leviticus 12— there is no realization that the main motif for the insertion of the two lines alluding to Leviticus was precisely the triptych, mentioned in the text: Paganism—*Old Law*—New Dispensation. Again, both writers are agreed that physical blindness is the "restraint" or "veil" which prevents the poet from seeing his wife fully in the dream—there is no realization with them that the vision in the dream serves only to foreshadow the reunion in Heaven and therefore must include "veils" and "restraint."

poems) to recognize only the motif of the poet's blindness as a second meaning added on to the first.

But in so doing, we must realize that the main theme and the only problem of the sonnet "Methought" is not, as Boas would make it appear, the problem of Milton's blindness (nor that of the death of his wife), but the generally human problem of the Ideal in our world (and in this respect, as we have seen, our sonnet is as greatly determined by literary tradition—this time the tradition of the *donna angelicata* borrowed from the Italian poets of the *dolce stil nuovo*, from Dante and Petrarch[14]—as are the love sonnets of Shakespeare, who "plucks the same strings as had been plucked by countless Italian poets before him"). And the detail of blindness, which in Milton's personal life was a cruel physical fact, is made to serve in our poem only a "metaphorical" function, suggesting, as it does, our actual world deprived of the Ideal—to serve as a metaphor not essentially different, in its subservience to the "general," from those used by Shakespeare in order to make "vivid," as Boas says, the "general" feeling of love.

That the true meaning of the poem "Methought" can be grasped only by a reader who has experienced blindness and that the specific physical sensations of a blind man were of any importance to the poet, is utterly refuted by the two sonnets devoted precisely to his blindness—wherein we find this condition referred to briefly and in the most general terms ("my sight is spent," the world has become "dark"), accessible to any member of the human community, the main emphasis being placed on the *moral* problems involved in this condition.[15] When faced with the sonnet "Methought,"

---

[14] Milton's sonnet shows its debt to this tradition also by the quite exterior detail of repeating in its first line the opening phrase of another famous English poem of a Petrarchian nature: Sir Walter Raleigh's "Methought I saw the grave where Laura lay."

[15] Even in the beginning of *Par. Lost*, canto III, where Milton does expatiate on the effects of his blindness, we are offered as it were a quite dispassionate inventory of outward objects he cannot see, from which he immediately turns, in what is equivalent to the traditional "invocation of the Muse," to an appeal to the "celestial light" which will allow him to grasp the "things invisible to mortal sight."

then, the "Poor-blind-twice-widowed-Milton-wrote-this-poem-in-a-dreary-apartment-alone-with-his-small-children" school of thought (Masson *et al*) must definitely yield to that of the less sentimental and more factual literary historians concerned with the *dolce stil nuovo* of Dante and Petrarch. Not only is the reader of the sonnet not obliged to speculate about the probable complexities of Milton's empirical life outside of the poem; he is obliged not to so speculate.

It is a quite illegitimate procedure, one most detrimental to any *explication de texte* (although widely current with our academic positivism),[16] to "utilize" indiscriminately "what we know of the poet's biography," because this may destroy the artistic framework carefully devised by the poet: the boundary between art and life which he perhaps may have wished to erect—and which any classical poet would be apt to erect. Professor Boas is disappointed by Shakespeare's "mathematical" generality in his love poems mainly because this poet has succeeded (aided therein by the fruitlessness of all "pedantic" investigations) in keeping us in the dark about the particular persons to whom he addressed his sonnets; Boas is more at home with Milton, who has at least himself half-lifted the veils from his autobiography (his biographers, also, having been successful in uncovering the facts of his life), but not quite happy because the singular experiences of the historical Milton make it difficult for us to know exactly what "he saw and felt when he dreamed of Katherine Woodcock." To me the brusque introduction of the matter-of-fact, opaque name Katherine Woodcock[17] into the transparent

[16] For the delicate art of reading, which consists in continuous acts of rejection and admission according to the context, we are prepared by our universities only insofar as word usage is concerned: that *late* in line 1 of Milton's sonnet must be interpreted in harmony with Milton's general word usage would be readily admitted by all our schools—which, however, biographically biased as they are, would not caution us against illicit usage of auctorial biography.

[17] This is a regression to the positivistic ideals of past generations who discussed Dante's Beatrice in terms of Beatrice Portinari. One may ask the biography-minded literary critic what he will do in cases when the poet has willfully distorted his own biography in his poems (for instance, in the case of Pontano, the austere and forbidding public servant who represents himself in his poetry as an erotomaniac)—or when he offers

and transcendent atmosphere of our poem is as shocking as the whole proposition of making the poem more empirically concrete than it has been conceived. The poem should, in my opinion, be apperceived *half-concretely* as it was intended to be. Such is the tact and discipline required from the reader, who should not indulge in unwarranted psychological or historical curiosity, but should abdicate such inquiry when it is nocive to artistic apperception.

Boas' thesis is tantamount to a repudiation of all classical art which prefers the general to the specific, a repudiation of the greater part of our Western tradition. One may justly appreciate the historical necessities which, since the period of Romanticism, have brought about the fascination with the specific and the concrete in art, and I fully share Boas' opinion, expressed in an eloquent page [p. 319], that the modern artist cannot go back in his production to the relatively simple patterns of Enlightenment and of the Middle Ages. But that the modern *appreciation* of the art of *former* times should be dictated by the tenets of art as our artists of today understand it, is to me a *non sequitur*. If Boas is to a certain extent justified in writing: "it is certainly false that all men and all societies and all times are essentially alike; they are superficially similar; all men, to be sure, fall in love and are born and die, but the way in which they fall in love and the things for which they are born and die are different," it is equally true that in all concrete loves and births and deaths the *general* facts of love, birth, and death are apperceived all over the world alike, in a somehow detachable fashion: the abstract is not blotted out by the concrete, it lives on in it, under it,

---

contradictory biographical evidence (the same Pontano who represents in *De amore conjugali* his marital life with Ariadna as ideal describes in the dialogue "Antonius" the same Ariadna as a replica of Xanthippe).

The biographical fallacy appears clearest in the case of writers and poets of whom the biographical fact of their homosexual leanings is known to the public: as is seen from the examples of Platen, George, Wilde, Gide, Proust, the esthetic judgment of the public is infallibly colored by moral aversion, while in the case of Shakespeare of whose private biography nearly nothing is known, the sonnets addressed to a certain youth may be freely enjoyed and even read in school, nor would there be any temptation to read his dramas as products of a homosexual.

as it were. The greatness of the classical poets—we remember Horace's precept *proprie communia dicere*—consists in giving a *second* (*artistic*) *concrete* form to the universally valid abstractions which they have extracted from the concrete facts[18] (this is somewhat shamefacedly realized by Boas when he says that Shakespeare expresses "general" feelings, "made vivid only [why "only"?] by his similes and metaphors and music"). It is absolutely untrue that the modern reader is impermeable to the abstract aspects of feelings and that he is forced to fill in the lacking concreteness of our classical poets by biographical data or by parallel personal experience. I deny most emphatically Boas' contention: "unless we are blind ourselves, unless we have suffered a similar loss, unless we have striven to justify the way of God to man, dictating the expression of our thoughts and emotions to rather indifferent daughters, how can we say that we have completely understood the meaning of those fourteen lines [of the sonnet *Methought*]?" Apart from the fact, pointed out above, that all these, as it were, technically required experiences would not be helpful for the understanding of a poem devoted, not to blindness, but to "the Ideal in this world," does Boas not confuse in his "unlesses" the understanding of the whole empirical psyche of the poet (as he reconstructs it) when he wrote the lines, with the understanding of the lines themselves (which certainly neither require, nor admit of, the detail of the "indifferent daughters")? The appreciation of the work of art seems here to be drowned out by the interests of the psychologist interested in the biology of the artist. An autonomous and self-sufficient artistic structure is subjected to an extraneous causal chain.

[18] Milton himself, as the sonnet on his blindness suggests, must have been aware of the abstract fact underlying his personal blindness. Was it not a *topos* of stoic Renaissance poetry to celebrate one's bodily affliction as an opportunity for showing one's courage and spirit of abnegation (cf. DuBellay's "Hymne de la Surdité" in which his own and Ronsard's deafness is praised as the source of studiousness, imagination, and judgment)? Milton's sonnet on his blindness, too, stands within a literary tradition which has shaped the empirical feelings of the blind poet in view of the literary use of this motif. Cf. on this point the general remarks of René Wellek and Austen Warren, *Theory of Literature*, 67-74.

Boas' negative attitude toward "meaning" in the literary art is, of course, based on a pessimistic philosophy of language which, as I said in the beginning, saps the basis of all philology. With this philosophy Champollion could never have deciphered the hieroglyphs nor Mommsen have understood the Romans nor the Schlegels have rediscovered medieval poetry. It is one thing to prophesy that the modern artist, in his growing isolation from his public, will become more and more unintelligible; it is another to infer from this modern experience that the art of the past, unless biographically supported, cannot be understood. Again, it is one thing to remind the philologian commenting on the meaning of the texts of remote cultural climates, of the possibility of failure inherent in the fallacies of language, another thing to despair radically about the meaning of the literary work of art in general. I wonder whether this (I fear, rather widespread) American disillusionment about "meaning" is not an exaggerated over-compensation for the even more general American tendency toward illusionistic optimism and whether Boas' radical negation of "meaning" is not an odd result of disappointed perfectionism. If it is not true that everyone can understand everyone, neither is it true that no one can understand any one.

••

Herrick's "Delight in Disorder"*

A sweet disorder in the dress
Kindles in clothes a wantonness:
A lawn about the shoulders thrown
Into a fine distraction:
An erring lace, which here and there
Enthralls the crimson stomacher:
A cuff neglectful, and thereby
Ribbands to flow confusedly:
A winning wave (deserving note)
In the tempestuous petticoat:
A careless shoe-string, in whose tie
I see a wild civility:
Do more bewitch me, than when art
Is too precise in every part.

••

THIS POEM has been commented upon by F. W. Bateson in his
book *English Poetry and the English Language* and by Cleanth
Brooks and Robert Penn Warren in their anthology *Understanding Poetry* (who quote Bateson's statements approvingly on pp.
188ff. and expand them pp. 572ff., proposing to replace Bateson's term "ambiguous associations" by "indirection"):

"The impression of a surprising richness, and almost grandeur
(as of a painting by Titian), with a certain tantalizing quality,
that Herrick's poem leaves, is primarily due to the skill with
which he has exploited the ambiguous associations of the epithets. On the surface his subject is the 'Delight in the Disorder'
of the title—a disorder, that is, of costume. But a second subject
is hinted at, though not protruded: a delight in disorder, not of
costume but of manners and morals. It is not only the clothes

---

*From *Modern Language Notes* (*MLN*), 1961, LXXVI, 209-14.

but their wearers too whom he would have sweet, wanton, distracted, erring, neglectful, winning, tempestuous, wild, and bewitching rather than precise. The poem, in fact, instead of being the mere *jeu d'esprit* that it would seem to be, is essentially a plea for paganism. There are three themes: (1) untidiness is becoming; (2) the clothes are the woman; (3) anti-Puritanism. But the success of the poem depends upon the fact that the themes are not isolated and contrasted but grow out of and into each other. The suspension between the various meanings produces a range of reference that none of them would have alone."

I think this analysis rests on a misconception and is in direct contrast with the text of the poem. I am unable to see any "ambiguity" or "indirection" in our poem nor do I believe in the "three themes" supposedly woven together by the poet.

To start with the latter assertion, the title of the poem is "Delight in Disorder" and this delight is throughout the poem exemplified by disorder in costume. But the "second subject" (or rather the same subject if we consider dress, and especially ladies' dress as an example of *art*) is not "disorder of manners and morals," but disorder in *art* (l. 13), a theme, well-known in 17th and 18th century art theory, which appears in Boileau (*un beau désordre*) and Pope (*brave disorder*).

Thus Bateson's theme 2 and 3 (which hangs on 2) must be discarded. As we know from our fashions of today, the clothes are not necessarily the woman: very civilized ladies may wear daring dresses that in some of their detail may make the impression of wantonness, neglectfulness, carelessness, etc. Bateson has obviously confused the metaphoric description of disorderly clothes by moral epithets applying to women, with a description of a woman by her clothes. If the poem describes clothes in terms of the human character of a woman, that is, endows them with a character of their own, we should enjoy this animization instead of seeing in it an allusion to a human reality *behind* them. I would say, not that the clothes are, but that the clothes behave like a woman (they are wanton, distracted, erring, neglectful, tempestuous, wild, bewitching), they have temperament, whims, caprices of their own and it is that motive power, that unpredictable quality ascribed to them which gives its animation to the enumeration, a procedure that could otherwise have become easily monotonous. The reader, by following the mischievous play of the various articles of feminine attire, may forget the mechanical device underlying the enumeration underlying the dance of the items of the wardrobe. Since each disorderly detail is connected with a clear-cut trait of character there prevails no ambiguity. The pieces of clothing are actors on a stage, acting out their specific well-defined parts. And the whimsicality of behavior praised as an ingredient of art is what permits the poet to present so many verbal variants, or avatars, of one basic character whereas obviously "precision" finds only one verbal representative.[1] I see, then, in the series of animated, or animized, pictures of pieces of clothing an anticipation of Walt Disney technique as they whirl around a figure of a woman who is not there. Now it is true that Herrick has described his ideal of a woman in terms of a parallelism between esthetic and moral creeds in the poem "What kind of Mistress he would have" ("The Poetical Works," ed. L. C. Martin, p. 232) where, after a description of that mistress—including lines reminiscent of our poem:

> Be she shewing in her dresse
> Like a civill Wilderness
> That the curious may detect
> order in a sweet neglect—

the poet exclaims:

> Let her Lucrece all day be,
> *Thais* in the night to me.

But that poem is not our poem and we should not confuse the two. Obviously, Bateson's supposition 3 ("antipuritanism," "a plea for paganism"), since, as we said, it hangs on supposition 2 "the clothes are the woman," has to fall (along with the latter).

Now is Bateson's supposition 1 true: "untidiness is becoming"? Is, according to our poem, *all* untidiness becoming? This is

[1] I am reminded of the sentence of Bernardin de St. Pierre (quoted by Littré, s. v. *désordre*) : "On se fait une idée précise de l'ordre, mais non pas du désordre."

surely not what Herrick says. Bateson has not taken into account the *restrictive* element in certain of the humanizing epithets of the dress:

1. While the title promises us a poem on delight in disorder the first line already restricts "disorder" to "sweet" disorder: not *all* disorder is pleasant.

2. The expression "kindles a wantonness" contains an indefinite article which is equal to "a kind of, a certain" (wantonness)—again, not *all* wantonness is pleasant.

3. ll. 2-3: "A lawn thrown into *fine* distraction"—distraction is praised insofar as it is a fine one.

4. ll. 4-5: "An erring lace which *here and there* enthralls"—only here and there does the lace not appear at its right place.

5. ll. 9-10: "A *winning wave* (*deserving note*) In the tempestuous petticoat"—only a wave is praised that is "remarkable" in the tempestuous petticoat.

Thus the required disorder in the dress is throughout subjected to the stipulation that it be pleasing. And just as in the beginning ("sweet disorder") the tension between opposite forces was suggested as the source of esthetic pleasure, so it will be in the end when the poet sees in the last detail mentioned, the shoe-lace, a "wild civility"—that is a tension between wildness and civility, wildness being accepted only as far as it is civil—as it should be in the classical art Herrick ultimately advocates.[2] For our commentators the multiple or ambiguous associations prompted by the epithets produce a "surprising richness, almost grandeur, as of a painting of Titian" (Bateson), "the concentration and condensation that we associate with dramatic presentation" (Brooks-Warren). While I grant the dramatic character (which in my opinion is based on the tension between opposite principles) I do not see the Titian-like quality of the pictorial effect: we are not offered heavy velvet in rich, statuesque folds, but evanescent frothiness. Nor do I believe in ambiguous associations as the source of the pictorial effect.

[2] We may think of Gide's definition of classicism as "romantisme dompté."

As to the form of our poem, I wonder why critics so eager to read poems "closely" and so alert to questions of structure have failed to see that the idea of wild civility is reflected by two features of our poem: its syntax and its rhymes. In this "sonnet of couplets" in each of which (except for the first and the last couplet) one piece of clothing is enumerated, six rhymes out of seven are only approximative (dress: wantonnéss; thrown: distractión; there: stomachér; thereby: confusedlý; note: petti-cóat; tie: civilitý), the final one being a perfect rhyme (art: part)—a rhyme structure and a syntactic structure, that shows in itself wildness tamed: the final couplet contains the predicate which the series of enumerated nouns made us wait for and formulates the artistic creed of the poet, the finality of which is reflected in the perfect rhyme. Metrical perfection (indeed "pre-cision" at the moment when "precision" is only half-heartedly endorsed in the couplet) wins out in the end over approximation.

Up to this point we have deliberately ignored other poems of Herrick's concerned with women's dress as well as the sources of "Delight in Disorder" (both categories are discussed in L. C. Martin's edition). As to the sources, the immediate model, Ben Jonson's "Song" inserted in the play "Epicoene or the Silent Woman" shows one indumentary detail (no enumeration of several pieces of clothing) in the service of a plea for natural simplicity addressed to his lady:

> Give me a look, give me a face,
> That makes *simplicity* a grace;
> *Robes loosely flowing*, hair as free;
> Such *sweet neglect* more taketh me
> Than all th'adulteries of art.

Here Ben Jonson is echoing similar pleas for simplicity found in Neo-Latin poems of the type (cf. the edition of Jonson's play in *Yale Studies in English*, XXXI, p. lv):

> *Neglectim* mihi se quae comit amica
>   Se det; et ornatus *simplicitate* valet.

We recognize as the central *topos* the paradox of "sweet neglect" which, whether applied to woman's appearance or not, has ancient precedents in Ovid's "neglecta decens" and Cicero's (advice to the orator) "quaedam etiam negligentia est diligens." But in contrast to the praise of the natural and the simple of the sources Herrick praises the art hiding behind apparent neglect-fulness.[3] For instance, another poem of his, "Art above Nature, to Julia" (p. 202) seems to be a direct rejoinder to Ben Jonson's poem, from the title to the proclamation in the end (in which the very rhymes of Jonson are used: heart: art) :

> I must confess, mine eye and heart
> Dotes less on Nature then on Art—

a point of view shared by Burton in a passage of his *Anatomy* in which there is also found an enumeration[4] of beautiful "coutre-ments" more tempting then "barbarian homelinesse." Thus Herrick sees art, if not in the barbaric, in the wild and his "wild civility" is, as it were, a synthesis of "art superior to nature" and "barbarian homlinesse." The next poem of Herrick's (p. 232) "What kind of Mistresse he would have" develops the idea of the "civil wildness" in dressing so as to confirm our con-tention that the two contrasting elements of this paradoxical expression were felt by the poet as limiting each other ("That the curious may detect / *Order* in a *sweet neglect*"). And, ac-cordingly, the poet will speak in terms of contrasts between which the ideal mistress finds a judicious mean: "witty more then wise, pure enough though not precise," "tempting all the

[3] This stand does, of course, not prevent Herrick from praising in other poem the "nak't simplicities" of his beloved (cf. "Clothes do but cheat and cousen us," p. 154).

[4] Such an enumeration of garments may ultimately be derived from the medieval and Renaissance habit (surviving in John Donne, Ben Jonson, and perhaps Herrick himself—cf. "The Description of a Woman," p. 404) of enumerating the parts of the beloved's body in their order from head to toe in order to show its total perfection. In our poem the enumeration of garments replaces the enumeration of parts of the body and must be seen as a conscious variation of that pattern. Of course, the accent lies not on a list of perfect, but (according to Herrick's artistic canon) of less-than-perfect items.

passersby . . . but herself held fast by none," "Lucrece all day, Thais in the night to me," "be she such as neither will famish me nor over-fill." Another step is taken by Herrick in the third poem to be mentioned here, "Julia's Petticoat" (p. 66) where animization of *one* piece of garment of the beloved takes place: the petticoat is described as "panting, sighing, heaving," "erring here and wandering there, / pleas'd with transgression ev'ry where." This summary, which is not intended as presenting an hypothesis about the chronological order in which the different poems about feminine garments were actually composed, but to suggest a possible psychological order in which they offered themselves to the poet's imagination, shows us that only in "Delight in Disorder" has Herrick entirely detached the garments from the woman, annihilating her in order to give life to them; only in this poem has he subordinated the description of womanly dress to an artistic canon so as to pit against each other the contrasting forces of wildness vs. civility (whose struggle is reflected in the rhyme structure of the poem). "Delight in Disorder," while using devices occurring in the other pieces, puts them to the service of a more universal experience, that of *art*.

CHAPTER IX

· ·

Three Poems on Ecstasy[*]

(JOHN DONNE, ST. JOHN OF THE CROSS,
RICHARD WAGNER)

· ·

IN AN ARTICLE entitled "A Farewell to Criticism," the American
poet Karl Shapiro has written (*Poetry*, Jan. 1948) : "I question
the principle underlying *explication de texte*. A poem should
not be used as a subject for linguistic, semantic, or psychological
study. . . . Poetry is not language, but a language *sui generis*
which can be understood, paraphrased, or translated only as
poetry. . . . The same word used in a line of prose and a line of
poetry are really two different words, not even similar, except
in appearance. I would designate the poetry word as 'not-word'
. . . a poem is a literary construct composed of not-words which,
in their retreat from meanings, arrive at a prosodic sense-beyond-
sense. The aim of a poem is not known." (By "prosody" Mr.
Shapiro means not only poetic rhythm but also poetic associations and figures of speech.)

Accordingly, what I wish to attempt in this series of lectures
(*explication de texte* applied to poetry) should, in the opinion
of a poet of real authority, be resolutely eschewed. Now the
literary critic who is able to draw on his historical knowledge
may discount the periodically recurring revolt of poets against
critics who would explain their poetry; this is a "poetic" attitude which dates from the period of Romanticism. It would not
have occurred to a Dante, a St. John of the Cross, a Racine, a
Milton, to doubt that their poetry, representative, or so they
thought, of universal feelings, could be explained by their fellowmen; indeed, these poets often took pains, themselves, to explain
their poetry. But, since the discovery, in the eighteenth century,

[*] From *A Method of Interpreting Literature* (Smith College, 1949),
pp. 1-63.

of the "original genius" who is supposed to speak not for mankind, but for himself alone—since that time the irrational meaning of their poetry has been stressed by the poets more and more; we have all heard of such stock situations as, for example, that of the professor of French literature explaining the meaning of Valéry's *Cimetière Marin* in one of the *amphithéâtres* of the Sorbonne, while the author was sitting in the gallery, his gentle smile expressing a skeptical *que sais-je?* as he listened to the positive statements of the commentator. It is, of course, the prerogative, perhaps the duty, of the poet of today to defend the irrational, the somehow "aimless" nature of his creation against any unilateral, rational, or behavioristic explanation. But there is also to be considered the undeniable fact that *language*, the particular medium of the poet, is itself a system both rational and irrational; it is lifted by him to a plane of still greater irrationalism while nevertheless maintaining its ties with the normal, mainly rational language. It is simply not true that poetry consists of "not-words" (except perhaps in the case of the *dadaistes*, or the recent sect of *lettristes*, who coin words nonexistent in their own or in any human language). Poetry generally consists of words belonging to a given language which have irrational as well as rational connotations, words which become transfigured by what Shapiro calls "prosody." If we pause to consider a stanza from one of the poems of Mr. Shapiro himself, the poem *Nostalgia* (which can hardly be called "aimless" since an aim, that of portraying nostalgia, is stated in the title and is so understood by the reader), we shall see that he makes a constant appeal to the usual connotations, that is, to the prose (but not entirely prose) connotations of English words:

> My soul stands at the window of my room
> And I ten thousand miles away;
> My days are filled with Ocean's sound of doom,
> Salt and cloud and the bitter spray,
> *Let the wind blow, for many a man shall die.*

Not only is the outward and the inner situation clear (the world-war soldier Karl Shapiro, who fought in the Pacific, looking out from his window upon the Ocean and thinking of the fate of so many fellow-soldiers who would not see their homeland again); it is true also that the prosody is assimilable and explainable: the fifth line, which happens to be the refrain of the whole poem, breaks the rhythm of the preceding quatrain with its initial anapaest and the subsequent shock of two tonic syllables ("let the wind blów"), thereby evoking the impact of the doom already foreshadowed in the static sense, but now emergent, actual: "for many a man shall die." But in this refrain the words *wind* and *blow, man* and *die* are still those of our language, which have preserved their usual connotations (and these connotations are in themselves not entirely rational); it is only by their arrangement in our causal sentence,—or rather pseudocausal sentence, for there is no necessary connection between the blowing of the wind and the death of many a man—and by the rhythm already described, that another plane is suggested, that of poetry. Thus, by means of words of our daily life, there is given the possibility of a logic beyond our human logic, the logic of the doom that wills the blowing of the wind in order that men may die. The experienced reader will immediately think of the technique of the folk-ballad, of Villon's "Mais où sont les neiges d'antan?" or of the song at the end of *Twelfth Night:* "The rain it raineth every day"—in which trivial-seeming sentences are given a new function: that of suggesting the necessity of submitting to fate as figured by the elements. Instead of saying that poetry consists of "not-words which, in their retreat from meaning, arrive at a prosodic sense-beyond-sense," I would offer the suggestion that it consists of *words,* with their meaning *preserved,* which, through the magic of the poet who works within a "prosodic" whole, arrive at a sense-beyond-sense; and that it is the task of the philologist to point out the manner in which the transfiguration just mentioned has been achieved. The irrationality of the poem need not lose anything at the hands of a discreet linguistic critic; on the contrary, he will work in accord with the poet (although with no regard to his approval), insofar as he will patiently and analytically retrace the way from the rational to the irrational: a distance which the poet may have covered in one bold leap.

I shall take up three poems dealing with approximately the same subject matter (the ecstatic union of a human ego with a non-ego), in order to study the magic transformation which actual words of the particular language have undergone at the hands of the poets who have succeeded in making their inner experience a poetic reality for the reader.

John Donne's poem "The Extasie" (published in 1633) begins by describing the outward situation of two lovers, reclining on a grassy, violet-scented mound near a river bank; against this background they experience mystic union of a Neo-Platonic order, without being diverted or disturbed by physical passion.[1]

> Where, like a pillow on a bed,
>   A pregnant banke swel'd up, to rest
> The violets reclining head,
>   Sat we two, one anothers best.
> Our hands were firmely cimented   5
>   With a fast balme, which thence did spring,
> Our eye-beames twisted, and did thred
>   Our eyes, upon one double string;
> So to'entergraft our hands, as yet
>   Was all the meanes to make us one,   10
> And pictures in our eyes to get
>   Was all our propagation.
> As 'twixt two equall Armies, Fate
>   Suspends uncertaine victorie,
> Our soules, (which to advance their state,   15
>   Were gone out,) hung 'twixt her, and mee.

[1] Professor Don Cameron Allen, who attracted my attention to Donne's poem, pointed out to me a similarity in décor with a poem found in Sir Philip Sidney (*The Complete Works*, ed. Feuillerat, II, 274).

And whil'st our soules negotiate there,
   Wee like sepulchrall statues lay;
All day, the same our postures were,
   And wee said nothing, all the day.   20
If any, so by love refin'd,
   That he soules language understood,
And by good love were growen all minde,
   Within convenient distance stood,
He (though he knew not which soule spake,   25
   Because both meant, both spake the same)
Might thence a new concoction take,
   And part farre purer then he came.
This Extasie doth unperplex
   (We said) and tell us what we love,   30
Wee see by this, it was not sexe,
   Wee see, we saw not what did move:
But as all severall soules containe
   Mixtures of things, they know not what,
Love, these mixt soules, doth mixe againe,   35
   And make both one, each this and that.
A single violet transplant,
   The strength, the colour, and the size,
(All which before was poore, and scant,)
   Redoubles still, and multiplies.   40
When love, with one another so
   Interinanimates two soules,
That abler soule, which thence doth flow,
   Defects of lonelinesse controules.
Wee then, who are this new soule, know,   45
   Of what we are compos'd, and made,
For, th' Atomies of which we grow,
   Are soules, whom no change can invade.
But O alas so long so farre
   Our bodies why doe wee forbeare?   50
They are ours, though they are not wee, Wee are
   The intelligences, they the spheare.

We owe them thankes, because they thus,
    Did us, to us, at first convay,
Yeelded their forces, sense, to us,   55
    Nor are drosse to us, but allay.
On man heavens influence workes not so,
    But that it first imprints the ayre,
Soe soule into the soule may flow,
    Though it to body first repaire.   60
As our blood labours to beget
    Spirits, as like soules as it can,
Because such fingers need to knit
    That subtile knot, which makes us man:
So must pure lovers soules descend   65
    T'affections, and to faculties,
Which sense may reach and apprehend,
    Else a great Prince in prison lies.
To'our bodies turne wee then, that so
    Weake men on love reveal'd may looke;   70
Loves mysteries in soules doe grow,
    But yet the body is his booke.
And if some lover, such as wee,
    Have heard this dialogue of one,
Let him still marke us, he shall see   75
    Small change, when we'are to bodies gone.

The author evidently intends to offer, in poetic guise, an intellectual definition of the ecstatic state of two souls, which emerge from their bodies and blend so completely that they become one. The Greek term *ekstasis*, "going forth," is literally paraphrased in lines 15-16: "Our soules, (which to advance their state, Were *gone out*,)," a line which must be contrasted with the final one: "Small change, when we'are *to bodies gone*"; *i.e.*, when we return to unecstatic normal life. Two phenomena must be described by the poet: the separation of soul from body (the *ekstasis* proper) and the union of the two souls. Both are explained by a technique of insisting and re-insisting on the same

facts which are described with a wealth of variations. I shall
list first the varied references to the idea: "two become one":

    4 we two, one anothers best
    5 our hands were firmely cimented
  7–8 thred our eyes upon one double string
 9–10 to'entergraft our hands, . . . to make us one
15–16 our soules . . . hung 'twixt her, and mee
   26 both meant, both spake the same
   35 (love these) mixt soules (doth mixe againe)
   36 make both one, each this and that
41–42 [love] with one another . . . interinanimates
        [= animates] two soules
   59 soule into the soule may flow
   74 this dialogue of one

The concept of "union" suggests the corollary idea of
"procreation"; and, indeed in our poem, we shall find references
to the fruit of the lovers' union—which must be on the same
spiritual plane as the union itself:

  5–6 [our hands were firmely cimented] with a fast balme,
        which *thence did spring*
11–12 [pictures . . . was all our] propagation
   15 our soules, (which to *advance their state* were gone
        out)
   27 [he who would be a witness to our union] thence
        a new concoction [=distillate, state of maturation]
        take
   43 that *abler* soule, which thence doth flow
   45 wee then, who are *this new soule*

And we may add further the first two lines: "Where, like a pil-
low on a bed, / A pregnant banke swel'd up," which give to the
intellectual procreation of the lovers a background of exuber-
antly fertile nature and vegetative life;[2] this passage should be

2 The "pregnant banke swel'd up, to rest the violets reclining head"
is obviously a feature belonging to the literary "ideal landscape," a

taken together with ll. 37-40 (though this quatrain may strike us as a later interpolation) : just as a single violet, transplanted into new soil, thrives with renewed life, so the single souls, offered a new soil by love (the soil of two-ness), will "redouble and multiply" their potentialities.

As for the idea of the ecstasy proper, this is taken up in the simile (ll. 13-16) of the two armies between which Fate hangs and for which the souls negotiate—a simile which is carried over into the following image of a double tombstone with recumbent figures from which the souls have fled. Again the idea of the unembodied souls recurs in line 23 ("by good love . . . growen all minde") and in ll. 47-48: "For th' Atomies of which we grow, / Are soules, whom no change can invade"; "Wee [our soules] are / The intelligences, they [our bodies] the spheare" (in medieval cosmology the spheres are moved by the angelic intelligences).

The last third of the poem is entirely given over to a justification of the body: since this must be abandoned if the soul would know ecstasy, one might assume that the body is only a hindrance for the spirit. And yet Donne insists on rehabilitating the body, describing the service it renders the spirit. By means

---

topos recently treated by E. R. Curtius, *Europäische Literatur und lateinisches Mittelalter* (Bern, 1948), p. 189 et seq.; the ultimate sources are such passages as Virgil, *Bucolics*, III, 55-57:

> Dicite, quandoquidem *in molli consedimus herba.*
> Et nunc omnis ager, nunc omnis *parturit* arbos;
> Nunc frondent silvae; nunc formosissimus annus.

This is exactly the *décor* to be found in Donne's poem: a spot in nature, made beautiful by exuberant vegetation, inviting repose and enjoyment. In another ideal landscape of Virgil (*Buc.*, II, 45 et seq.), we find eight species of flowers mentioned and with the late Roman poet Tiberianus, four (among them also the violets: "tum nemus fragrabat omne violarum spiritu") ; Donne, however, mentions only the violet, probably because he wished to emphasize the climate of love, for, with the ancients, the violet is the flower symbolic of love: "tinctus viola pallor amantium" (Horace, *Odes*, III, 10) : "palleat omnis amans, hic est color aptus amanti" (Ovid, *Ars amatoria*, I, 727). Cf. in Petrarch "S'un *pallor di viola e d'amor* tinto," *"Amorosette et pallide viole"* (*Concordanza delle Rime di Fr. Petrarca*, ed. McKenzie, s.v. *viola*) ; in Camoens "Pintando estava alí Zéfiro e Flora/*As violas da côr dos amadores*" (*Lusiads*, IX, 61 ; cf. Richard F. Burton, "Camoens," IV, 657).

of the senses the body mediates between the affianced souls: the body is not "drosse," but "allay" (1. 56). Moreover, it produces the blood-spirits (*spiritelli, esprits vitaux*) which are closely knit to the soul and produce those sensuous images that lead toward the revelation of love: "Loves mysteries in soules doe grow, / But yet the body is his booke." Donne ends by repeating the motif of the changelessness of souls that have once united in ecstasy.

We cannot escape the impression that the poet proceeds in the whole poem in the manner of a believer who has, firmly established in his mind, a conception of which he wishes to convince his audience. Indeed, so conscious is he of the need to *convince* others that, not content with the audience of his readers, he would introduce (1. 21) into the poem itself, "within convenient distance" of the lovers, a witness, or a listener, able to understand the language of love, who would listen to the "dialogue of one" (1. 74). Such a one, he assures us, could not but testify both to the purity of the mystic act and to the lasting effect of ecstasy, even after the return of the ecstatic souls to the bodies.

As for his audience of readers, the technique the poet adopts in order to convince us is a quantitative one: he must multiply his evidence in order to hammer home his conviction. With ever-new similes (*to ciment, to graft, balm, concoction, to string, violet*), or with new coinages (*entergraft, interinanimate*) he forges the idea "two become one," and with accumulation of similes (negotiators for armies, sepulchral figures, intelligences not spheres, alloy not dross, mystery not book) the idea of ecstasy is given form. This revelation itself is portrayed from an intellectual point of view, as the paradoxical mathematical reduction: "2 becomes 1." The depth of the mystic experience, the feeling of its ever-increasing depth, is not expressed: nothing is revealed of the genesis of this experience, of the development up to the culminating moment of trance. The ecstasy has existed from the beginning: it is clearly named "this Extasie" in line 29: it lasts not a moment, but the whole day through. We are allowed to share only the enduring state of bliss-without-desire. Statuesque calm prevails throughout the poem. We see before us an allegorical statue of Ecstasis which stands unveiled from the beginning, while the flexible figures of speech circle about it, weaving ethereal wreaths around it, casting ever-new shadows upon it—a composite allegorical figure indeed, of which are predicated attributes belonging to different realms of life. To express the same observation by varying the well-known couplet of Robert Frost:

> They all dance around in a circle and suppose,
> But the *concept* sits in the middle, and knows.

All the sciences and crafts are allowed to enter our poem in the form of metaphors and to testify to the central concept: the craft of the perfumer, of the jeweller who strings pearls, of the gardener who transplants, of the military negotiator, of the sculptor, of the alchemist who distills "concoctions," of the cosmologist who deals with the atomic structure of the universe—they all parade before the statue in a pageant, a Petrarchian *triumphus pudicitiae.*

Connected with Donne's quantitative procedure is his use of hyperbole, often misunderstood by the critics: he tells us that so great was the ecstasy, that (ll. 7-8) "Our eye-beames twisted, and did thred / Our eyes, upon one double string"—a feat none too easily visualized. But he means, of course, to predicate the impossible. According to the requirements of metaphysical wit, he must ascribe to what he praises the physically impossible as well as the limitless: not only must he marshal all the kaleidoscopic richness of the earth, he must introduce the unvisualizable possibilities of the impossible—well aware that with all his effort his panegyric must, in the end, still be an approximation. Of course, this type of eulogy has the effect of distancing the object of praise: Donne does not re-enact what is within him, but points us to something above him. Instead of the re-creation of the intuitive experience the poet actually had, with its particular quality, we are offered an encyclopedic, discursive analysis. Yet this is informed by rhythmic beauty: the beauty of the rhythm of simple spoken speech with all its convincingness—a rhythm that echoes the inner event and testifies to the veracity of the report. Notice the rhythm (indicating "sameness" by chiastic "return to the same"), which accompanies the simile of the "sepulchre" (ll. 18-20):

> Wee like sepulchrall statues lay;
> *All day*, the same our postures were,
> And wee said nothing, *all the day*.

The rhythm by which the "new soul" is portrayed as beyond change (ll. 45-48):

> Wee then, who are this new soule, know,
> Of what we are compos'd, and made,
> For, th' Atomies of which we grow,
> Are soules, *whom no change can invade*.

or the meditative rhythm of the lines that indicate the non-sexual nature of that love (ll. 31-32):

> *Wee see* by this, it was not sexe,
> *Wee see, we saw* not what did move. . . .

It can be no chance that the rhythm chosen by the poet is most convincing where the immutability of the union is contrasted with transient phenomena.

After having noted that in our poem the intellectual kernel of an intuitive state of mind has been made concrete and that an experience which must have developed in time has been reduced to timelessness, we may observe that the last part, that in which the justification of the body is offered (love begins in the body and will continue when the souls have returned to the body), is poetically less successful than the rest—and this, in spite of occasional poetic gems, such as (l. 64) "That subtile knot, which makes us man" (a line which turns the succinct definition of the psycho-physical nature of man into poetry), or (l. 68) "Else a great Prince in prison lies," where for one moment we seem to see the Segismundo of Calderón in his tower, deprived of the light of his senses. The final part of the poem verges on a scientific treatise of physiology, that is, of seventeenth-century physiology. Any reader must feel here a poetic anti-climax (he may even suspect composition of that last part at a different time) : after we have known of the ecstasy of two souls become one, the idea of their return or "descent" to that body is disconcerting. For mortal man is so constituted that he can visualize a state of bliss only as an apex that must stand out in isolation, a death within life followed by silence; Goethe's Egmont exclaims: "Let me die, the world has no joy greater than this," and the curtain must fall. Donne, however, wished to make the ecstatic vision tributary to the daily life which must follow—and which could be enhanced by the remembrance thereof. But this very noble moral thought, so deeply connected with religious reformation and regeneration, has not come to poetic fruition; for, after having shared an ecstasy which is beyond time and change, we are not ready to return to the world where change, however slight, is possible. And the repetition of the motif of the witness who would observe the lovers in their post-ecstatic life is an indication that here Donne's poetic imagination was lagging.

Moreover, we feel somehow that Donne himself, in spite of his endeavor to justify the flesh, was more intimately convinced of the reality and beauty of the spiritual union than of the necessity of the body for that union. It may well be that the basically Protestant mind of Donne is responsible for this self-contradictory attitude. For estrangement from the body may be said to be characteristic of Protestantism, whereas in the Jewish faith the rights of the body can easily coexist with the claims of the Creator on man's immortal soul, and, in the Catholic religion, a bridge from soul to body is afforded by the church sacrament according to which Christ is present in the bodily union of the believers, who are *membra Christi*. In the Protestant monument erected by Donne to the mystic union, the figures impersonating this union show the touch of a firmer hand than does the pedestal of clay by which he would have them supported. Donne knows, in fact, no true answer to that tormenting question: "But O alas so long so farre / Our bodies why doe wee forbeare?" It is no chance that the word *sex* (l. 31) is used in our poem for the first time in European literature in the modern sense of the specific, objective, definable, but questionable, urge that conditions the life of man and woman.[3] Again in his poem *The Primrose* Donne says: ". . . should she / Be more then woman, shee would get above / All thought of sexe . . ."; to "get above all thought of sexe" goes hand in hand with "Wee see by this, it was not sexe": in both cases, "sex" is treated as a lesser factor which exists to be transcended.

However, if sex is envisaged (so sharply!) as a thing to be dismissed, we can, of course, not expect to find in Donne a representative of religious mysticism, which (as we know from Evelyn Underhill's studies on mystical psychology) borrows from sex the raw material of psycho-physical sensitivity with which to welcome, on a higher plane, *but still in one's body* as well as in one's soul, the invasion of the divine.

It is the Spanish mystics who, in their procedure of giving flesh to spiritual experience (while sharing Donne's ultimate attitude of disillusion, *desengaño*, toward the body), have found the most direct way to reconcile the splendor of the body, rediscovered by the Renaissance, and the supernatural beauty of divine grace, experienced in medieval meditation. And yet, our poem, with its clear demarcation between body and soul, will remain a monument of intellectual clarity. How characteristic is the verb *unperplex* (l. 29) which Donne has coined (and allowed to rhyme with *sex*—a counterbalance!), how revelatory of Donne's passionate desire for intellectual clarification of emotions! And it is this urge which has made John Donne so dear to our age, an age sore perplexed, mistrusting instinctual emotion—preferring, perhaps, clarity of analysis to syntheses which it can no longer wholeheartedly ratify.

In view of the interpretation I have just suggested for Donne's poem, it is hardly necessary to state that I am utterly opposed to the opinion offered by the late Professor Legouis in his *Histoire de la littérature anglaise*. Legouis, who evidently has in mind the numerous poems in which Donne has ridiculed the theme of Platonic love (think of *The Flea!*), sees

[3] A suggestion I owe to Professor Allen.

in our poem a "sophistical" and "insidious" plea for physical consummation. The two lovers, after having enjoyed for a full day the sensation of having formed one soul, "sentent qu'ils sont devenus de purs esprits. De la hauteur où ils planent, que le corps est peu de chose! Pauvre corps, mais qui pourtant mérite sa récompense pour les avoir menés l'un vers l'autre. Il n'est que juste de penser à lui! 'Pourquoi s'abstiennent nos corps si longtemps?... Sans cela un grand prince gît en prison.'" Now, in order to justify such a carnal interpretation, Legouis has interpreted line 50 ("Our bodies why doe wee forbeare?") as if *forbear* meant, not "endure, tolerate," as I have understood it, but "restrain, control" ("pourquoi s'abstiennent nos corps si longtemps?"). Furthermore, in the last line: "Small change, when we'are to bodies gone," which I have explained as referring to the inevitable return from ecstasy to everyday life, he evidently sees an allusion to physical love. And what we have taken as a description of the beginning of love (which must start with the body), as a point from which to reach the ecstasy —he assumes to constitute an invitation, *hic et nunc*, to indulge the body; and the noble line 68: "Else a great Prince in prison lies," descriptive of the mortal condition of man, he brings in, somehow, as the climax of the carnal invitation: the individual man's eternal self-pitying plea to the woman.

Before such Gallic worldly wisdom, such familiarity with the age-old stratagems of a resourceful seducer (of a Valmont in the *Liaisons Dangereuses*), how naïve my own earnest remarks may appear! It sometimes happens, however, that candor is the most direct way of understanding; I have chosen simply to believe the poet when he speaks, at the beginning, with the unmistakable voice of truth, of the beauty, and reality, of the spiritual *ekstasis*: and if we do believe him here, we cannot, then, see in the last part an invitation to carnality—which could only mean that the first part was a mere stratagem. And the lines with their sincere and final ring, "Wee see by this, it was not sexe, / Wee see, we saw not what did move"—is this the tone of hypocrisy? We should suspect that the speaker knew at the time that sex *did* move (or would move)? And that witness upon whom Donne calls at the end, "When we'are to bodies gone"—incredible to think that Donne is calling upon him to witness the physical act: he whom the poet has described as "by good love . . . growen all minde" (notice the lofty Augustinian phrase *good love = amor bonus*)!

No, I still prefer to see in our poem a glorification of true *ekstasis* (lacking perhaps in artistic convincingness, for the noble reason earlier suggested) rather than a circuitous exhibition of lofty Neo-Platonic philosophy destined only to bring about the inevitable earthy dénouement: I see in it, not an *argumentum ad hominem*, or rather . . . *ad feminam*, but, in accord with Donne himself, a "dialogue of one"—of, if you wish, a monologue of two.

We have said that the Jewish sensibility—and I believe this to be as true today as in the days of the patriarchs—admits the coexistence of the body and the soul in the presence of God, but with no attempt at fusing them. It is then not surprising that a sensuous Oriental epithalamium that had found access to the Jewish biblical canon, the *Song of Songs* (that "herrlichste Sammlung Liebeslieder, die *Gott geschaffen hat*," as Goethe called it), should have been, by Christian exegesis, transformed into an allegorical treatise of mystic union. And it is this mystical theme that we find in the Spanish poem *En una noche escura*—which might be described as a Catholic *Song of Songs* (for, indeed, it derives its inspiration from the re-interpreted Hebrew canticle). This poem, written about 1577 by the Carmelite monk San Juan de la Cruz, is a perfect example of the manner in which the body can be made artistically tributary to the mystic experience. The Catholic saint treats no lesser subject than the ecstatic union, not with a human being, but with the divine, in terms that constantly fuse soul and body:

> 1. En una noche escura,
>   Con ansias en amores inflamada,
>   ¡Oh dichosa ventura!

Salí sin ser notada,
Estando ya mi casa sosegada;

2. A escuras y segura,
Por la secreta escala, disfrazada,
¡Oh dichosa ventura!
A escuras, y en celada,
Estando ya mi casa sosegada.

3. En la noche dichosa,
En secreto, que nadie me veía,
Ni yo miraba cosa,
Sin otra luz y guía,
Sino la que en el corazon ardía,

4. Aquesta me guiaba
Más cierto que la luz del mediodía,
Adonde me esperaba
Quien yo bien me sabía
En parte donde nadie parecía.

5. ¡Oh noche, que guiaste,
Oh noche amable más que el alborada,
Oh noche, que juntaste
Amado con Amada,
Amada en el Amado transformada!

6. En mi pecho florido,
Que entero para él sólo se guardaba,
Allí quedó dormido,
Y yo le regalaba,
Y el ventalle de cedros aire daba.

7. El aire del almena,
Cuando yo sus cabellos esparcía,
Con su mano serena
En mi cuello hería
Y todos mis sentidos suspendía.

8. Quedéme y olvidéme,
El rostro recliné sobre el Amado;
Cesó todo, y dejéme,
Dejando mi cuidado
Entre las azucenas olvidado.

This poem, as has been recognized by its finest commentators, the Frenchman Baruzi[4] and the Spaniard Dámaso Alonso,[5] falls into three parts: the beginning of the soul's pilgrimage, stanzas 1-4; the arrival and the announcement of the mystic union, stanza 5; and the scene of the union itself, stanzas 6-8. In order to gain insight into the poetic organism, let us begin again by a "list," as we have done before in the explanation of Donne's poem. There it was the sequence of similes that allowed us to penetrate into the poet's procedure of composition; here, however, we shall start with an (at first glance) trivial linguistic detail: starting from the point of view of tense usage, let us draw up a list of the preterites used in our short narrative, because it is by these that the action is carried forward: they form, as it were, the dramatic framework, expressing an unbroken development. We shall see them increase at the end of the poem: in Part I there is only *salí*, "I started forth" (stanza 1); in Part II (stanza 5) only *guiaste*, "you [the night] led me," and *juntaste*, "you joined us"; in Part III, in addition to *allí quedó dormido*, "my love fell asleep," of stanza 6, we find five preterites in the last stanza, four of them verbs of bodily movement; the action, as I said, is conceived in bodily terms. This climactic increase in dramatic tenses toward the end coincides, strangely enough, with a decrease in voluntary or dynamic action on the part of the protagonist: the loving soul that in Part I started forth resolutely on its pilgrimage, is, in Part II, led forward by the night, and it is the night that joins the soul with its Beloved (who is himself passive: *quedó dormido*)—whereupon all striving ceases; and the activity of the soul in the last stanza is one of gradual self-extinction: *cesó todo*. This contrast between the accumulation of dramatic tenses and the *smorzando* of the activities they express is paradoxical:[6] the climax of action is reached in non-

---

[4] Jean Baruzi, *Saint Jean de la Croix et le problème de l'expérience mystique*, 2nd ed., Paris, 1931.

[5] Dámaso Alonso, *La poesía de San Juan de la Cruz*, Madrid, 1946.

[6] This observation has not been made by Dámaso Alonso, who speaks only of the "scarcity of verbs" in the first part of the poem (p. 184); according to Alonso, if I have understood him correctly, the nominal constructions predominate.

I would say that, not to speak of the last stanza in which the verbs

action, in the receiving of the mystic invasion (which can be only a gift of divine grace), in self-annihilation. The first preterite *sali* was an élan motivated "con ansias en amores inflamada," by the burning anxiety of the flame of love; the *dejéme* of the end, though expressing self-abandonment, melts immediately into "dejando mi cuidado . . . olvidado" ("leaving my sorrow forgotten") : the cessation of all perturbation. The action of the Spanish poem, which begins with a movement dictated by pain and by the will to still pain, ends with the achievement of self-forgetfulness free from pain.

After having gained a bird's-eye view of the whole and of the salient features of its structure, let us now return to the beginning and seek to analyze in their turn the three parts we have isolated.

In the first stanza, as has already been said, the outstanding word which starts the movement of the poem is *sali*. But we may ask ourselves: who is it that started forth? Who is the protagonist of the poem? The participle *inflamada* (stanza 1), followed by *notada* and later by *amada* and *transformada* (stanza 5), would seem to indicate a feminine being; and since this being speaks of joining her Beloved (*Amado*), we might be justified in seeing the action in terms of an earthly love. Or is this feminine aspect predicated only of that spiritual being, the soul (Spanish *alma*, a word never mentioned in our poem), eternally conceived as feminine? This ambiguity is obviously intended by the author not only because of his desire to express figuratively the spiritual by the physical: it is true also that, just because the identity of the protagonist is presented as self-evident, as needing no elucidation, we are drawn immediately into the atmosphere of the one who speaks of her love, and we can share, unquestioningly, in her experience, as this develops in the poem.

---

undoubtedly predominate, even in the first three stanzas the strength of the one verb *sali*, on which, according to Alonso's own analysis, all the circumstantial adverbs and parentheses hang, is rather increased: the main verb is not "absent"; on the contrary, it makes itself felt in the sustaining power it has, in the support it gives to the nominal phrases: the *sali* symbolizes the calm will-power of that soul that makes its way toward its goal, unperturbed by loneliness and night.

To return again to *salí*: whence was this departure? From what background does this sudden movement emerge? But it is only the first two stanzas *taken together* that give us this background; indeed, these two stanzas must, as Dámaso Alonso has pointed out, be taken as one sentence (not to be separated by a period, as is done in all the editions) : they contain the same rhymes, and, if considered as a unit, the opening period will show that *parellelismus membrorum* characteristic of the Hebrew model (the *Song of Songs*) : compare the parallelisms in

> By night on my bed I sought him whom my soul loveth:
> I sought him, but I found him not.
> I said, I will rise now, and go about the city,
> In the streets and in the broad ways,
> I will seek him whom my soul loveth.
> I sought him, but I found him not.

and in our poem:

> En una noche escura,
> Con ansias en amores inflamada,
> ¡Oh dichosa ventura!
> Salí sin ser notada,
> Estando ya mi casa sosegada;
>
> A escuras y segura,
> Por la secreta escala, disfrazada,
> ¡Oh dichosa ventura!
> A escuras, y en celada,
> Estando ya mi casa sosegada.

These musical, even dance-like cadences help situate our poem in the climate of Biblical mystery, in which movements that would seem erratic to the uninitiated are guided by Providence. In the stillness of the night we hear those mysterious accents, supported, as it were, by *word-motifs* which repeat themselves with a consistency suggestive of continuity of will and purpose. Here the repetitions are not destined to bring one concept to full clarity by ever-new similes, as were those of Donne; instead, we find a few very simple word-motifs parsimoniously repeated with only slight variation: indeed "¡Oh dichosa ventura!" is repeated without change, as is also "estando ya mi casa sosegada": these establish the homology of the two stanzas. Again in the sequence "en una noche escura—a escuras y segura—a escuras y en celada" we find one word (*escuro*) thrice repeated—while in the sequence "sin ser notada—secreta escala disfrazada—en celada" we have only thematic affinity, but still affinity. Not that there is always a musical *echo*: gentle contrasts may be heard: it is a soul stirred by passion that leaves the house now wrapped in silence (*inflamada—sosegada*); the darkness of the night (*a escuras*) is in opposition to the sureness of the purpose (*segura*). And the rhyming of *ventura* with *segura* also suggests a contradiction—though this is softened by the fact that the adventure is called *dichosa* ("blessed"). The decision of the soul is, indeed, a *venture* into the unknown, an *adventure*, not in the trivial sense of today (a capricious interruption of everyday life), but in the sense in which it has been said that in the Middle Ages all of life was an adventure: man's venturesome quest for the *advent* of the divine. The soul that has here decided to meet the divine has engaged itself in an existential adventure, and we are assured of a response from the divine by the epithet *dichosa*. And the word *escala*, with its suggestion of height, is the symbol of the upward development of the soul (we may remember the mystic ladder of Bernard de Clairvaux).

The next two stanzas (which I would translate as follows: "In the happy night, in secrecy—for no one saw me nor saw I aught but the light of my heart—, this light, brighter than the noon-day sun, did guide me to the one whom I knew to be in a place accessible to none other") should also be taken together (though this suggestion has not been made by others) because of the same rhymes in -*ía* and also because of a discreet parallelism which runs through them. Here we find again the alternation of motifs which assures the continuous flow of the poem: the words *dichosa* and *secreta* of stanza 2 re-appear; *sin ser notada* of stanza 1 is continued by *nadie me veía*, and *en celada* of stanza

2 by *en parte donde nadie parecía*. We may also note that in this pair of stanzas the one main verb is the imperfect *guiaba*. Once the decision is made, announced dramatically by the preterite *salí*, the action may subside to a calm, steady, prolonged rhythm, suggestive of firm direction. And we sense a new note of serenity and clarity: *en una noche escura* has given way to *en la noche dichosa*; night has now become a familiar medium in which the soul knows its way. In this darkness a light appears which shines from the heart; and this light is first introduced negatively (*"without* a light . . . save that . . ."), as if, thereby, made to emerge out of darkness. It is this radiance by which the soul is guided (*guía—guiaba*) more surely than by the brightness of noon-day. And with the first line of stanza 4 there is suggested an outburst of glad relief: *aquesta me guiaba*, "this, this was my guide." Out of the maze of the third stanza, which suggests the movement of the soul as it feels its way through the darkness, there emerges, like a clearing, the sure guide; the wondrous light, which was first suggested tentatively (negatively as we have said) in a dependent clause, is now, in the main clause, hailed openly: *aquesta. . . .* The sentence structure is thus allowed to translate the consistent progress of the soul that has striven, encouraged by an inner hope (*segura—dichosa*), until now the light within her shines around her, beyond her, toward the goal, now well discerned (*adonde*), toward that one (*quien*) whose dwelling-place is instinctively known to her ("one whom I knew to be in a place accessible to none other"). Here we have the idea of secret, exclusive knowledge, just as earlier there were suggestions of a secret, clandestine journey (the mystic ladder was "camouflaged," *disfrazada*). This motif of surreptitious love may be ultimately a remnant of the social-poetic conventions of the Troubadour love-poetry,[7] but it has acquired with

---

[7] Cf. the didactic exposition of this convention in Old Provençal passages, such as:

> Fals amador mi fant gran destorbier,
> Car son janglos, enojos, mal parlier;
> Mas ieu pero tenc *la dreita carrau*
> E vauc avan *suavet* e *a frau*.
> Qu'eu l'auzi dir en un ver reprovier:

Juan de la Cruz a mystical sense; since Christian mysticism represents the highest development of the Christian belief in a personal God, Who conditions the immortal soul of man, as this, in turn, presupposes God—the *mystic* soul, then, is able to affirm its knowledge of that individual God, as it were, as its *personal* possession in isolation, even in secrecy. With these last lines the pilgrimage has come to an end: with the allusion to *quien* "one who" (that ambiguous pronoun which posits an individual without revealing his identity). Later, this beloved individual here alluded to by *quien* will appear as *amado* (line 4, stanza 5) and finally as *el Amado* (in the following line).

We have been led, by the technique of musical variation and of a gradual syntactical unfolding, from the *noche escura* to the light that is brighter than day, from loneliness to the meeting with Him who is the divine goal—from what the Greeks would call στέρησις ("privation") to ἕξις ("possession"). These are basically terms of logic and indeed we find the idea of privation, of absence of positive characteristics, rendered by such negative grammatical elements as *sin, nadie, ni . . . cosa, sin, nadie*, which lead to the positive *aquesta* and *quien*, to fulfilment: "seeing nothing" leads to seeing the Beloved. Mysticism, indeed, posits privation, renunciation, and purgation as the starting-point toward fulfilment: expanding the Christian tenet that to have-not is ultimately to have, that only by closing one's eyes to the outward world does one truly see (the eyes of the heart, *oculi cordis*, are keener than the eyes of the senses), and that the light of the heart shines brighter than any other light.[8]

Per trop parlar creisson maint encombrier;
Per qu'eu *m'en cel* a tot homen carnau.

(translated by Shepard and Chambers, *Romance Philology*, II [1948], 86: "False lovers irritate me greatly, for they are indiscreet, tiresome, evil speakers; nonetheless, I keep to the straight road and go forward gently and secretly. I have heard it said in a true saying: Many evils come from over-much talk; wherefore I hide my secret from every mortal man"). I have italicized the Old Provençal expressions which foreshadow those of Juan de la Cruz; the lonely path of the loving soul quietly wandering toward its sure goal is already anticipated here.

[8] For this quite unclassical and un-Platonic conception of darkness cf. the masterly article of Rudolf Bultmann, "Zur Geschichte der Licht-

And now we understand the jubilant exclamations with which the next part (consisting of one stanza alone) begins:

> ¡Oh noche, que guiaste,
> Oh noche amable más que el alborada,
> Oh noche, que juntaste . . . !

Here, too, there is a paradox: "night that didst guide." It is more natural to think of the light that guides: but, then, as we know, the night has become light ($\sigma\tau\acute{\epsilon}\rho\eta\sigma\iota\varsigma$ appears in the splendor of $\acute{\epsilon}\xi\iota\varsigma$). And this radiant night has also "joined together" (*juntaste*). This *juntaste* is the climax of the sequence *guiaba—guiaste—juntaste*; we have already noted that in *aquesta me guiaba* there was a new note of tranquillity (the momentum of will-power, originally announced by *salí*, has subsided, as the soul yields to the inner light); now with *¡oh noche que juntaste!* the guidance has become a successfully accomplished fact, and the initiative passes from the light of the heart to the *night* itself; and it is the night alone which brings about the union. This poetic symbol of the night, as the mediator of the spiritual marriage, is original with Juan de la Cruz, as Baruzi has pointed out—who would also distinguish between the *symbol* of the night as it is used in our poem, and the *allegory* of the night as we find this elaborated in the prose commentaries of our author.[9]

---

symbolik im Altertum" (*Philologus*, XCVII [1948], 1-36), who dates the loss of the classical Greek conception of light from the downfall of the Greek Polis: whereas in classical Greece the light of day was considered not only the perfect means of orientation, but also a primary source of mental enlightenment, in later mystery religions man who, become dualistic, had lost confidence in the light of day, thought that supreme knowledge is revealed to him only by the intervention of supernal powers shining in the darkness. In gnostic texts light of day is said to be "dark light"; Plotinus recognizes in the ecstatic vision alone the "true light"; Dionysius the Areopagite speaks of the "divine darkness." The Greek temple, which stands in the full light of day and of which every detail can be perceived clearly by the believer who stands before it, is contrasted by Bultmann with the dark Christian church, which deprives the believer, who stands within its enclosure, of the light of day, while an artificial light, an image of divine inspiration that invades his heart, must be lit for him. The Christian mystics purposely expand the views of Dionysius on divine darkness.

[9] I do not believe, for example, that in stanzas 1 and 2 we have to do with "two" nights: "noche de los sentidos, noche del entendimiento."

For whereas allegory consists of an intellectual play wherein a series of fixed qualities belonging to one realm are made to correspond to a series of fixed qualities belonging to another realm (so that a literal "translation" is possible at any stage), a symbol represents an emotional identification of a complex of feelings with one outward object which, once the initial identification has been achieved, produces itself ever-new images, with their own rhythm and their own development, not always translatable. The symbol continually unfolds before us in time, while the allegory once developed is fixed forever, as is the relationship of its details. The allegory of love in the *Roman de la Rose* can be translated step by step; for example, the rose is characterized by thorns, by a delightful odor, etc., the allegorical implications of all of which are obvious. But the cross of Christ is a symbol: once Christ's suffering has been symbolized by that particular wooden instrument of torture, once Christ has "taken the cross on Himself," this Cross may become, in time, the "balance" on whose scales the sins of the world are weighed, the "tree" of life that conquers death, the "lyre" of Orpheus, etc. And with Juan de la Cruz the night is a similarly untranslatable symbol, generative of new situations and emotions which must be grasped as they unfold in time: it was first only the medium in which the lonely soul started its venturesome journey; now it has become the guide and (here no "translation" is actually possible) even the mediator between the Lover and the Beloved. Indeed the night itself is drawn into the atmosphere of *amar: noche amable*. Perhaps there is suggested an equation between night and love; surely it is love which joins the lovers, and yet it has been said of the night: "¡oh noche que juntaste. . . !" Therefore night = love. And, together with *amado* and *amada*, our *noche amable* forms a triangle (implying the triune relationship).[10] The three variations of the stem *amar* are symbolical of this mystic alchemy.[11]

[10] The device of indicating the reciprocity of love by the repetition of the stem of *amare* is well-known from Dante's line: "Amor che a nullo amato amar perdona."

[11] Cf. Ramon Lull's *Llibre de Amich e Amat*, where the relationship between the protagonists (Soul and God) is similarly expressed by two

The *noche amable* which figures as the basic essence of the union, of the transformation of the *amada* into the *amado*, is actually referred to in line 2 of stanza 5 as "amable más que la alborada" (more lovely than the dawn). Here we may see a continuation of the motif (stanza 4), "más cierto que la luz del mediodía" (night more precious than day), in which the normal evaluation of night and day is reversed. The praise of the night at the expense of the day is also quite contrary to the tendency in the Christian hymns, of hailing the morning star or the crowing of the cock as signs of the defeat of the powers of darkness and evil by those of good. Nor, obviously, is our apostrophe: "¡oh noche amable más que la alborada!" to be compared to the "o vere beata nox!" of the Holy Saturday liturgy, which prepares the believer for the more important, the all-important resurrection of the Lord, which will take place on Easter Sunday. Perhaps the poetic inspiration may be traced here not only to the general tradition of Christian mysticism (v. note 8), but also (again) to the Troubadour genre called the *alba*, in which so often the glory of the night, the night of love, is extolled to the disparagement of dawn.[12] Of course, the dramatic situation is not the same: there is no friendly guard posted on the tower to warn the lovers (often in vain) of the danger of approaching dawn—for here no danger need be feared by the lovers.

And here it should be remarked that the mystical metamorphosis as described by Juan de la Cruz (*Amada* becoming one with *el Amado*) implies no complementary transformation (*Amado* > *Amada*); that is, no equality between the lovers, as was the case with Donne. The love described by Donne, even on a spiritual plane, is still the love which could never invite a

---

variations of the stem *am*—though the "marital simile" does not become equally clear, owing to the masculine gender of both nouns.

Cf. also in Juan de la Cruz' *Romance*, I, the similar wording that depicts the Trinity: " . . . tres personas y un amado / entre todos tres había / Y un amor en todas ellas / y un amante las hacía; / y el amante es el amado / en que cada cual vivía. . . ."

[12] Cf. the scene in *Llibre de Amich e Amat* (25): "Cantaven los aucells l'alba, e despertà's l'amic, qui es l'alba; e los aucells feniren llur cant, e l'amic morí per l'amat, en l'alba"—where the prose refrain *l'alba* indicates the original situation.

metaphorical interpretation of union with the divine, because of his (very modern) concept of basic equality between the two lovers. If our Catholic poet is able to use human love as a figuration of love for the divine, this is because human love itself, according to age-old tradition, implies no equality: the bride submits to the bridegroom.

We have treated stanza 5 as representing the lyrical culmination of the poem, an interpretation borne out linguistically by the sequence of three apostrophes to the night. This exclamatory style has already been foreshadowed by the repetition of "¡oh dichosa ventura!", parenthetically inserted. But now the exultant note comes to full *épanouissement*—and is expressed in a pattern which, in Judeo-Christian liturgy (it is not to be found in pagan liturgy, according to Eduard Norden), was reserved for addressing the deity: a vocative, followed by relative clauses describing the triumphs or the favors of God, and usually followed in turn by a request for further favors[13] (though, in our poem, no additional divine favor can be desired; the soul wishes only to pour forth its gratefulness to the charismatic power of love).

And now the scene of the *unio mystica:* with the first lines of stanza 6, we sense immediately a new stillness and composure—after the exultant, ringing notes of the preceding stanza. Let us note first the word *pecho* ("breast")—a word capable of both a moral meaning (here, perhaps, "the heart") and, of course, a physical meaning.[14] It is surely in the moral sense that we must understand line 2: "que entero para él solo se guardaba" (which kept itself entire for Him alone), a line which makes explicit for the first time the motivation, the monogamic motivation, of the pilgrimage: of that *salí* which may have first appeared prompted by sudden passion, but is now revealed as springing

[13] Cf. in the *Chanson de Roland*, l. 2384 et seq.: "*Veire Paterne, ki unkes ne mentis, / Seint Lazaron de mort resurrexis / E Daniel des leons guaresis, / Guaris de mei l'anme de tuz perilz . . . !*"

[14] This double meaning was made possible only by the substitution of the singular *pecho* for the "betwixt my breasts" of the *Song of Songs*. Notice also that in the Hebrew poem it is the Bridegroom from whom the perfumes emanate; "as a bundle of myrrh, that lieth betwixt my breasts."

from deep-set faithfulness to the divine. And yet with *pecho florido* of the first line, which means, no doubt, "flower-scented breast," a suggestion of the sensuous is inescapable; here the disembodied soul whose progress we have followed acquires a mystical body. The prepositional phrase "en mi pecho florido" may remind us of the similar phrases "en una noche oscura" and "en la noche dichosa": the framework of the background of the dark night gives way to that flower-scented breast on which the Beloved reposes: "En mi pecho florido . . . Allí quedó dormido."

But in this *allí* ("on my breast, *there* he rested"), in this logically superfluous, somehow idiomatic adverb, do we not feel an emotional insistence ("there, in this place") as if on the breast as a goal attained—by the Beloved? So far, we have treated the pilgrimage only as a striving of the soul toward her own goal. And in describing her expectation we have, perhaps, passed over too easily the reference, in stanza 4, to the Bridegroom who was waiting (*esperaba*), waiting at the trysting-place. By now, in this one word *allí* we may catch the delicate suggestion of the quiet, steadfast yearning of the divine for the human soul[15]—whose relief from longing is now declared in the gently climactic *allí* (surely an echo of that *aquesta*, that sigh of relief with which the Bride greeted the guiding light). There the divine sleeps. And it is while he sleeps that the soul knows its final mystic rapture (described only in the last stanza). This sleep of Christ, how is it to be understood? (The critics, all of them silent on this point, must have thought only of the Bridegroom of the *Song of Songs*, who is shown "as a bundle of myrrh, that lieth betwixt my breasts"; but it is not said there that he is sleeping.) The only suggestion that seems satisfactory to me is the hallowed medieval legend of the Unicorn, who, as the symbol of Christ, falls to sleep on the sweet-smelling breast of a virgin. Against this background, the *pecho florido* "that kept itself entire for Him alone" acquires a particular significance. And, in the idyllic scene centered about the quiescent divine, all activity is subdued, all the participants are

[15] Cf. in the *Song of Songs*: "I am my beloved's, and *his desire is toward me*."

hushed: divinity, the human soul, and Nature—the latter figured by the cedar trees (suggesting a Biblical landscape) gently fanned by the air. The idyllic quality of the scene is enhanced by the repetition of *and* which suggests never-ending tenderness: ("y yo le regalaba / y el ventalle de cedros aire daba"). The word *aire* is repeated in the first line of the next stanza; we seem still to be in the same gentle atmosphere lulled by a soft breeze—which perhaps plays with the hair of the Beloved as the Bride spreads it to the air. But let us not be deceived; it is "el aire del almena," the air from the battlement (*almena*, the Spanish word of Arabic origin, implies a medieval castle and its tower). Does this not suggest warfare, sudden attack, hostile arrows? Dámaso Alonso has not sensed this military note: to him the tower is a place of pleasant refuge to which the lovers have ascended, to enjoy, according to him, the air gently blowing between the turrets.[16] But between these two contradictory pictures evoked by two interpreters let common sense decide: are even the cedars of Lebanon tall enough to reach up to the turrets? And the lilies of the last stanza— would they be growing on the tower? No, surely the lovers are at the *foot* of the tower (among the lilies), beneath the cedar trees.

[16] Dámaso Alonso, p. 70, suggests that *almena* came to Juan de la Cruz from the *Egloga segunda* of Sebastián de Córdoba, wherein he transformed an eclogue of Garcilaso's *a lo divino*: in this poem the desperate Silvanio, who had been jilted by his Celia, visits a tower: "Allí (!) en otras noches de verano había gozado los favores de amor de su Celia, del alma," and there, sitting "entre almena y almena," he remembers "las noches de verano al fresco viento." But only the two last quoted Spanish phrases are to be found in the original of Sebastián de Córdoba, the sentence beginning with "allí en otras noches" being without support in that poem: for Sebastián de Córdoba outspokenly says: "Mis ojos el lugar reconocieron, / que alguna vez miré, de allí contento, / los favores de amor que se me dieron"—in other words, the place where former love-scenes took place is not the tower, but a place upon which the lover looked down from the tower. And, in any case, the *almena* of *En una noche escura* has nothing whatsoever to do with the *entre almena y almena* in the quite different scene described by Sebastián de Córdoba. The desire to find missing links between Garcilaso and Juan de la Cruz made the literary historian believe in a similarity of situations for which there is no evidence in the texts.

And from this turreted tower, something strikes and wounds (*hería*) ; it must be, though this has been suggested by no other critic, *the arrow of love*, the arrow by which Saint Teresa was pierced, in the scene made graphically familiar to us by the statue of Bernini. Our scene, of course, is not to be visualized so concretely, so plastically, or with such harrowing effect; the arrow that strikes the unprotected neck is still only the air, and it strikes gently "con su mano serena"—but it finds its mark and leaves sweet death in its wake. This is the moment of ecstasy and annihilation ("todos mis sentidos suspendía"), the familiar "theopathic" state experienced by all mystics and often described by them as a blend of heavenly sweetness and piercing pain.[17] And the gentle hand that wounds suggests a bold personification which does not, however, quite materialize: the "aire del almena" does not harden into a figure of definable contours (least of all into the figure of the gay archer Cupid of Bernini) : it remains in the state of that *vaporoso* atmosphere of a Murillo. It is an intangible, an immaterial agent which, by an imperceptible activity, produces the climactic effect—while Christ sleeps. Is this air that wounds with serenity a symbol of the Holy Ghost, who is often compared, in Juan de la Cruz' commentaries, with air (cf. the relationship of Latin *spiritus* with *spirare*, "to breathe") ? Perhaps we cannot hope to penetrate the veil of mystery with which the Spanish Saint has wished to conceal as well as to reveal the mystery of the inactive activity, the Nature-like activity of the deity.

And now the last stanza, which may be said to render acoustically the gradual extinction of life: a love-death. Even before we come to this stanza we have learned that all the senses are suspended—as ours too must be: the sensations which had been

---

[17] Cf. Crashaw's poem *In memory of the Vertuous and Learned Lady Madre de Teresa:* "Oh how oft shalt thou complaine / Of a sweet and subtile paine? / Of intollerable joyes? / Of a death in which who dyes / Loves his death, and dyes againe, / And would for ever so be slaine! And lives and dyes, and knows not why / To live, that he still may dy." The mystic martyr who "loves his death" must not be confused with the "lover of death" Richard Wagner, of whom we shall speak later.—It must be borne in mind also that Crashaw's poem is a eulogy of Saint Teresa, not a re-enactment of her mystic experiences.

earlier aroused (the olfactory sense [the flowers], the sense
of touch [the air]) by now are numbed; the life of the senses,
which came to its highest intensity in the mystic union, recedes;
these have been stimulated by the poet only to make us realize
the *spiritual* eroticism experienced by the mystic soul that will
abandon the life of the senses. And this condition of deprivation
or στέρησις is very aptly symbolized by the immaculately white
lilies (*azucenas*), delicately profiled against the dawn, which
lack a positive color (unlike the pomegranate of the love-scene
in the *Song of Songs*); the Umbrian mystic Jacopone da Todi
says of the mystic soul engulfed in the sea of God: "en ben sí
va notando / belleza contemplando la qual non ha colore," "all
its feeling swims in sweetness: it contemplates a beauty which
has no color."[18] The suggestion of beatific nothingness, of
gradual Lethean self-forgetfulness, is achieved in our poem by
a combination of two devices: we are offered a picture of bodily
relaxation, leading to psychic extinction (*recliné mi rostro,
dejéme*), together with an acoustic effect of lulling incantation,
produced by the monotonous repetitions of sounds. As for the
first, *el rostro recliné*, "I let my face fall," suggests clearly the
physical; *dejéme*, "I abandoned myself," perhaps a blend of
the physical and the spiritual; while, of course, *dejando mi
cuidado*, "leaving my sorrow forgotten . . . ," describes purely
a state of the soul. The psycho-physical and the active-inactive
aspect of the mystic experience could not be better expressed
than by this ambivalent *dejar*. As for the acoustic devices, we
may note the two variations on the verb *dejar* (*dejéme—
dejando*) and the two on *olvidar*, "to forget" (*olvidéme—
olvidado*), and particularly the repetition of the rhyme in *-éme*
(*quedéme—olvidéme—dejéme*), which suggests a gradual sinking into the abyss of forgetfulness. And in the words "dejéme, /
Dejando mi cuidado / Entre las azucenas olvidado," which
offer a final, lingering cadence, we have a transition from the
act of abandoning the world to the state resulting from this

[18] I assume that the mention of *alborada* in stanza 5 (contrasting with
"estando ya mi casa sosegada") is intended to prepare us for a further
progress in time: for the coming of dawn (when the world will still be
somewhat blurred).

act: oblivion attained. In the final word *olvidado*, "already forgotten," this state is presented as an accomplished fact which must have taken place, somehow, before—so that when we actually come to the word *olvidado*, we know we have left it behind. The soul *is* already resolved in God. And this "already," the temporal adverb that I see implied in *dejando*, is the counterpart to the explicit *ya*, "already," of the first stanzas ("estando ya mi casa sosegada"): from the beginning to the end of the poem we are reminded of the progress in time of the mystic experience.

Juan de la Cruz has been able to transcribe the unbroken line, the parabola of that experience in its evolution from energetic pursuit to self-annihilation, from human to divine action—and this is a short poem of eight stanzas (as though the poet would suggest that what happened with such intensity cannot be measured by man-devised clock-time), a poem in which mystery is presented with the greatest clarity and simplicity (as though he felt that his experience, which may be given only to the elect, has nevertheless a limpid quality that even a child could understand).

For, unlike such a German mystic as Jacob Böhme, who resorts to new coinages in the attempt to express the inexpressible, adding the mystery of words to the mysterious experience, our poet, following the sober Latin tradition of all religious writing in Romance languages, is content with the stock of words already given by the language and, even here, limits himself to a restricted number. At the same time, however, he multiplies, by repetition, variation, and syntactical disposition, the density of the web of semantic interrelations, resuscitating the memories (memories of the soul and of the flesh) that are latent in popular terms. Thus, although the poem contains only familiar Spanish words which can be understood by the Spaniards of today as well as they were in the sixteenth century (perhaps with the exception of the Gallicism *ventalle*, "fan"), these words have become endowed with a mystical depth which makes them appear as new words (though they *are*, *pace* Mr. Shapiro, the old words). And we have again a suggestion of profundity coupled with simplicity in the easy, though far from trivial, musicality of our poem. This is written in the meter of the *lira*, that solemn, ode-like form which, however, becomes singable thanks to the predominance of *one* rhyme in each stanza—in our poem of a feminine rhyme by which the musicality of the Spanish verse is still more enhanced; nor do the consonants that occur in these bisyllabic rhymes, mainly evanescent spirants [-b- and -d-], detract from the vocalic character of this language, but rather suggest the soft breathing of the "aire del almena."

It could be said that, in Juan de la Cruz' mystic poetry, there is to be seen a development of Spanish Renaissance lyricism away from its learned, verbally ornate character[19]—perhaps through the influence of the sublime Biblical poetry of the *Song of Songs*, which, in turn, we find with him desensualized: the sensual world of that epithalamium has become with him a borderland between the realm of the senses and that of the soul.[20] Such a poetic blend was possible for a poet in whom the Renaissance poetic ideal of outward beauty and clarity has met with the tradition of medieval mysticism centered in inward contemplation.

But there is, perhaps, an important problem to be faced before we leave this poem: the expression of mystic experience in a manner that appeals to the sensuous realm, the presentation of mystic love in terms that could be taken as describing erotic pleasure—is this not sacrilegious? Is it not the pagan subsoil of Catholicism that comes here to the surface?[21] Many of you, while listening to my explanation, must have asked yourselves, more or less explicitly, such questions—since, in our own age, to which few religious geniuses have been given, the Saint's

---

[19] Dámaso Alonso has contrasted the *epitheta ornantia* of Garcilaso and the epithet-less nouns of Juan de la Cruz.

[20] An expression such as "ninfas de Judea" in another poem of San Juan's shows well the convergence of the two poetic traditions.

[21] I believe that the Spaniards feel more than other nations the carnal part in Christ's personality, and among the three divine persons they are apt to emphasize more the second ("verbum *caro* factum"). Hence their mystic glorification of the blood—which somehow reminds them of the blood of Christ. It is an error to ascribe to them a *pagan* cult of sensuous deities—they are Christian in that the sensuous reminds them of the descent of the deity to the flesh.

psychophysic or theopathic experience is not self-evident. I would say simply that the description of the mystical event in physical terms gives a graphic effect of *actuality* which might not have been achieved otherwise. Here, too, though in another sense, the body serves as a necessary "alloy": that which gives concreteness to the elusive emotion. The documentary value of our poem we must accept with reverence. Here, truly, beauty is truth and truth beauty: the beauty of the mystic's description testifies to its veracity, and the evidence with which that concrete happening develops before us in time is undoubtable: we know that this event *has happened*. We may remember that the capacity of giving the evidence of the flesh and of temporal development to spiritual experience is first found with the greatest medieval poet, Dante, who, in the place of timeless allegories of the perfect Beloved, substituted the graphic image of a Beatrice who actually walks, smiles, sighs, within a poem that has a beginning, a middle and an end[22] (unlike the "Extasie" of Donne, where we were thrown back to the pre-Dantean timeless allegory). Modern lyricism, even of a worldly kind, is indebted to such religious poets as Dante and Juan de la Cruz for the evidence (evidence of the flesh and evidence of time) which they have given forever to the description of inner feeling.

And now, for our third poetic picture of ecstasy, let us consider the scene of Isolde's *Liebestod*, at the end of Richard Wagner's "music-drama," *Tristan und Isolde*.

This choice may seem surprising at first glance, since Wagner's text has always been considered to require association with music—that art which by definition transcends words. And it is true that here the "text" of our *explication de texte* will have to be wrenched from the context with which it was destined to be forever fused. Since, however, Wagner himself has included the texts of all his operas within his collected works, thus giving to understand that he believed his poetry alone would stand examination, we are justified in analyzing it critically. And per-

---

[22] This difference was pointed out by E. Auerbach, *Dante als Dichter der irdischen Welt*.

haps it is with just such a poet, whose texts we ordinarily hear
mixed with, or drowned out by, an intoxicating music, that a
sober philological interpretation of the words might be considered most necessary.[23]

The scene is a high cliff in Brittany overlooking the ocean,
where we see Isolde by the dead body of Tristan, whom she has
found too late. In her monologue, which is addressed to Marke,
Brangäne, and Kurwenal, and which will be followed by her
transfiguration and death, there occur variations of the words
of the love-scene from the second act: indeed the monologue is
sung to the same air, to that melodious *Liebestod*-motif, orgi-
astically developed by the instruments, which in the score is
counterpart to the disharmoniously grating monody of the
Sehnsuchtsmotiv:

Mild und leise		Wie das Herz ihm	15
wie er lächelt,		muthig schwillt,	
wie das Auge		voll und hehr	
hold er öffnet:		im Busen quillt;	
seht ihr, Freunde,	5	wie den Lippen	
säh't ihr's nicht?		wonnig mild	20
Immer lichter		süsser Athem	
wie er leuchtet,		sanft entweht:—	
wie er minnig		Freunde, seht—	
immer mächt'ger	10	fühlt und seht ihr's	
Stern-umstrahlet		nicht?	
hoch sich hebt:		Höre ich nur	
seht ihr, Freunde,		diese Weise,	
säh't ihr's nicht?		die so wunder—	

[23] Thomas Mann in his essay on Wagner (*Leiden und Grösse der
Meister*, Berlin, 1935, p. 89 et seq.), an essay on which I shall draw
heavily in the following discussion, has quoted our passage as an example
of excellent craftsmanship: the German equivalent of the poetry of the
paradis artificiels of Baudelaire and Poe.

In Mann's comparison of Wagner with other great writers of the 19th
century, I miss the name of Victor Hugo, with whose *Légende des siècles*
the myths invented by Wagner can well be compared—except for
Wagner's procedure of limiting himself to medieval Germanic myths; in
this, he is rather a companion of German "philological poets" of doubtful
value, such as Felix Dahn.

voll und leise,
Wonne klagend
Alles sagend,   30
mild versöhnend
aus ihm tönend,
auf sich schwingt,
in mich dringt,
hold erhallend   35
um mich klingt?
Heller schallend,
mich unwallend,
sind es Wellen
sanfter Lüfte?   40
Sind es Wogen
wonniger Düfte?
Wie sie schwellen,
mich umrauschen,

soll ich athmen,   45
soll ich lauschen?
Soll ich schlürfen,
untertauchen,
süss in Düften
mich verhauchen?   50
In des Wonnemeeres
wogendem Schwall,
in der Duft-Wellen
tönendem Schall,
in des Welt-Athems   55
wehendem All—
ertrinken—
versinken—
unbewusst—
höchste Lust!   60

It is with the dead Tristan that the dying Isolde becomes united in an ecstasy which marks the final separation of the soul from the body. Isolde senses the transfigured state of Tristan: she feels the light that radiates from his still open eye ("immer lichter / wie er leuchtet"), the perfume of his breath still exhaled from his lips ("wie den Lippen / wonnig mild / süsser Athem / sanft entweht"), the music that emanates from his still rising and falling breast ("Höre ich nur / diese Weise / . . ."); note again the synthesis of sensations characteristic of the state of ecstasy, but this time emphasized with the programmatic insistence of an Edgar Allan Poe or a Baudelaire.[24] We must believe that in Wagner's ideology of "eroticism sanctified" the dead lover Tristan is presented, not only as alive in death, but

[24] The synaesthetic devices are also at the basis of the idea, dear to Wagner, of the *Gesamtkunstwerk* to which all arts should contribute. The latter idea is attacked by Thomas Mann as typically "bad 19th Century"—as if, he argues, quantitative addition of the different arts should produce greater effect! The fact is, however, that any Catholic mass is a *Gesamtkunstwerk* and that already the first hymns of Ambrose show a tendency in that direction (cf. my article in *Traditio*, III).

as having become a *saint* whose body, contrary to natural processes, has acquired miraculous qualities that make it a delight
to the senses. That Wagner himself realized the difficulty of this
philosophy for the audience is suggested by the fact that Isolde
feels compelled to call upon her companions for corroboration:
"säh't ihr's nicht?" (witnesses are appealed to, just as in
Donne's poem). The somewhat turgid lines 7-24 give way to
true poetry when Wagner has Isolde describe the song which
she, and she alone, hears coming from Tristan's body ("Höre ich
nur / diese Weise / . . .?"). The mystic ecstasy is incited (and
this is a trait characteristic of Wagner) not through the eye that
is bent on light,[25] but through the ear that hears a supernatural
melody—through the music, joyful and painful, strong and
serene at the same time, which pierces Isolde like a dart and
envelops her like a cloud ("in mich dringt / . . . / um mich
klingt? / . . . / mich umwallend"). Gradually, in Isolde, the
faculties become blurred—so that she can no longer distinguish
the lines of demarcation between the senses: ". . . sind es Wellen/
sanfter Lüfte? / Sind es Wogen / wonniger Düfte?" And when
she must question: ". . . soll ich athmen, / soll ich lauschen? /
Soll ich schlürfen / . . .?" we have also, perhaps, an indication
of the gradual recession of the will—though the very fact of
self-questioning shows that all reason is not yet extinct. But
soon, a curious syntactical disintegration, echoing the relaxation
of the will, takes place: the infinitives will detach themselves
from the verb "shall I?" to appear, in the final period as semi-
independent, as no longer belonging to a question imposed by
the consciousness, but as free lyrical effusions—which are at
the same time impersonal, suggesting the process itself, without
personal agent: *ertrinken—versinken*. These infinitives, somehow released from the tutelage of *sollen* and *wollen* (that is, of
the will), suggest sighs of relief and joy as the soul immerses
itself in the sea of nothingness. In the sequence which begins by
questioning the reality of the miracle ("Höre ich nur / diese
Weise"?), which continues by questioning the identity of the

[25] Wagner himself wrote (Thomas Mann, p. 104): "Es scheint, dass
das Auge mir als Sinn der Wahrnehmung der Welt nicht genügt."

miraculous phenomena ("sind es Wellen / ... / Sind es Wogen / ...?"), which leads then to the questions showing the gradual disintegration of the will ("soll ich ...?"), and which ends with the gentle sighs of liberation, *ertrinken—versinken,* Wagner has found an inimitably graphic device of syntactic onomatopoea by which to render the final stages toward the ecstatic union.

But though there is here, as with Juan de la Cruz, a suggestion of "todos los sentidos suspendidos," the ecstasy which Wagner is describing differs in one most essential point. The union for which Isolde yearns is a union no longer directly with Tristan (who is lost sight of after l. 32), but with the elements into which he himself has dissolved: the emanation of perfume, breath, and sound elicit from Isolde the desire for a similar dissolution (*"mich verhauchen"*) in the scented, breathing, sounding medium (note how the preposition *um* [*"um mich klingt,"* *"mich umwallend,"* *"mich umrauschen"*] suggests a circumambient medium), which is figured as a sea: "untertauchen / ... / In des Wonnemeeres / wogendem Schwall / ... / ertrinken— / versinken."[26] Here we have the pantheistic idea of the melting into the universe of two souls who have consumed themselves in longing for each other. In the words of Isolde—which we hear sung in a deep contralto—there is no suggestion of upward movement (two souls mounting heavenward in an apotheosis, as at the end of the *Flying Dutchman*); rather, that of sinking, ever deeper, into the sea of nothingness. Only in the soaring music of the orchestra, which Isolde's voice will finally join in her last note (the note *Lust* that suddenly rises, *pianissimo*), is

---

[26] Thomas Mann (p. 132) has pointed out a passage from the dialogue of the lovers in Friedrich Schlegel's *Lucinde*, which seems to anticipate the *Tristan*-mood, and which Wagner must have known: "O ewige Sehnsucht!—Doch endlich wird des Tages fruchtlos Sehnen, eitles Blenden sinken und erlöschen, und eine grosse Liebesnacht sich ewig ruhig fühlen." These lines, supposedly belonging to a prose dialogue, are in fact already poetry, but Wagner has enhanced their poetic character by his syntactical onomatopoea.

Our passage showing the progression of infinitives from questions to exclamations is foreshadowed in Act II by the lines of the love-scene: "Wie es fassen / wie sie lassen / diese Wonne! / ... / ohne Wähnen / sanftes Sehnen, / ohne Bangen / süss Verlangen / ...."

there an anticipation of apotheosis and the sense of height—as though through depth the freedom of height could be won.

This sea of nothingness is not that void described by Jacopone and other mystics (including Juan de la Cruz): an emptiness created by the soul in order that it may be filled by God; it appears as a turbulent mass of waves, perfumes, breaths ("In des Wonnemeeres / wogendem Schwall, / in der Duft-Wellen / tönendem Schall, / in des Welt-Athems / wehendem All"), ruled over not by a personal God, but by the violent forces of Nature. According to Wagner's system, the world-spirit, figured here as the "world-breath" (*Welt-Athem*), is identified with the universe itself (*das All*): it is no longer the spirit of God that breathes upon the waters: rather *Deus sive natura*. This *All* of Nature, as it appears at the climax of the ecstatic vision, is the true Bridegroom of Isolde. The participles *wogendem, tönendem, wehendem*, with their onomatopoeic quality and their dactylic rhythm, add their impact to the evocation of the chaos that is infinite movement. We have seen that in our Spanish poem a poetic effect was achieved by simple, popular words and phrases; Wagner, however, in accordance with the spirit of the German language, must accumulate new word-combinations and compounds (*wogendem Schwall, Wonnemeer, Duft-Wellen*, as well as that tremendous hapax *Welt-Athem*, which swells the lungs of any German), in order to mirror linguistically the multitude of ever-new shapes. Again, whereas with Juan de la Cruz the genuine vocalic richness of Spanish was exploited as an invitation to linger on the serene feelings expressed in the words, with Wagner the consonantic quality of German is reinforced by the introduction of the medieval device of alliteration (in des *W*elt-*A*thems / *w*ehendem *A*ll—the '*a*'s with their glottal stop have a consonantic flavor), as if to render the dynamism of a swelling and pulsating universe. And this pulsating effect is further enhanced by the insistent multiplication of the reverberating rhyme-words which punctuate the lengthy period that extends from line 26 to 50—and which serve, somehow, at the same time to echo also the throbbing intensity of Isolde's own feelings—those of a freedom-seek-

RICHARD WAGNER

ing soul, hammering at the walls of its own individuation, beyond which may be heard the surging of the cosmic forces that
promise liberation. The dynamism of dissolution which we
find in Wagner's poem, describing the passionate strivings of
the ego to lose its identity, contrasts strongly with the quiet
control that informs the Spanish poem, wherein the soul is
allowed to remain individualized—just as we have the contrast between union with the ungraspable forces of the universe,
and union with a personal God: indeed, these contrasts are
interdependent.

We come now to the last two lines: "unbewusst— / höchste
Lust!" where we find an epigrammatically isolated equation
(soldered by the rhyme) between the two terms on which is
built the philosophy of Wagner (which is not that of Descartes
or Kant, but that of Schopenhauer) : the highest rapture (*Lust*)
is freedom from consciousness and individuation: Nirvana. But
it is only an *expectation* of rapture that is suggested by the final
word *Lust* (which, as we have said, rises unexpectedly above
the low notes of "ertrinken— / versinken"). In the Spanish
poem all expectations have been fulfilled when we come, or
even before we come, to the final *olvidado*—on which the voice
may only sink; but here we must leave the soul on the threshold
of new experiences, or paradises, timidly, hesitatingly glimpsed:
"unendliche Werdelust" which lingers after the close of the
poem.

We may note also that this "unbewusst— / höchste Lust"
is a significant variation on the passage from the love-duet of
the second act: "ein-bewusst: / . . . / höchste Liebes-Lust!"
Ein-bewusst (= "uni-conscious"), said of the two lovers, is
replaced by *unbewusst* (= "unconscious"), said of Isolde
alone; and *höchste Liebeslust* has become simply *höchste Lust*.
By this parallelism of words (reenforced by the identity of the
musical motif) Wagner is obviously suggesting that for him
the ecstasy of death is a consummation of the ecstasy of love:
for love, as portrayed in the second act, was associated with
night and death (the expression *Liebes-Tod* itself is found in
this scene) and was already defined as an extinction of indi-

· 177 ·

viduation: an extinction achieved not in the light of day, which outlines sharply the separate individualities, but in the night of love, which makes them one: "ewig einig, / ungetrennt"; "ohne Nennen, / ohne Trennen." Thus Death represents only a more radical process by which individuality is dissolved; Death is an eternal night of Love. And just as in Wagner's idea of love the craving for death is implied, so, with him, death itself has the quality of erotic ecstasy. That the love-scene and the death-scene should be set to the same voluptuous music suggests that in the former there is stressed death-in-love, in the latter love-in-death: thus the expression *Liebestod* is ambivalent. It may even have a third meaning: "death *to* love"— a farewell to love; for is not the dying Isolde freeing herself from the fetters of that murderous instinct of sex? Perhaps the Wagner of the Wesendonk period, who himself could not find rest from the obsession of passion, has let Isolde, that Valkyrie of the senses, die a vicarious death *for him*?

We have already mentioned several differences of detail between the German and the Spanish poem: we see now that they are diametrically opposed in their treatment of love. Wagner would glorify eroticism by raising it to the height of a new mysticism; Juan de la Cruz would glorify (that is, make actual) the spiritual mystic union by descending to the medium of the flesh. Wagner's is a pantheistic, pan-erotic universe; the world of Juan de la Cruz is ruled by the love of God.

Whereas to the Church Fathers erotic love was only a lowly reflection of love for God, to Wagner, a Freudian before Freud, it is the erotic which is the source of all varieties of love.[27] But it cannot be said that the erotic pantheism of Wagner is rooted in naïve, healthy confidence in the senses, as was true of the Greeks, or of a Goethe, or a Walt Whitman: it is tinged with melancholy and pessimism. Wagner is inspired by the desire

[27] It is the same attitude toward love which Augustine has called *amabam amare*, and which he rejected as a youthful aberration, that makes up Wagner's whole concept of love: indeed the wording *amabam amare* itself appears, with a far from pejorative connotation, in the first (non-versified) draft of *Tristan und Isolde*, in the form: "Könnte ich die *Liebe* je nicht mehr *lieben* wollen?"

to drown the burden of life and of his individuality in love, death—and in the music of the love-death. He would not have sung of the blades of grass.[28] His flowers are opium-scented *fleurs du mal*, in contrast to the delicate white lilies of Juan de la Cruz and the fresh violets of Donne.

Aesthetically considered, it must be said that the poetic form chosen by Wagner as an expression of his philosophy is just as convincing as is that of Juan de la Cruz (and surely the German master has conquered with his Dionysiac music more souls than has any artist of any other nation). But underlying the artistic form of Wagner's poetry (and the "unendliche Melodie" of his music), there is the ultimate formlessness of his philosophy. For the desire to escape from one's individuality, whether through love, through death, or through music—a tendency which has led to tragic consequences in the German history of the 19th and 20th centuries—is an essentially formless and nihilistic desire to succumb to the chaos of the universe. But the mystic philosophy that would preserve and purify the personality, which should be annihilated only before the Creator, is a triumph of inward form over the chaos of the world.

The climax of desire is represented in our two poems by the two reflexive verbs *mich verhauchen* and *dejéme*: it is characteristic that the first refers to the sheer physical process of evaporation, the second to a deliberate act willed by a moral being.

---

[28] It must be granted, however, that Walt Whitman, too, has at times sacrificed on the altar of the deified Love-Death; cf. the poem *Scented Herbage of My Breast:*

> . . . you [the leaves] make me think of death.
> Death is beautiful from you (what indeed is
>   beautiful except death and love?)
> Oh I think it is not for life I am chanting here
>   my chant of lovers.
> I think it must be for death . . .
> Death or life I am then indifferent, my soul
>   declines to prefer, (I am not sure but the
>   high soul of lovers welcomes death most).

The concurrence of dates (the poem of Whitman is written in 1860, Baudelaire's *Invitation* in 1857, and *Tristan und Isolde* in 1857) is striking.

Spenser, *"Shepheardes Calender, March"**
(Lines 61-114)
and the Variorum Edition

THE PASSAGE in Spenser's *Shepheardes Calender* in which the story of the fowler boy and Cupid is treated seems to me to have been wrongly appraised in the Variorum edition (*The Works of Edmund Spenser, The Minor Poems*, Johns Hopkins Press, 1943, I, 272). As a background for my own interpretation of the passage in Spenser, I may summarize the story as originally told by Bion in his *Idyll*, IV and adapted by Ronsard in his *Ode* of 1556, later (1660-1672) called *L'Amour oyseau* (P. de Ronsard, *Oeuvres complètes*, ed. Chamard, VII, 259), which Spenser is generally assumed to have used.

With Bion the fowler boy seeks to capture what seems to him to be a huge bird, though the poet has informed the reader that the creature is Cupid ($\tau\grave{o}\nu$ $\text{"E}\rho\omega\tau\alpha$). When the youth, his forces spent, finally gives up the chase, he goes to seek advice from the old plowman who has taught him the art of fowling—to learn only that he should shy away from that particular bird ($\tau\acute{o}\delta\epsilon$ $\tau\H{\omega}\rho\nu\epsilon\text{o}\nu$), that evil creature ($\kappa\alpha\kappa\grave{o}\nu$ $\theta\eta\rho\acute{\iota}\text{o}\nu$): "this one ($\text{o}\H{\upsilon}\tau\text{o}\varsigma$) who now eludes you, hopping hither and thither, will one day suddenly, of his own accord ($\alpha\dot{\upsilon}\tau\grave{o}\varsigma$ $\dot{\alpha}\phi'$ $\alpha\dot{\upsilon}\tau\H{\omega}$) attack and overpower you." Thus the boy learns only that the "bird," the "animal" he tried to catch in vain ("bird" and "animal" are expressed by neuter nouns) is a personal being ($\text{o}\H{\upsilon}\tau\text{o}\varsigma$ and $\alpha\dot{\upsilon}\tau\acute{o}\varsigma$ are masculine pronouns)—it is only the reader who knows that this $\text{o}\H{\upsilon}\tau\text{o}\varsigma$ is the demigod $\dot{o}$ $\text{"E}\rho\omega\varsigma$ ("the well-known Eros") and that the plowman's warning contains an epigram such

*From *Studies in Philology*, 1950, XLVII, 494-505.

as: "do not prematurely seek to fall in love; Love, the ruthless
god, will conquer you in due time." A similar delicate play with
psychological and linguistic perspectives is also to be noticed
in the ambiguous use of the epithet ἀπότροπος, said of Eros
when he is being pursued by the lad: this may mean simply
"turning away (from the boy)" (active use), or else, in passive use, "the one from whom one turns away (because of his
dangerousness), the dangerous one": from the boy's point of
view, the epithet may have been intended to have the first meaning, from that of the reader the second. We shall see that the
double perspective deliberately introduced by Bion in that
serene εἰδύλλιον or picture-poem that paraphrases an intellectual
epigram quietly addressed, over the head of the child, to the
adult mind, will not be continued by the two modern poets
who, more emotional or sentimental, leave nothing to the imagination of the reader and have the boy learn (Ronsard) or
know by himself (Spenser) the outspoken lesson: "this is
Love."

The first difference to be noted with Ronsard is his graphic
description of the physical appearance of Cupid (with Bion we
learned only the fact that the boy saw him as a huge bird):
Ronsard's *Amour emplumé* is thus described:

> Son plumage luisoit plus beau
> Que n'est du paon la queue estrange,
> Et sa face sembloit un Ange,
> Qu'on voit portrait en un tableau.

This hybrid if magnificent outward appearance ("half angel
and half bird") is the contribution of Ronsard—whom Spenser
will follow—and indeed if he would give us an "objective" picture of Cupid the Winged One-Become-a-Bird, there remained
no other way for him than mythological invention (invention,
of course, with the help of well-known classical motifs: the
peacock is the bird of Venus). Obviously, then, "cet enfant,
qui ne sçavoit pas, que c'estoit," must seek an explanation: an
explanation not of a technical nature ("why was I not able to
catch the bird?"), for which the boy in the Greek poem had

sought out the old man who had taught him the art of fowling, but the explanation of the event itself: his meeting with such a strange and elusive zoological species ("Il luy va le fait expliquer . . . L'oiseau de mauvaise rencontre"). And for this, he goes to a fortune-teller—who begins by identifying the "bird":

> Cet oyseau, c'est Amour qui vole,   33
> Qui toujours les hommes affole
> Et jamais ne fait que du mal . . .
> Ce malheureux oyseau volage . . .   43
> Sans y penser te surprendra . . .
> Et foullant de ses pieds ta teste   47
> Que c'est que d'aimer t'apprendra.

The fortune-teller is characterized by Ronsard as "une vieille mère qui se mesloit de deviner" (ll. 23-24), as an "amateur" fortune-teller (qui se mesloit . . .), a garrulous commère, a public adviser, who could hand out information to whosoever came her way. She is by no means an oracle whose veracity is beyond doubt, rather a slightly comical and frustrated old woman who pours out her own pessimism. We may notice that she makes the picture of love even blacker than had the plowman: "Qui toujours les hommes affole Et jamais ne fait que du mal." But, indeed, even before we hear the old woman's explanation wherein Cupid is represented as "Ce malheureux oyseau volage," the idea "bird of ill omen" has twice been suggested, the boy himself has seen the bird flying about "comme oiseau de mauvais augure," and seeks an explanation of "l'oiseau de mauvaise rencontre." (Obviously, Ronsard is translating and expanding only the pejorative meaning of Bion's ambiguous epithet ἀπότροπος.)

But if Ronsard has, on the one hand, multiplied the pejorative allusions to Love, on the other he has chosen to describe Cupid's physical appearance as dazzlingly beautiful: beautiful as only art can depict it (l. 12). In this contrast between fair exterior and sinister essence, do we not have the familiar baroque pattern of "sensuous beauty unmasked": a pattern in which illusion and disillusionment (desengaño) are presented with equal insistence, as if maintained in polar tension? The serenity of Bion disappears with Ronsard, who points up extremes (though softening these with a touch of humor).

Another important difference between Bion and Ronsard is the stage of enlightenment reached by the boy. On the one hand, in the French poem he is told outright the identity of the being he had been pursuing: "Cet oyseau c'est Amour." Ronsard rejects the device by which the boy is kept in ignorance and the reader alone informed. On the other hand, though he learns immediately the *name* of "Love," he is told by his informer that the *meaning* of love ("que c'est que d'aimer") will become clear to him only in the future, through personal experience which he cannot have at his age. Thus the oracular suspense of the Greek poem is somehow maintained with Ronsard: the meaning of the word "love" becomes no clearer to the boy than is to Rabelais' travellers the meaning of the word *Trinc*! that they hear from the priestess Bacbuc.

With Spenser it is the lad himself who learns the identity of the winged being—as the result of being pierced, in his pursuit, by Cupid's shaft. And, indeed, the incident of the pursuit is brought into the larger framework of the eclogue, only in order that Thomalin may prove to his companion Willye that he knows about Love's game. As the eclogue begins, we find the two youths speaking freely of Nature now awakening, and of her divinities; Flora, Maia, and "little Love" whose statue, incidentally, can be seen "shrouded" in a bush: line 68. Here we find the well-known pastoral convention of young shepherds discoursing familiarly about the figures of age-old mythology, a familiarity, however, which may be only theoretical, just as children understand only theoretically the concepts of the words they hear their elders use.

Willye speaks of "little Love" as on the same level with the mythological figures of Flora, Maia; and, though, in connection with "Love," he mentions a particular girl, the rustic lass Lettice, with whom he would "sporten with delight," we feel that he knows only of the word-world to which Cupid belongs.

Not so Thomalin, who rudely interrupts his companion's poetic embroidering: when Willye speaks of awakening "little Love that now sleepeth in Lethe Lake," Thomalyn takes him sharply to task: "Willye, I wene thou bee assott / For lustie Love still sleepeth not / But is abroad at his game." For, as he remarks in answer to Willye's ironic question ("How kenst thou, that he is awoke? / Or hast thy selfe his slomber broke . . . ?"): "No, but happely I hym spyde, / Where in a bush he did him hide, / With winges of purple and blewe." In these lines, we hear the voice of personal experience which rejects poetic paraphrase. This means that just before we are told the full story of the lad's encounter with the winged being (the episode of Greek origin which concerns us), we are given to understand that the problem of identity has already been solved. Thus the element of suspense, present in the Greek poem and the French, is eliminated by Spenser, who, from the beginning, presents the boy as informed; and the story which we are soon to hear will be told in retrospect.

> It was upon a holiday,   61
> When shepheardes groomes han leave to playe,
>> I cast to goe a shooting.
> Long wandring up and downe the land,
> With bowe and bolts in either hand,
>> For birds in bushes tooting:
> At length within an Yuie todde
> (There shrouded was the little God)
>> I heard a busie bustling.
> I bent my bolt against the bush,   70
> Listening if any thing did rushe,
>> But then heard no more rustling.
> Tho peeping close into the thicke,
> Might see the moving of some quicke,
>> Whose shape appeared not:
> But were it faerie, feend, or snake,
> My courage earnd it to awake,
>> And manfully thereat shotte.

With that sprong forth a naked swayne,
With spotted winges like Peacocks trayne,   80
   And laughing lope to a tree.
His gylden quiver at his backe,
And silver bowe, which was but slacke,
   Which lightly he bent at me.
That seeing I, levelde againe,
And shott at him with might and maine,
   As thicke, as it had hayled.
So long I shott, that al was spent:
Tho pumie stones I hastly hent,
   And threwe: but nought availed: 90
He was so wimble, and so wight,
From bough to bough he lepped light,
   And oft the pumies latched.
Therewith affrayed I ranne away:
But he, that earst seemd but to playe,
   A shaft in earnest snatched,
And hit me running in the heele:
For then I little smart did feele:
   But soone it sore encreased.
And now it ranckleth more and more,   100
And inwardly it festreth sore,
Ne wote I, how to cease it.

And here we see that Thomalin has not only solved the "problem of identity": his encounter has taught him the *meaning* of Love: by himself he has learned more than had Bion's lad from the plowman or Ronsard's from the fortune-teller (though, as we shall see later, we do find with Spenser a comment on the central incident, by Thomalin's interlocutor, Willye). In spite of his denial ("or hast thy selfe *his slomber broke*?"—"*No* . . ."), Thomalin has awakened Love (". . . my courage earned it to *awake*"), but he has done so unwittingly. He had gone out into nature carefree and sportive at the first signs of its awakening from the sleep of winter, in order just to play as is fitting on a holiday in spring, to wander about and let fly at birds. Suddenly he hears a "bustling" noise in a near-by bush, which could indicate the presence of a bird, and he makes himself ready to take aim. When nothing appears to view and the rustling of the bush subsides, the lad still cannot give up the chase; now it has become for him a matter of "manly" honor and "courage" to run down his quarry, fairy, fiend or snake— and he must now shoot at the bush. The original aimlessness of the lad has given way to the true hunter's instinct, to the spirit of adventure, attack, and challenge. This is his hybris: he "manfully thereat shotte," shot at an undefined "it" and thereby awakened Love. The natural restlessness and adventurousness of the adolescent who thinks it his duty "to act like a man," will fatally lead to love. And from the moment the war with Cupid has begun Thomalin's fate is sealed: the would-be captor will become Cupid's captive. In vain are his thrusts at the god; the disproportion between the efforts of the sturdy attacker (the hail of arrows, the "pumie-stones" thrown) and the elusiveness of the light-footed, laughing god are humorously described. So much so that the boy himself becomes alarmed at this strange game and, suddenly defeated, turns to flee— whereat the god that had seemed but to play sends a shaft "in earnest" into the heel of the fleeing lad: an erstwhile hero whose "Achilles heel" was only his normal youthful restlessness and spirit of aimless adventure. In this inimitable *poetic description of puberty*, we are led, in an uninterrupted sequence, from careless sporting in nature to the chase of an elusive something, which turns out to be Love, then to the struggle with the god which ends in defeat, and to a lasting wound. We find here no moral formulated, as with Bion ("keep away from Love!"); indeed, the only moral to be deduced would be: "Rejoice not in spring, be not young!—for this is hybris, and nemesis must follow!"

In the light of the inner logic underlying the chain of events here described, we may easily understand the contrast between the realism of the sporting episode (which in turn brought with it as a consequence the use of the "old rusticke language," the dialectal terms of Lancashire) and the appearance of the

Mediterranean god Cupid with his bow and quiver: Thomalin, who does only what any lad (and any English lad) would do, is suddenly faced with a supernatural ancient force—a force older than civilization which we may call by its ancient name Eros, in the realization that the mythological force with which the ancients invested this figure is still alive among us. Spenser, by exploiting the native dialect and choosing brisk rhythms and forceful alliterations, has described, with all the freshness of an English month of March, the restlessness and pains of adolescence—a description which becomes all the more universal in meaning the more it has the genuine English ring.

We must, however, dwell for a moment on the motif of the statue of Cupid that is "shrouded" by an ivy-bush. It is another convention of pastoral poetry that nature, highly stylized, is mingled with art: the Renaissance-gardens of bucolic poetry are nature-plus-art because pantheistic nature must contain the pagan gods of nature in their omnipresence—how could they be made more "present" than by statues generously distributed throughout the landscape? The statue of the god Cupid clad with ivy is then the symbol of that mythical weddedness of nature and art that is presented as an age-old or timeless element in the pastoral convention. But the presence of Cupid in nature in the form of a statue has a dormant quality—the god is potentially, not actually present as if still sleeping "in Lethe lake." And it is perhaps in order to emphasize the state of oblivion in which the god dwells before he has become actual and "awake" that Spenser has introduced the ivy instead of the Greek box-tree (which Ronsard has preserved, but Baïf, in his otherwise literal translation of Bion's poem *L'Amour oiseau*, has changed into a holly-bush, more genuine in France). Surely Spenser's change is to be explained by a desire not only to acclimate our episode in England, but also to enforce the "dormant" aspect of Love: the evergreen ivy which is independent of the seasons is usually associated by us with the past, with ruin, with the grave: it represents nature spinning its age-old web of oblivion over the slowly decaying works of man; the statue of Cupid covered with ivy represents then the minimum of Love's effectual force. But out of this state of sleep, Thomalin will "awake" the god[1]—he who had wanted only to capture birds will unwittingly force the god to come forth from his statue: the statue will release its living content—and the word "Love" will fill itself with meaning.

To state all this should be superfluous—were it not that the critical utterances about our poem, quoted in the Variorum edition, read like the minutes of a symposium of grumblers and fault-finders[2] unanimously bent on condemning the eclogue beforehand. Not one of the critics quoted has taken the pains to analyze it from within, from within the poetic logic that binds

---

[1] One could mention here the many passages in which Spenser uses the "wanton yvie" as the symbol of lust, cf. for example *Shepheardes Calender, August,* l. 30 (*Variorum,* note of the editor: "By 'wanton' he meant luxuriance plus luxury in the old sense"), *Faerie Queene,* book II, canto V, 29 and canto XII, 60-62 (note of C. W. Lemmi: "Ivy is the plant of Bacchus, and Bacchus, identified with the sun, was familiar to the Stoics, to Plutarch, to the Neo-Platonists, as the embodiment of the masculine principle in nature"—to this, I would add that the most immediate source of Spenser's "wanton yvie" must be Horace's *lasciva hedera*). In our own passage, however, where the general emphasis is on Nature still asleep, and where the ivy is represented without the epithet "wanton," and as serving to "shroud"—I would stress the idea of dormancy rather than lust: or, perhaps, dormant lust.

[2] A typical example of what I should term misplaced erudition is offered by Renwick's remark on the expression *Lethe lake*: "Lethe was, of course [!], not a lake, but a river, and souls drank of it. Spenser probably had in mind Virgil's use of 'lacus' for Styx in *Aeneid* 6. The second error [!!] may have arisen from a memory of Achilles being dipped in Styx by his mother. . . ." Our learned critic is thinking solely in terms of the category of "historical accuracy" on the poet's part: that the poet could freely fabulate, using the ancient tradition for new combinations—that, indeed, he could do what the ancient poets themselves have often done, evidently does not occur to the "scholarly mind." Spenser's "errors" are, of course, poetically motivated: Love is at first, as we have said, represented as dormant in our poem, and *therefore* Lethe becomes a stagnant lake, not a flowing river: that is, for the same reason that the box-tree became an ivy-bush. (Incidentally, in medieval English, *lake* meant, as my colleague Professor Malone points out to me, a "slowly flowing river," so that Spenser's term could be justified also on linguistic grounds.) And why should Spenser not have thought of the dormant Cupid as comparable to one of those pale souls whose pathetic fate in the Tartarus the ancients have so vividly described? The paler, the "deader" Cupid is first depicted, the more striking will be his later awakening.

its parts organically together: they all judge from without, from preconceived general ideas about Spenser's mythological poetry. Moreover, their procedure in dealing with a particular poem is to extract certain features which offer parallels and contrasts with Spenser's sources, thereby proceeding in a horizontal direction; never have they proceeded vertically, showing the organic unit formed by Spenser's poem, as opposed to the quite different poetic organisms created by Ronsard and Bion. It is my general experience that the gaze of the commentator, when divided between a poem and its source, is unable truly to concentrate on either of them.

Here are three samples, as listed by our edition, of the dogmatic and throughout negative criticism to which our poem has been subjected:

HERFORD: Spenser here attempts to add another new note to the pastoral flute. In the *February* he pastoralized the Aesopian fable; here he pastoralizes the delicate mythology of the idyllists Bion and Moschus. The task was harder, and the result is not altogether pleasing. The homely popular wisdom of the fable sat well on the lips of the old shepherd, and accorded with the old-fashioned gait of the verse. But Bion's choice artificialities have an exotic air in Spenser's shepherd world, notwithstanding the evident endeavor to harmonize them. We resent this winged Cupid hunting with golden quiver and silver bow in the English woods; and the matter is little mended by the "pumie stones" which Thomalin throws at him, or by the realistic detail of the fowling-net set for carrion crows, in which, he tells us, the "winged lad" had once been caught.

RENWICK: The result is not of the happiest. This sort of confection depends for its effect on lightness of touch, and Spenser's tastes overcame his judgment in leading him to make a full descriptive painting of what at best is only a decoration. . . . The sporting episode is too realistic—too good, indeed—for such a quarry as this playful lyric convention of a Cupid. Spenser felt the requirements of the idyll sufficiently to make him simplify his style, but that simplification was in the direction of realistic conversation, and he did not realize that simplification of detail was also necessary. This sort of thing was not really in Spenser's line: he required more room, and subjects that would stand his habitual solidity of construction. . . . Spenser visualizes the whole affair, and makes his fowler hear, before he sees the quarry. The point is good and natural, but not useful[3] here.

BUSH: The mythologizing of nature is not quite the same as the naturalizing of mythology, and the latter, which is the healthier instinct, is responsible for much of the most attractive verse of the period, both dramatic and non-dramatic. Whatever foreign influences, ancient or modern, contributed in the way of motives or polished workmanship, the native pastoral tradition (like the native drama) was strong enough to undergo refinement without losing its own color and sap. Lyrical poems which were subdued by mythology we do not read; those that subdued mythology everyone knows. In the former category might be placed, for example, Spenser's eclogue for March, which hardly succeeds in acclimatizing Cupid.

But is not the purpose of all classicism to "acclimate" the Greco-Roman gods in our modern world ("die Sonne Homers, sie scheinet auch uns," as Schiller has formulated it)? Was not the whole literary movement of the Renaissance inspired by the idea that Greco-Roman mythology has an eternal metaphorical validity for all people?[4] In our case, it is ironical that the critics have failed to recognize that Spenser has succeeded precisely

[3] Why should it not be "useful" to show the eager lad—who is a hunter! —sensitive to and interested in every sound he hears in nature? This acoustic detail was a necessary stage in the sequence leading up to the dénouement.

[4] The critics who indict Spenser for introducing Cupid into English scenes succeed in revealing their own dogmatic approach to poetry. And it may be feared that their pedantic prejudices have already eaten deep into literary history as this is taught in schools: it seems to me that an anti-mythological bias of this sort, quite unknown in non-Anglo-Saxon countries, is forwarded quite mechanically to succeeding generations of

in showing the transformation, in a youthful mind, of a purely
verbal mythological entity into a living reality, that he has
"naturalized" (and humanized) ancient mythology which for
him is no empty "decoration." All theoretical contentions as to
the impossibility of making mythology come alive in English
poetry must vanish before the fact that here the theme of a
superbly beautiful English poem is none other than the coming
alive of mythology. Thus the traditional verdict that Spenser's
Shepheardes Calender is an "experiment that has failed" should
be drastically revised.

Now let us turn, belatedly, to Willye's comment on Thomalin's story, which we have not yet discussed:

> Thomalin, I pittie thy plight.   103
> Perdie with love thou diddest fight:
>   I know him by a token.
> For once I heard my father say,
> How he him caught upon a day,
>   (Whereof he wilbe wroken)
> Entangled in a fowling net,
> Which he for carrion Crowes had set,   110
>   That in our Peeretree haunted.
> Tho sayd, he was a winged lad,
> But bowe and shafts as then none had:
>   Els had he sore be daunted.

On this passage Renwick comments as follows: "The ending
is rather feeble, for Cupid has already been recognized. Spenser
makes a story of what is really an epigram, and the point of
the epigram has been anticipated." As we have pointed out above,
Spenser has, from the beginning of our episode, rejected the
device of suspense; he has deliberately presented Thomalin
from the start as one who knows of Love: thus the function
of his narrative is only to explain to the reader how he has
come by his knowledge. And this shift in presentation, as was

---

students, so that the situation which the schoolmasters unwarrantedly
take already for granted may (secondarily) become an historical fact
through their ministrations.

also pointed out above, means that the function of the interlocutor's comment must be different with Spenser: what Willye offers, in the words "Perdie, with love thou diddest fight" (l. 104) is, obviously, not explanation, but a confirmation of Thomalin's experience to which Willye is brought by his familiarity with his father's experience: confirmation and, in a sense, expansion. If Renwick has found Willye's statement anti-climactic, this is because he has failed to see that Spenser has used Bion's episode[5] to begin at the end and work his way backwards.

But what of the "expansion" offered by Willye's words just cited: the parallel experience of his father? The older commentator "E. K." has rightly said, "In this tale is sette out the simplicitye of shepheards opinion of love." Willye's father had set his fowling-net in his pear-tree for quite utilitarian purposes: to trap the carrion crows that molested him; absent, here, is the spirit of adventure and challenge which brought about Thomalin's doom. Yet the simple farmer, too, had unwittingly captured Love and, though temporarily spared by the "winged lad" (who, this time, was without his weapons) will evidently not remain unpunished ("whereof he wilbe wroken"). Thus Love, who is no respector of persons, avenges himself alike on those who seek and those who avoid adventure. However, in this picture of a paterfamilias awaiting Cupid's persecution, we must admit that Willye's parallel has been somewhat laboriously contrived by Spenser—who perhaps felt constrained to repeat the diptych of young lad and graybeard found with Bion.

---

[5] I offer this possibility of influence (whether direct or indirect) from Bion's poem, in opposition to the general opinion. But to imagine that Spenser had known only Ronsard's version is to postulate the almost impossible coincidence of his replacing Ronsard's old woman by Bion's old man! Moreover, the very laboriousness of the episode of Willye's father suggests a constraint exercised by the classical model.

CHAPTER XI

Explication de Texte Applied to Three Great Middle English Poems*

IN HIS "Introduction aux études de philologie romane" (Frankfurt a/M, 1949), pp. 33-37, Professor Erich Auerbach has characterized the method known as *explication de texte* as "the healthiest and most fertile" among the different types of literary scholarship now in use, as the one method which from the start prevents the isolation of literary phenomena from their context (thereby avoiding the mechanical and compilatory aspect so often offered by literary studies) and allows the literary phenomena under study to remain in their natural environment, their individual particularity continuing intact. Professor Auerbach distinguishes three stages in the historical development of *explication*:

(1) The practice of commenting upon literary works, continuing from antiquity through the Middle Ages and Renaissance to our days, which involved only the removal of difficulties for the benefit of the reader, by providing the factual data (historical, linguistic, cultural, exegetic) necessary for the correct and complete understanding of the text.

(2) The French school practice of *explication de texte* which serves to replace the "passive" study of handbooks by an activity on the part of the student which allows him to discover for himself and from the text itself the general features of an author or work.

(3) The practice of commenting—"developed and enriched by certain modern philologists (among the scholars in Romance particularly by L. Spitzer)" [to whom should be added Prof.

* From *Archivum Linguisticum*, 1951, III, 1-22, 157-65.

Auerbach himself]—which seeks, not to rediscover in the texts things already known, but to reach "new first-hand observations" which must then be integrated to the known and may lead to re-evaluation of the particular author or work.[1]

[1] Auerbach finds the philosophical background of this new type of *explication* in Croce's aesthetics as "scienza dell'espressione"; Husserl's phenomenology with its insistence on the particular phenomenon in which its essence can be grasped; Wölfflin's parallel concrete analysis of works of art; and in "many other currents"—among which I personally would list Freud's analysis of the psychological laws governing the expression of the subconscious. In René Wellek and Austen Warren's *Theory of Literature* (New York, 1949), 1887, I find, in spite of their friendly attitude toward my work, my activity in the field of stylistics somewhat distorted: contrary to Auerbach, who has not mentioned the contribution of Freud, the authors have only taken into consideration my earlier Freudian beginnings in which mental deviation from the normal in modern, mostly pathologically warped writers was shown to explain linguistic deviation or innovation, not my maturer work in *explication de texte* which deals with writers of all periods and attempts to explain particular stylistic traits by their historical or cultural background (Wellek and Warren, while complete in their bibliography, mention in their text only an earlier article of mine on Racine, published in 1928). I regret to say that the objections voiced against what the authors call "psychological stylistics" (a term, incidentally, which they seem to apply only to the study of "pathological" writers) show a complete misunderstanding (or ignorance?) of the "circular procedure" characteristic of the humanities (as pointed out by Dilthey—of whose ideas they discuss only the theory of *Erlebnis*—and as used in all my studies, including the present one). Wellek and Warren argue, in the manner that has become traditional with the school of unregenerate positivists from which these critics are usually miles away, (1) that "many relationships professing to be thus established [i.e. by inference from style to psyche of a writer] are not based on conclusions really drawn from the linguistic material, but rather start with a psychological and ideological analysis and seek for confirmation in the language"; (2) that "the linguistic confirmation . . . itself seem[s] frequently strained or based on very slight evidence." In reality, my procedure involves two separate movements (both of which, taken together, serve to complete the "philological circle") : I first draw from one detail (which need not always be linguistic or stylistic, but may also be compositional in nature) of incontrovertible factual evidence, an inference as to the (at this stage still hypothetic) psyche of the author or the period, which hypothesis is then, in a second movement, controlled by a scrutiny of (to the degree that this is feasible) *all* other striking details (stylistic or compositional) which occur in the same author or period. From the first poem under study in this article, for example, I shall isolate first an undeniably factual linguistic observation (the number of repetitions, the repeated occurrence of expressions, especially of totality and number, of

Thanks to an invitation of the English department of the Johns Hopkins University to lecture on my method, I have enjoyed an opportunity of applying it to certain Middle English poems and I am publishing these modest attempts in a field not my own with the hope that some of the points of view applied here, derived as they are from a long study of medieval Romance texts, may not prove without benefit to scholars in the English field.

I

The first poem I shall treat is "Blow, northerne wynd" (published critically by Böddeker, *Altenglische Dichtungen des Ms. Harley 2253*, and by Carleton Brown, *English Lyrics of the Thirteenth Century*, under no. 83).

> Blow, northerne wynd,
> sent þou me my suetyng!
> blow, norþerne wynd,
> blou! blou! blou!   4
>
> 1. Ichot a burde in boure bryht
> þat fully semly is on syht,
> menskful maiden of myht,
> feir ant fre to fonde;   8

---

enumerations, anaphoras, etc.), then to draw a hypothetical line to the medieval psyche (the idea of *summa*), finally to corroborate this hypothesis by other (non-linguistic) traits which seem to me to corroborate my tentative assumption (the complete synthetic portrait, the accumulation of medieval motifs, the coupling of courtly and popular poetic forms, the insistence on total sacrifice, etc.). I challenge Messrs. Wellek and Warren to show that the evidence from which I start (the number of repetitions, etc.) is not pure "linguistic material," but conclusions derived from a previous "psychological and ideological analysis" and that either the linguistic evidence (the repetitions) or its analysis (the idea of *summa*) are "strained" or "based on very slight evidence." (In the explanation of the second poem, I start not with linguistic but with ideational material: the idea of the closeness of the three realms; for the third I choose as basis a compositional element: "time" as a poetic device.) It is a pity that critics of critics such as the authors of the very useful book *Theory of Literature* fall into the most familiar trap of critics in general: not to understand what they criticize and thus to allow themselves an ultimately sterile fault-finding attitude, thereby making necessary tedious rectifications on the part of critics of the "critics of critics." . . .

In al þis wurhliche won,
a burde of blod & of bon
neuer ȝete y nuste non
Lussomore in londe.   12
   Blow, &c.

2. Wiþ lokkes lefliche & longe,
   wiþ frount & face feir to fonde,
   wiþ murþes monie mote heo monge—
   þat brid so breme in boure,   16
   wiþ lossom eye grete ant gode,
   wiþ browen blysfol vnder hode.
   he þat reste him on þe rode
   þat leflich lyf honoure!   20
      Blou, &c.

3. Hire lure lumes liht
   ase a launterne a-nyht,
   hire bleo blykyeþ so bryht,
   so feyr heo is ant fyn.   24
   a suetly suyre heo haþ to holde,
   wiþ armes, shuldre ase mon wolde
   ant fyngres feyre forte folde.
   god wolde hue were myn!   28

4. Middel heo haþ menskful, smal,
   hire loueliche chere as cristal:
   þeȝes, legges, fet, ant al
   ywraht wes of þe beste.   32
   a lussum ledy lasteles
   þat sweting is & euer wes;
   a betere burde neuer nes,
   yheryed wiþ þe beste.   36

5. Heo is dereworþe in day,
   graciouse, stout, & gay
   gentil, iolyf so þe Iay,
   worhliche when heo wakeþ.   40
   Maiden murgest of mouþ;

bi est, bi west, by norþ & souþ,
þer nis fiele ne crouþ
þat such murþes makeþ.   44

6. Heo is coral of godnesse,
   heo is rubie of ryhtfulnesse,
   heo is cristal of clannesse
   ant baner of bealte,   48
   heo is lilie of largesse,
   heo is paruenke of prouesse,
   heo is solsecle of suetnesse
   ant ledy of lealte.   52

7. To loue, þat loflich is in londe,
   y tolde him as ych vnderstonde
   hou þis hende haþ hent in honde
   on huerte þat myn wes;   56
   ant hire knyhtes me han so soht,
   sykyng, sorewyng, & þoht,
   þo þre me han in bale broht
   aჳeyn þe poer of péés.   60

8. To loue y putte pleyntes mo,
   hou sykyng me haþ siwed so,
   ant eke þoht me þrat to slo
   wiþ maistry ჳef he myhte,   64
   ant serewe, sore in balful bende
   þat he wolde, for þis hende,
   me lede to my lyues ende
   vnlahfulliche in lyhte.   68

9. Hire loue me lustnede vch word
   ant beh him to me ouer bord,
   ant bed me hente þat hord
   of myne huerte hele   72
   ant bisecheþ þat swete ant swote,
   'er þen þou falle ase fen of fote
   þat heo wiþ þe wolle of bote
   dereworþliche dele'.   76

10. For hire loue y carke ant care,
    for hire loue y droupne ant dare,
    for hire loue my blisse is bare,
    ant al ich waxe won;   80
    for hire loue in slep y slake,
    for hire loue al nyht ich wake,
    for hire loue mournyng y make
    More þen eny mon.   84

The commentaries of Böddeker and Brown, obviously conceived according to Auerbach's type I, offer us factual explanation of difficult passages, literary parallels, and an approximate localization of the anonymous 13th century author of our poem —which, because of textual concordances with three other poems contained in the same manuscript, one of which shows "acquaintance with Wales and Welsh folklore," must originate from a poet familiar with that particular country. About the particular art of our poem the two commentators have nothing to say. It may be then fitting to attempt a commentary of the type III described by Auerbach—by endeavouring to offer "new first-hand observations" which must be, of course, immediately integrated to our previous knowledge of medieval poetry.

Our poem falls into two parts: the "courtly" love-poem and the refrain or burden, of a "popular" character. As to the first, three obvious observations, perhaps apparently disjointed, suggest themselves from direct observation of the text: (1) the purpose of the poet is to prove his Beloved to be the absolute Paragon of Excellence; (2) his stylistic treatment seems to depend for effect to a large extent on repetitive devices; (3) the procedure of description is to break down the "totality" of the figure of the Beloved into minute details.

(1) That the poet sees his Lady as a paragon means that he singles out for praise not individualistic traits of personality but qualities of objective validity which she possesses to a superlative degree (her uniqueness consisting in the potentiated generic). And yet the poem entitled by Brown "The Loveliest Lady in Land" offers only one (doubtful[2]) example of the gram-

---

[2] Doubtful, because this example could also be interpreted as an elative—

matical superlative ("maiden murgest of mouth," l. 41): the idea of the superlative is more consistently expressed:

(a) By a negative comparison which excludes the possibility of any equal in time or in space: cf. the types "never was there found a maiden . . .": ll. 9-12, 35-36 (the same pattern is also applied to the "exemplary" love of the poet, ll. 83-84) and "nowhere in the world is there found a maiden . . .": ll. 42-44.

(b) By affirmative comparison (simile) with an object traditionally representing an ideal object: cf. the type "hire loueliche chere as cristal," ll. 20-21, 30, 39, etc.

(c) By identification with an object (metaphor) representing a superlative degree of excellence: cf. the type "heo is coral of godnesse" (repeated throughout stanza 6).

(d) By presenting a feature as universally desired: "wiþ armes, shuldre ase mon wolde," l. 26.

(2) The repetitive devices mentioned above are illustrated in the following ways:

(a) Repetition of certain laudatory epithets: *lussom*, ll. 12, 17, 33; *feyr*, ll. 8, 14, 24, 27; *leflich* (*louelich*), ll. 13, 20, 30, 53; *suet* and its family, ll. 25, 34, 51, 73; *mirth* and its family, ll. 15, 41, 44; each of the epithets *menskful, hende, dereworþe, bryht*, appears twice in the poem.

(b) Accumulation of synonyms (repetition by synonymy): *feyr and fin*, l. 24; *graciouse, stout & gay, gentil, jolyf*, ll. 38-39; *swete and swote*, l. 73.

(c) Rhetorical anaphoras: *wiþ* (five times in stanza 2), *heo* (6 times in stanza 6), *for hire loue* (6 times in stanza 10)—and we may perhaps also mention as a repetitive phenomenon:

(d) The alliterations present in every line of the poem.

(3) The detailed description offered by the poet falls into two parts, required by medieval canons: body and soul. In the description of the Lady's virtues (stanzas 5-7) we find simply a loose-joined enumeration of qualities; in the physical description, however, we find a systematic procedure "from head to foot" (stanzas 2-4).

---

of which there are more examples: "of þe beste," 32, "wiþ þe beste," 36, "fully semly," 6.

Surely there must be a common denominator for the three features just mentioned; and this would be a concern with the *quantitative* presentation of ideal beauty. This is quite obvious in the case of (2) (repetitive devices) and (3) (enumeration of the parts of the body); and it may also be said that (1) the emphasis on the superlative is ultimately an emphasis on quantity. That in all (analytical) languages the superlative construction is formed by means of a word designating quantity ("the most," etc.) shows that this concept is always underlying that of the superlative degree. But in our poem this latent suggestion of the quantitative is reinforced precisely by the accumulation of superlatives [which in itself would fall under our feature number (2)]—which means that the quantitative itself is treated quantitatively: cf. for instance the pattern "heo is coral of godnesse" (quoted above under 1c) which appears, as we have said, repeated throughout stanza 6.

We have already suggested that the additive use of superlatives implies a normative attitude toward the Beloved which is peculiarly medieval, and may create a chilling effect upon the modern reader (we do not see the individual portrait of a particular lady with that mole on her neck, that peculiar lilt of voice, that slightly bent head of hers which we may have come to cherish more than anything in the world, but a synthetic lady composed of all the excellences theoretically conceivable in woman). Even more aberrant from modern taste is the application of the additive procedure to a lyrical description of physical loveliness—in accord with medieval canons: the medieval rhetorician Mathieu de Vendôme, for example (cf. Faral, *Les sources latines des contes et romans courtois*, p. 103), teaches his pupils how a—uniform—beauty should be described by enumerating the excellences of the different bodily parts, always observing the regular order downward from head or hair to legs and feet (and, it might be added, with no attempt to fuse these independently perfect *disjecta membra* into a visualizable whole); and such precepts continue to be observed in Renaissance descriptions of beautiful ladies: Ariosto, Spenser (and Donne who parodies them).

It is this "canonic" description by Ariosto of the enchantress Alcina which provoked the famous attack of Lessing (*Laokoon*, chs. XX-XXI), inspired by his belief that, since poetry is an art "in time" (not "in space," as is that of painting), the poet Ariosto has, in his description, transgressed the boundary of poetry. According to the German critic, Ariosto should have chosen either to depict the *effect* of Alcina's beauty on others, as Homer has done for his Helen, or, in a direct description, to present beauty *in movement* which is necessary for appeal ("Reiz") ; in spite of certain ripples of movement in the portrait of Alcina, such as the rise and fall, like waves of the ocean, of the "apples of ivory" of her breasts, the total effect must be a static one, depending on the enumeration, continuing through five stanzas full of "cold statements about beautiful form" which cannot be visualized by the reader who must proceed "in time" and is denied the possibility of remembering at the end all the detail he has read before ("bei dem Dichter sehe ich nichts, und empfinde mit Verdruss die Vergeblichkeit meiner besten Anstrengung, etwas sehen zu wollen"). Lessing, mainly concerned with the problem of visualization in poetry of pictorial beauty, gives expression to a creed of his time which sees beauty in the characteristic and can therefore not be our guide for medieval (or for that Renaissance) art according to whose canons beauty must conform to timeless, universal precepts. The emphasis of the medieval poet is on *perfection*—and in our poem, as pointed out above, on perfection quantitatively demonstrated. The perfect is complete (I would say in German, with a play on words : "Das Vollkommene ist vollständig") and the reader (or listener) must be given the opportunity to verify the sum total of completeness by adding deduction to deduction (the lovely long locks = the hair is perfect; the lovely eye great and good = the eye is perfect; the face lovely as crystal = the face is perfect), finally to arrive at the conclusion (or sum total of the addition) : "*everything* in the Beloved is perfect" ("lasteles" is the term used by our poem). Nor was it tedious to the medieval public to be forced to consider, in preordained succession, each limb and feature, for at each point of the enumeration assurance grows that nothing imperfect is to be found with the Beloved; and conviction of the perfect was for them visualization of the perfect—visualization of the principle of perfection to which, alone, the variety of expressions throughout the enumeration has contributed. What Lessing had failed to consider was the ability of earlier readers to enjoy the monotone of perfection—with its religious and moral overtones.

Perhaps the general medieval insistence on absolute perfection is indeed a reflection of the theological thinking expressed by Anselm of Canterbury in his (quantitative) definition of God as that being "quo majus nihil cogitari potest." Such Old French verses as . . . "plus bele creature / ne forma onques Nature" and the parallel lines in our poem: "a burde of blod & of bon / neuer ȝete y nuste non / lussomore in londe (a betere burde neuer nes)" are, perhaps, ultimately patterned on the Anselmian definition of God. Now just as the medieval writer of apologiae (or theodicies) must "prove" the perfection of God by displaying before us "the wonders of the world,"[3] the beauty and fullness of creation (in bestiaries, lapidaries, etc.), so the medieval poet of love, himself an apologetic writer in essence, must prove didactically the excellence of the Beloved in all her parts. In our poem the relationship between God and His creature, the Beloved, is outspokenly affirmed (l. 19, "he þat reste him on þe rode / þat leflich lyf honoure")—the implication being that since "that lovely life" is perfect in all its parts, it partakes of the divine.

The perfect being rests in its own static beauty, but potentially it is able to elicit action from the beholder at any moment. I see the Aristotelian and medieval idea of actualization of the potential expressed in expressions such as:

8   feir ant fre *to fonde*
14 face feir *to fonde*
25 a suetly suyre heo haþ *to holde*
27 fyngres feyre *forte folde*.

That the lovely maiden's beautiful body asks for actualization of its abstract efficacy—this we see in these phrases suggesting

[3] An expression coined by Raimundus Lullus.

the lover's tentative reaction (which is of her doing without any action on her part being involved). How much does he covet the possibility of folding those beautiful fingers that seem created in order to be folded! If with Homer (so perfectly conscious, according to Lessing, of the limits of poetic art) the beauty of Helen is shown in the immediate reaction on the elders of Troy, in our poem the Beloved, too, acts on her lover, if only *in potentia*.

For he is no sensuous Greek, but a Christian courtly lover who has deliberately decided to stay within that limbo of gratuitous sensuous-suprasensuous love which shuns consummation while not abating in its fervour for the sensuous beauty which enraptures his eye. The English courtly poem shows us a lover even more modest in his desires than do certain Provençal troubadour poems in which the poet dreams to meet his love "en vergier o sotz cortina": the beauty of his maiden is for the day, not for the night: (1. 37) "heo is dereworþe *in day* . . . worhliche *when heo wakeþ*" (the comparison of her face with a lantern "a-nyht" is not intended to suggest the situation of the Provençal *alba*). Indeed the maiden is, in accordance with the courtly ideal, a "lady in society." She is presented from the start "in boure" (1. 5, cf. 16), that is within the framework of a noble environment;[4] "vnder hode" (1. 18), that is in the chaste costume of honourable medieval womanhood ("che porta le bende," as Dante would say), in a surrounding worthy of her (1. 9 "in al þis wurhliche won," 1. 36 "yheryed wiþ þe beste") and endowed with that courtly mastery of ceremony and circumstance that is gaiety (1. 38 "gay"), with the "social smile" (1. 15 "wiþ murþes monie mote heo monge") and the gift of conversation (1. 41 "maiden murgest of mouþ"). In short, she is the woman of Christian society, not the object of lust, depending for respect only on her womanhood (apart from her possible role as wife and mother), worshipped with that *amor* or *hohe Minne* in which sexual attraction is included, but sexual con-

---

4 From the year 1000 on we find *bower* (a generic term for "dwelling") used to refer to "an inner apartment . . . in ancient mansions . . . especially applied to a lady's private apartment" (*NED*).

summation excluded. Here, too, the *ut in pluribus* plays its part: the conviction of the lover that she is the best on earth immediately implies her (potential) action on society.

Now it is well known that since the 12th century the Virgin comes to appear more and more, in literature as well as in art, as a lady (as Our Lady, *Notre Dame, Unsere Liebfrauen*), that is, as a noble woman with social attributes. It will then not surprise us to learn (from the commentary of Carleton Brown) that the attributes bestowed on the loveliest lady in land ("coral of godnesse, rubie of ryhtfulnesse," etc.) are those usually ascribed to the Virgin, who is said to be, in the Old French poem he quotes, "Safir esprové, / Jaspes alosé, / Amirande pure, / Lubis alumez, / Diamaunt amez / De noble nature" (Brown does not, however, elaborate on the parallel treatment accorded to the Virgin and to the perfect lady of society). There is one particular feature in the description of stanza 6 which can only be explained by a certain device practised in the hymns in honor of the Virgin: the selection of eulogistic terms from quite different semantic areas. In this single stanza, minerals and precious stones (coral, ruby, crystal) appear side by side with flowers (lily, perrywinkle, sun-flower)—and with symbols of earthly power ("banner"—"ruler").[5] How is such eclecticism to be explained (again a problem left undiscussed by Brown)? In an article entitled "Fleur et rose, synonymes par position hiérarchique" (which has appeared in the *Estudios dedicados a Menéndez Pidal*), I have attempted to explain the general medieval practice of coupling, in hymns to Mary, not only (the generic) "flower" and (the specific) "rose," but also "rose" and "ruby," "rose and pearl," etc. The "polyonomasia" of the Virgin which is based on her identification with the Beloved of the Song of Songs, to whom manifold sensuous epithets were ascribed, is a requirement of those hymns. In the lists of periphrases for Mary (which are also applied in courtly poetry to the Beloved) each single periphrase must consist of a metaphor expressing excellence, the different realms of nature (and of society) being scanned for representatives worthy to serve as

[5] About "lady" in the last line of stanza 6, see the discussion below.

comparata: the ruby, the diamond, etc., among gems, the lily, the rose, etc., among flowers (in our stanza, "banner" and "queen" have a similarly high distinction in the social world). The choice, now of ruby, now of crystal, etc., depends on their ability to reflect the various virtues of the lady; those objects exist not in their own right but only as so many embodiments of (her) perfection. The more gems and flowers are accumulated in the panegyric, the more complete the ideal moral portrait of the maiden will appear (we find here again the idea of *Vollkommenheit-Vollständigkeit*). Thus we need not be surprised if in our poem the natural boundaries of e.g. gem *vs.* flower are annihilated in favor of their common character (symbols of excellence), so that we find in the same stanza the ruby side by side with the lily (even "flower" may be coupled with "rose," as I show in my article, since the flower [bloom] is the most excellent part of the plant). If we take into account this medieval pattern of "synonymy on the basis of equal hierarchic position," the apparent disorder[6] in our stanza becomes order: we have before us a transversal cut through the "wonders of the world."

A short discussion of the syntactical construction "*x* of *y*" used eight times in our stanza seems here in order. The majority of the "of" expressions in our stanza and more specifically those of lines 1, 2, 3 and 5, 6, 7 could perhaps be thought of as "metaphorical appositions" (not literal appositions as in "the city of London," "the game of tennis" [= London, a city; tennis, a game], but metaphorical ones of the type "the sword of truth," "the wine of victory") with an "of" genitive that is

---

[6] This "disorder" is not a necessary consequence of the author's eclectic procedure: for, in another poem ("Annot and Johon," Brown, *loc.cit.*, no. 76) which is even richer in the choice of metaphors, our poet, in the words of the editor, "follows a simple and orderly arrangement: he praises his mistress by a series of comparisons, introducing into each stanza a list of names from some special branch of knowledge. The first stanza is devoted to gems, the second to flowers, the third to birds, the fourth to medicaments and spices, while the fifth . . . is made up of names from [Welsh] romance and folklore." The accumulation of gems, flowers, and symbols of power in stanza 6 of our poem seems to aim toward an effect of condensation or concentration.

generally called "definitional." But, looking more closely, we
will find that only the "crystal of cleanness" of line 3 has the
sensuous basis underlying the type "the sword of truth" (cleanness is [metaphorically] a crystal just as truth is [metaphorical-
ly] a sword). For example, "goodness" is no more closely associated with coral than with any other object. Indeed, if we
remember that such terms as "coral," "ruby" are intended to
represent primarily excellence in the abstract ("coral," "ruby"
being so many paraphrases for "the best"), we may then consider all six lines (including 3) as representing the partitive
genitive: "coral of goodness" = "the best part of goodness,"
etc. But surely the "of" constructions in lines 4 and 8 differ
syntactically from lines 1-3 and lines 5-7 just as these same lines
differ from the others in rhythmical length (lines 4 and 8 are
shorter lines), in character of rhyme (male rhymes), syntax
(the anaphoras *heo is* . . . are interrupted)—and in content in
that we have to do here with human society, not with nature. To
begin with line 4: "baner of bealte" could only with difficulty be
considered as another case of a partitive construction (*baner*
being "the best, the top part of beauty"?). It would be more
convincing to define the phrase as metaphorical apposition (very
similar to "the sword of truth": the maiden's beauty is a banner
around which all lovers of beauty can rally). As for line 8, the
phrase "ledy of lealte" can be explained neither as "the best part
of loyalty" (partitive *of*) nor as apposition ("loyalty [is] the
lady"). For this phrase I see two positive possibilities: either
we have to do with the qualifying *of* equal to an adjective (ultimately of Hebrew origin: "God of Majesty" = "the majestic
God"): "lady of loyalty" = "loyal lady," or, if we take "lady"
to mean "queen, ruler" (and the latter solution seems to be
preferable), we would translate "ruler *over* loyalty" (objective
genitive as in "King of France")—and, *qua* ruler, she would
still be "the best in the realm of loyalty"! Our poet would
then have interrupted the regular partitive "of" constructions
in lines 1-3 and 5-7 which ultimately express only abstract
excellence ("coral of godness," etc.) by (l. 4) a truly sensuous
metaphor ("banner of beauty") and (l. 8) an idea of ruling

power, majesty, sovereignty, which *in the end* is equivalent to "excellence," to the superlative. To the eye, the 8-fold repetition of "*x* of *y*" offers unrelieved continuity; when logically analyzed, the lines present variation—variation, however, on the one theme: "perfection."[7]

As for the syntactic repetition represented by *heo is . . .* which, as we have said, coincides in part with the "of" constructions, this is of the type that Hatzfeld (*ZRPh*, LII, 707) has called "einhämmernde Metaphorik" (in *heo is . . . heo is . . .* we hear the "hammers of didaxis"), a feature found in many Latin hymns. Here is an example of "anaphora" as used by Adam of St. Victor (coupled this time with the Hebrew genitive construction):

> *Vas* electum, *vas* honoris,
> *Vas* caelestis gratiae,
> Ab aeterno *vas* provisum,
> *Vas* insigne, *vas* excisum
> Manu sapientiae.

Again in our poem secularization of devices of religious exegesis has taken place.

We may note that the description of the maiden's character is somewhat less developed than the description of her body: the first requires two stanzas only, in comparison with three

---

[7] Dunbar's poem "In Honour of the City of London" shows us a similar display of *of* constructions:

> Gemme of all joy, jasper of jocunditie,
>   Most myghty carbuncle of vertue and valour;
> Strong Troy in vigour and strenuytie;
>   Of royall cities rose and geraflour;
> Empress of townes, exalt in honour;
>   In beawtie beryng the crone imperiall;
> Swete paradise precelling in pleasure;
>   London, thou art the flour of Cities all.

But here the phrase "empress of townes," which one might be tempted to compare with our "ledy of lealte," is exactly equal to the type "jasper of jocunditie"—"empress" being again "the best" and "of" clearly partitive. (The type "Troy *in* vigor" resembles somewhat the rhetorical pattern "*En* ventura Octavjano; / Julio César *en* vencer / e batallar" in Jorge Manrique's poem on the death of his father, a pattern whose ancient models E. R. Curtius [*ZRPh*, LII, 129 *seq*.] has pointed out.)

given to the latter, and the order of arrangement of the virtues is not as methodically convincing as is the procedure "from top to bottom" used for the beautiful body. This discrepancy between the description of the *homo exterior* and that of the *homo interior* is characteristic of similar medieval descriptions in general where occasionally the *homo interior* is even sacrificed—a circumstance the more startling in that in the Middle Ages spiritual beauty was believed to be superior to physical beauty (cf. the emphasis in the first line of the Old French *Chanson de Sainte Eulalie*: "*bel* auret cors, *belezour* anima"). This is doubtless to be explained by the dependence of the medieval writer on preordained patterns: whereas for the methodical description of bodily beauty there was a model at hand (first attested by Faral in the 5th century erotic Latin poet Maximian), the courtly poet of the 13th century would not have looked for a pattern of spiritual beauty in the Fathers whose catalogues of virtues do not square with the secular-social ideal of courtly poetry. In our poem, for example, a whole stanza will be given to the social virtue of "gaiety" in the maiden and a second stanza to a rather indiscriminate assortment of virtues and accomplishments, not easily identifiable with the classification of the moral world offered by the Fathers.

Whereas the first part of the poem (stanzas 1-6) is devoted mainly to the praise of the ideal lady seen as a static power (with potentialities toward *action* of this paragon of beauty and virtue [καλοκαγαθία] upon the lover) quite contrary to Homer's practice, the description of the *effect* of love comes only after the power ("myght") of the Beloved has been accurately described and defined. We must not *guess* her beauty from her influence, rather, as in a syllogism, does her actual influence derive from her general potentialities which from the start appear as given (just as God is the immediately given in a theocracy). The method of our—apological—poet is deductive. An unspoken "hence" is suggested at the beginning of the poet's dialogue with the Allegory of Love. To quote Brown's paraphrase of stanzas 7-9: "The poet complains to Cupid[8]

[8] I am not sure whether the translation "Cupid" does not substantially

('Love') that his lady has seized into her hand a heart that belonged to him, and that her three knights, Sighing, Sorrow, and Thought, pursue him 'against the power of Peace' and threaten to follow him to his life's end. Cupid listens to the complaint, and advises him to offer to his lady the treasure of his 'huerte hele' and beseech her to show kindness to him before he 'falle ase fen of fote.'"

Just as the portrait of the lady offered by our poet was an objective summary of all virtues conceivable in a lady, so the lovers' feeling is objectified. He appears possessed by that objective force, Love, which is said to be "loflich in londe," the impersonation, that is, of loveliness on earth, as clearly perceptible and real as the lady is "in al þis wurhliche won." The medieval psychology of love is not based on the individual's belief in the singularity of this feeling (Montaigne: [we were friends] "parce que c'estoit lui, parce que c'estoit moi"), but on the contrary on its universality. Allegories represent objectified forces present in the individual soul. This is borne out by line 69: "Hire loue [= love for her] me lustnede vch word" (where Böddeker corrected "Hire loue" to "Love," while Brown, without giving reasons, re-established the reading of the manuscript). Here we find personified the particular love of the poet (his "love for her") which partakes of the universality of Love itself. The modern reader, who is still capable of visualizing a personification of Love in general, would find it difficult indeed to imagine the personification of a feeling of his own in the form of a figure outside of him, endowed with a body (who bends over toward him while listening, etc.). The modern reader is able perhaps to understand a personification of Love in general, less so of "my, your, the poet's love." It must here be borne in mind that the Middle Ages conceived of the human psyche as participating in the *universalia realia* (*my* love is part and parcel of Love). It is precisely by this participation in objectively real abstract ideas that the human psyche as such, in medieval opinion, is ennobled (medieval allegories

---

alter the figure of that gentle and judicious judge Love whom our poet has presented.

are always presented as noble, princely figures, even *Synagoga* is as noble a princess as *Ecclesia*). And since man shares in different suprapersonal psychic forces which may antagonize each other, the psychomachic or dialectic element is, since the time of Prudentius, inherent to medieval allegory, as C. S. Lewis has pointed out: man is ever torn between two opposing forces and the abstractions fight out their battles within him. His soul is the field of operation, the battleground for these abstract forces. And it may even occur, as it does in our poem, that *one* psychological force may split into two opposing tendencies. In our case, the poet's love develops the two dialectically contrary tendencies: his will to serve his love and his rebellion against the sufferings entailed by this service. The psychomachic allegory takes then the characteristically medieval forms of feudalism (not only because the devotion of the poet to his lady from whom he expects a reward shows analogies with the relationship of the retainer with his overlord who, in exchange for the loyalty and faithfulness offered to him, grants protection). The poet is a retainer of the lady. But it is also true that the lady has other retainers who are purely allegorical figures: Sighing, Sorrow, and Thought, who, as it happens in feudal society, are antagonistic to the fellow retainer (sometimes because they may think to ingratiate themselves with the overlord by their persecution of their fellow retainer). The lady, then, who occupies the central position between the two opposed parties who both claim to execute her will, becomes a mysterious entity susceptible of different actualizations.[9] In the eyes of the poet, the lady, who is guilty of stealing the heart which was his and of letting her three servants persecute him to the death, is therefore guilty of a "breach of peace," of a penal crime. The ensuing lawsuit against her, with the speeches of the plaintiff and

[9] The possibility, realized in our poem, of manifold actualizations of a single abstract entity, together with the tendency to attribute to the allegory princely status (note, here, the suggestion of a retinue)—these two factors help to explain the fact that in medieval and Renaissance poetry we so often find the (allegorical) protagonist surrounded by a "court of allegories" (the expression "court of allegories" was coined for the baroque drama by Walter Benjamin).

the judge (the defendant is conspicuous by her noble and mysterious absence) is then the inner struggle in the heart of the poet made explicit: the voices in his heart become the voices of the litigating parties before the tribunal. However difficult it may be for the modern reader to understand how the sighing, the sorrow, and the thinking of the poet can become personified figures outside of him, the medieval mind was easily able to see inner psychological forces as isolable, objective *realia*. To complicate things even more, the lady is shown as the "unlawful" overlord against whom a complaint is lodged before "his Love for Her" as a judge—which must mean that the love within the poet is called upon to pass judgment on the consequences of love (sighing, sorrow, thought), on inward impulses in the poet ultimately caused by his love—obviously, for medieval hierarchic thought, the abstraction Love was located higher up on the hierarchic ladder than the consequences of love and these were subjected to Love's verdict. We may find for this exteriorized inner debate French models, e.g. in Thibaut de Champagne's poems numbers XLVII, XLVIII, and appendix number X, in Wallensköld's edition: there, the allegory of Love, *Amors* (a feminine noun in Old French) is confused with the Beloved and it is this composite "Love" who challenges, again in a juridical debate, the supposed defection of the poet in her service. In Middle English the abstraction Love being conceived as masculine, the Beloved was able to remain a person distinct from the abstraction: she becomes the defendant, "he" the judge so that the trial may assume the requisite triangular proportion[10]—but we are not quite sure whether this defendant, too, is not seen somehow as an abstraction: as the impersonation of that aspect of Love

[10] With Thibaut de Champagne, in spite of even more frequent allusions to feudal law ("mes hom," "tort," "forfait et mesprixon," "querreis . . . ochoison," "avez fait de moi autrui garson," "vos ai porté loiaul tesmoing"), the debate remains purely on the level of personal discussion. Especially the word "paix" (peace) is not allowed to come to its full legal meaning: "Por ceu vers vos ne demant se paix non" (app. X, 2, cf. in the Provençal model of Thibaut: "bona patz") since it only means "a lull in the sufferings of the poet," not the "public peace (that is broken by the lady)" which is able to serve as a tangible reason for a lawsuit.

that harms the lover. The lines of demarcation between concrete and abstract, between a person who has the universality of an abstraction and an abstraction which takes on personal features, are blurred in the Middle Ages.[11]

In the end, as we learn, the verdict of Love the judge is in favour of the Beloved and amounts to a denial of any right to the lover: he should give his "whole" heart to her who has stolen it, that is, acknowledge the legitimacy of her crime, in other words: this crime is legalized and justified. The basis of feudalism, *mutual* love and service between retainer and overlord, is *de facto* destroyed. The feudalistic law-suit, revealed in the end to be an anodyne metaphor, has served only to disclose the absence of any valid law that would protect the lover: the gentle judge is called upon to proclaim the permanent rule of the most terrible anarchy. Courtly love must remain a one-sided, gratuitous feeling, and the lady would even be justified in dropping the lover "like dirt from the foot." The reward of the lover consists in his feeling of love *per se*. The Christian radicalism of establishing the love of God as a gratuitous feeling which takes possession of the entire soul of the believer has here found its secular foil: earthly love for earthly love's sake (*hohe Minne*). The idea of totality and completeness, present in the whole poem, dominates also our stanza: the gift of the treasure of the *whole* heart is the only means of redemption. Toward the all-perfect being that had been described in the first part of the poem, only total self-denial, as depicted in the second part, is the fitting attitude. The parallel with the all-exacting love of God against whom there is no appeal possible is obvious. The legalism of our stanza ultimately reveals a basically Christian anti-legalist *caritas* which gives everything for nothing.

[11] We may observe that the noble maiden has been shown surrounded by abstractions already earlier in the poem (l. 15): "wiþ murþes monie mote heo monge"—shown, that is, communing ("mixing") socially with the Graces, since the abstraction "mirth" ("grace") was conceived to be as sensuously perceptible and as real as is the living figure. As Jacob Burckhardt has pointed out in his essay on Allegory, we may find historical figures side by side with allegorical ones as late as in Rubens' paintings for Maria de Medici.

And in the last stanza the litany built on the anaphora *For hire loue* "hammers" into us the necessity of continuous self-sacrifice on the part of the lover who heeds the advice given to him by the judge "Hire Love" (it is for this gentle judge, seen as a person, at least as much as for the Beloved that he will undergo pain), and this service through suffering is proclaimed with the resounding rhetoric of a heroic decision. We are left in the end with the impression, conveyed by the rich flow of words, the lilt of the sentence structure and the firm prosodic articulation of the stanza, that the suffering in itself bears its own glory and its own bliss. The rhetorical enumeration in our final stanza is reminiscent of the final declaration of love in the scene of Chrétien's *Yvain*, where the protagonist and Laudine meet: that triumphant aria, studded with rhetorical anaphora:

[Laudine has asked Yvein *an quel manière*, in what manner he loves her.]

> An tel que graindre estre ne puet [= quo majus . . .],
> An tel que de vos ne se muet
> Mes cors n'onques aillors nel truis,
> An tel qu'aillors penser ne puis,
> An tel que toz a vos m'otroi,
> An tel que plus vos aim que moi,
> An tel, se vos plaist, a delivre,
> Que por vos vuel morir et vivre.

Our own stanza, however, has the particular function of relieving us, by its enthusiastic ring, from the depressing burden actually described in its lines: the inner victory of the lover who has deliberately taken up the cross of suffering has found its adequate verbal expression.

As for the exact nature of this burden, the description given is a condensation of the phenomenology of courtly love ultimately derived from Ovid and first developed in the Old French *Roman d'Eneas*. Faral (p. 133) has codified in the following paragraph the different traditional manifestations of lovesickness to be found in the Old French romances: "Celui qui aime change de couleur et pâlit: il tremble, frémit, tressaille; il souffle, il

bâille; il a froid et il transpire; il se pâme; il se 'demente,' sou-
pire, pleure, geint, sanglote, se plaint, crie, vocifère; il perd le
boire et le manger; il 'se travaille' et songe; il veille, s'étire et se
retourne sur son lit; il se démène, se 'degete'; il est comme en
rage." We may recognize in our stanza the same art of condensation that we have admired in stanza 6: out of the wealth of details given by poetic tradition, here as there, the poet has chosen
only a few, to enforce them by the devices of alliteration and
anaphora which come to suggest here the continuity and totality
("*al* ich waxe won," "*more* þen eny mon") of his submission to
the chosen suffering.

Looking back at the body of the poem as a whole, we must
emphasize the variety of medieval motifs which the poet has
brought together in order to impress his love upon us: the physical and the interior portrait (with all their different traditional
devices), the debate with its allegory of Love, the detailed picture of the gratuitously suffering lover. This poem is indeed a
résumé of the possible medieval variants of courtly love poetry.
The enumerative and numeric element, so often emphasized by
me, is represented also in the choice of this totality of devices.
Quite appropriately, the lengthy poem has 10 stanzas—the perfect number![12]

Turning now to the burden "Blow, northerne wynd," we must
first remark that its inspiration is quite different from the courtly body of the poem: it is a refrain of popular origin, with all the
significant features of the folksong. In opposition to that carefully worked-out harness of the stanzas (provided with a refined rhyme-scheme and alliteration), the burden has no rhyme,
only (perhaps) an assonance (*wynd-sweting*); it seems to belong, like the refrains found since the 13th century in Old French

---

[12] It is therefore preposterous to shorten the poem as has been done in
the new edition of *The Oxford Book of English Verse* from which stanzas
4-5 and 7-9 have been omitted. Not only does this procedure violate the
spirit of numeric totality informing our poem: it also introduces the
quite arbitrary conception of a poem with omissible ("less poetic") parts
(obviously the allegorical debate had to fall under the shears of the
modern editor while the "complete" portrait of the lady was mutilated)—
thereby destroying a perfect work whose *raison d'être* is that of "completeness."

lyrical poetry, to another poem, which is lost, whose rhymes it may reproduce, but from which it has been detached: poetic gossamer floating in the wind. While the body of the poem is conceived intellectually, the burden is an outburst of lyrical emotion, of what we moderns would call "true lyricism": no justification, on moral and aesthetic grounds, is offered here for the poet's love; quite simply, his heart sends out the melancholy sigh, justified in its directness: "Blow, northerne wynd. . . ." The insistent syntactical construction in this part is the abrupt imperative ("blow . . . send . . .") as is fitting for a longing that seeks relief, whereas in the courtly part the calm, objective indicative prevails. Only at the end of stanza 2 ("he þat reste him on þe rode / þat leflich lyf honoure!") and stanza 3 ("god wolde hue were myn") do we find imperatives, or rather desideratives, in the body of the poem, and in both cases these wishes serve as prelude to the burden which follows immediately.[13]

The poet's command to the wind originates in a naïve identification with the forces of nature. Folk-poetry often shows the lyrical ego embedded in nature whose influence may run parallel, or counter, to the former. This primitive longing for (and with) nature (it is the strength of his nostalgia that makes the poet identify it with the powerful North wind) is a far cry from the stylization of nature in the courtly part of the poem, where nature figures only in the form of ideal representatives ("coral of godnesse," etc.), that is, intellectually interpreted. In his naïve confidence in the favourable element of the wind, the poet repeats in the burden the imperative "blow!" five times (not the imperative "send!" because the "blowing" includes the "sending"): he dwells on the activity of the wind with the same insistence with which he would like to linger on his own feeling; we infer the monotonous continuity of his feeling from the repeated monosyllable—which becomes an onomatopœia of the wind.

Directness of feeling is also reflected in the choice of words displayed in the burden: not one Gallicism or Latinism occurs

[13] After stanza 3 the lyrical note becomes extinct in the courtly stanzas and the intellectualized feeling alone prevails (compare "Sighing," personified as a knight, line 58, with the actual and prolonged sigh expressed in the burden).

in its four lines, whereas a quatrain chosen at random in the courtly part such as ll. 37-40 shows us six Gallicisms. And one may also compare the direct simplicity of the phrase "my suet-yng" (l. 2) with the recherché elaborateness of "heo is solsecle of suetnesse" (l. 51). No doubt, the musicality of the burden was enhanced by the (not preserved) melody which must have been more emotional than that of the declamatory and rhetorical courtly part.

If we realize that the short, popular, simple, emotional, vio-lent, dynamic, natural, and musical burden is intended to be heard again and again after every one of the ten lengthy, courtly, elaborate, intellectualized (generally) calm, static, didactic, and rhetorical stanzas, we must conclude that in our poem a continu-ous opposition of two strata of human nature, and also of two social levels, has been achieved. The eclectic or syncretistic poet must have sought to couple two approaches to love: one the lyri-cal (popular), the other the didactic (courtly). Out of the so-phisticated reflection that no one type of poetry would suffice for the unfathomable subject matter of love, he must have striven toward synthesis and (again) totality. His poem was to be a *summa* of medieval love lyrics. That there is little or no attempt to fuse the two parts of quite different inspiration (as in ll. 19-20 and 28), may be due to the sociological structure of medieval society whose rigid hierarchy had created different equally rigid poetic forms. Enough that he, like his predecessors in 13th cen-tury French lyricism, felt the implicit need for integration: he was allowed only to juxtapose, not to fuse, the popular and the courtly inspiration. His poem is "great" in that it offers an overly rich condensation of the whole wealth of medieval thought and feeling about one of the basic forces of mankind.

II

We shall turn now to a poem of religious inspiration, an anonymous carol written about 1400, in which the integration of the popular and the learned (if not courtly) element has been achieved,—a devotional poem in which the elements de-rived from the dogma and the Scriptures are couched in a style that has the popular ring. The fact that this was possible is an illustration of the truth that Christian dogma was able to reach the whole of the people while the courtly theory of Love was a prerogative only of the upper classes.

> Of a rose, a lovely rose,
> Of a rose is al myn song!

1. Lestenyt, lordynges, both elde and yinge,
   How this rose began to sprynge;
   Swych a rose to myn lykynge
       In al this world ne knowe I non.

2. The aungil came fro hevene tour   5
   To grete Marye with gret honour,
   And seyde sche xuld bere the flour
       That xulde breke the fyndes bond.

3. The flour sprong in heye Bedlem,
   That is bothe bryht and schen: 10
   The rose is Mary, hevene qwen,
       Out of here bosum the blosme sprong.

4. The ferste braunche is ful of myht,
   That sprong on Cyrstemesse nyht,
   The sterre schon over Bedlem bryht   15
       That is bothe brod and long.

5. The secunde braunche sprong to helle,
   The fendys power doun to felle:
   Therein myht non sowle dwelle;
       Blyssid be the time the rose sprong!   20

6. The thredde braunche is good and swote,
   It sprang to hevene, crop and rote,
   Therein to dwellyn and ben our bote;
       Every day it schewit in prystes hond.

7. Prey we to here with gret honour,   25
   She that bar the blyssid flowr,
   She be our helpe and our socour
       And schyld us fro the fyndes bond.

This devotional poem (in the vernacular) has the practical aim of encouraging a prayerful spirit in a community (which is explicitly addressed in the *exordium*, l. 1) in preparation for the (Latin) church service of the Nativity and, more specifically, for the communion on that feast day (as is slightly suggested by l. 24). This didactic or strategic aim does not prevent the poem from being poetic. If poetry is characterized by the vision it opens up before us of a world radically different from our everyday and workaday world of ratiocination and practicality and by the relief it offers us from the daily burden of our environment—then the Christian dogma as such is poetic, in that it reveals to us the existence of an irrational world based on God's love for man, an aspect totally different from our everyday experience of a life in the midst of human egotism and calculation. The idea of a God-Messiah who, in order to reveal to his believers his love, must needs share their earthly life, obviously entails the idea of an earthly (if not entirely earthly) birth of this deity. From this the idea of a miraculous birth (from a virgin) came to suggest itself.[14] This dogma as such is poetic[15] because of its suggestion of a possible other world in which the normal laws of causation and of procreation are by exception suspended. Any representation, in poetry or the arts, of the homely and at the same time supernatural scenes centering around the Child and his Mother is poetic—not necessarily artistic (not all paintings representing the Madonna are artistic),[16]

[14] With this step, the Holy Family makes its entrance into Christian art—while Greek gods were generally portrayed as figures standing alone in space.

[15] I would say that, while poetry is not always of a religious character, religion is generally poetic (because of the evocation of "another world" implied by religious speculation). And while to believe religious truths is more than to be swayed by their poetic appeal, it is still not certain whether the greatest religious geniuses (Dante, for example) did not often apperceive religious truth in the form of poetic truth. Perhaps, just as Galileo thought that mathematics was God's intellectual truth as revealed to man, we may also believe that poetry is the form best fitted to convince man emotionally of supernal verities. Apperception of poetry may be, then, to a certain extent, religious service.

[16] Similarly it can be said that we find in nature many poetic, not always artistic, phenomena: the squirrel is poetic (because it suggests a way of

if the work of art is characterized by its self-sufficiency and organic perfection which allow it to stand out as an independent whole. We shall have to investigate in detail the way in our poem the poetic has become artistic.

Considering our poem then as a reflection of Christian dogma as manifested in the sacrament of the communion, it is clear that the basis of this sacrament is the belief in the potential closeness of man to God (the particular Christian *numinosum*, to speak in terms of Rudolf Otto, is *fascinans*, gently attractive, not *tremendum*, frightening, as was the attitude of the Old Testament God). Christ having descended into the flesh, the believer is allowed symbolically to take unto himself the flesh of Christ. Now since our poem, as we have said, is written in the service of the communion, we should expect to find here expressed the theme of the closeness between man and God. Let this be our working hypothesis as we analyze our poem in search of "new observations" (just as the concept of totality was our working hypothesis in the interpretation of the poem, "Blow, northerne wynd"). And, indeed, in our poem the birth of the Saviour is presented as the connecting link between Heaven (whence He came), Earth (where He was born and dwelt) and Hell (where He went as a conqueror);[17] and the three realms are shown in their close connection (with man on earth being himself placed, in the words of Swedenborg, in the fields of attraction both of heaven and hell). If we consider for the moment only stanzas 2 and 7, we sense in each case that the three realms are indeed made to converge:

stanza 2:
   1. The aungil came fro
      hevene tour

stanza 7:
   1. Prey we to here . . . [in
      Heaven]

---

locomotion not given to man), but not artistic (it is not "beautiful"). But the rose is a work of art of Nature.

[17] The motif of the Harrowing of Hell, derived from the Evangelium Nicodemi, is foreshadowed by Joseph's dream in Matthew 1:21: "ipse enim salvum faciet populum suum a peccatis eorum." The Angel in the scene of the Annunciation (in Luke 1) prophesies only Christ's rule as a successor of David. Our poem is based on a legend in which the two reports were telescoped.

II. And said sche xuld bere the
flour [on *this earth*]

III. That xulde breke the
fyndes bond [= *Hell*]

II. She that bar the blyssed
flowr [on *this earth*]

III. And schyld us fro the
fyndes bond [*Hell*]

Again we may note the contrary parallelism of the first lines of stanzas 2 and 3: in line 5 Heaven is brought down to earth as the Angel comes downward from "hevene tour": in line 9 ("The flour sprong in *heye* Bedlem") we see earthly pinnacles reaching toward heaven (the heavenly Jerusalem and the earthly Bethlehem[18] are evidently visualized anachronistically as medieval castles or fortresses): the distance between heaven and earth has been here as there diminished.

But there is in evidence a still closer tie between this and the other world. This is the plant that in our poem grows miraculously to encompass and unite earth, heaven and hell: the rosebush (Middle English *rose* = rose-bush, rose-tree; cf. Latin *rosa sine spina*, Middle High German *rôs âne dorn*, etc.) which bore the flower Christ.[19] In the first three stanzas three links in a genealogical chain are suggested. The relation between the last two is obvious: the flower Christ springs from the rose (-bush) that is Mary. As for the source of the rose-bush, this is hinted at in line 2 as being the theme of the poem ("how this rose began[20] to sprynge"), but never mentioned or referred to again. We supply from our knowledge of tradition that the root from which Mary sprang is the root of Jesse. Had not

[18] The phrase "Heye Bedlem that is bothe bryht and schen" may, of course, be inspired by the passage of the Sermon of the Mount (Matt. 5: 14-15): "Ye are the light of the world. A city that is set on a hill cannot be hid. Neither do men light a candle and put it under a bushel, but on a candlestick; and it giveth light unto all that are in the house." The ideas of the city on the hill, visible from everywhere, and of the shining chandelier seem to be combined in our two lines 9-10.

[19] We may imagine our poem as it may have been presented in the original manuscript: the letters of the text embedded in a luxuriant foliage so that the whole page would have the appearance of a flowering thicket.

[20] This auxiliary verb marks only the ingressive aspect of the action of "springing" (just as do the similar Old French verbs *prendre a, comencier*): there is no question in our poem of a "beginning" to which continuation and termination of the action would be opposed.

Isaiah prophesied (7:14) : "Ecce virgo concipiet et pariet filium" and (11:1) : "Et egredietur virga de radice Jesse et flos de radice eius ascendet"? On the basis of this prophecy of the birth of the *virga-virgo* (Mary) and of the flower (Christ) the Church Fathers (cf. E. Auerbach, *Romance Philology*, III, 12) were able to establish a historical hypothesis which binds the Old and the New Testament together, the former being made to fore-shadow the latter, and which makes the miraculous and super-natural story of the Messiah-King appear under the form of or-ganic growth in time from a natural root. The dogmatic histori-cal speculation that He who was to bring the New Dispensation is a descendant of the Jewish kings who carries in his blood the promise made by the God of Abraham, Isaac, and Jacob to Israel, has been made poetic in our poem (or in poetic legend that pre-ceded it) by the substitution of the more specific rose-bush in-stead of the *virgo-virga* (we may remember that in Christian hymns the "rose" is one of the traditional attributes of the Virgin, originally ascribed to the Beloved in the *Song of Songs*). Our poet does not proceed, as would perhaps a patristic writer, from the dogmatic kernel of the story of Christ to the external symbol, but in reverse from the symbolic object in nature to its recondite meanings. We have before us again an allegory. The object in nature we are allowed to see is first only "*a* rose, a *lovely* rose"; the cunning dogmatic strategist that was our poet purports to speak "only" of a rose ("of a rose . . . is *al* myn song") ; the rose becomes more and more identifiable (*"this* rose"—"*swych* a rose") and grows before us ("began to sprynge")—reminding us of modern cinematic techniques. Only after the beauty of this particular rose-bush has been praised (which beauty is described by reference to the medieval pattern "quo maius nihil cogitari potest") is the name of Mary men-tioned and somehow implicitly identified with the rose-bush in a courtly Annunciation scene ("The aungil came fro hevene tour/To grete Mary with gret honour"). At this point the listen-er must hesitate, then, to assume that the rose-bush he has been visualizing can be nothing but a woman, Mary, who will bear the Child. Yet, this child itself is a flower ("bere the flour")—

whose function, described in the next line, is dogmatically understandable, but not poetically visualizable. Again it is only after the birth of Christ on earth ("Bedlem") that Mary is finally identified with the rose-bush: "The rose is Mary"—with the explicit explanation of the allegory according to the formula "A is B." The gradual approximation to the allegorical significance of the object in nature has now come to an end. In spite of so clear-cut an explanation, however, the religious paradox is allowed to persist: Mary is a rose-bush, but she is also the Queen of Heaven. We are in presence of a Christian metamorphosis on a divine plane. The poet chooses his own way of presenting the idea of Christ's praeternatural birth, uncontaminated by the flesh, of reconciling, that is, the circumstance of Mary's obumbration by the Holy Ghost with the fleshly birth of Christ. According to the traditional version, Christ is born from the womb of his virginal mother: the Fathers, faced with the same problem, had chosen now to poeticize the virginal uterus itself, now to replace the womb by the ear (from which the "Verbum caro factum" must spring), or else by a symbolic parallel such as the pure pane of glass pierced by light. The two last procedures are somehow fused in our poet's explanation of the birth of Christ: Christ is a flower which blossomed from Mary's bosom and Mary is, at the same time, goddess-like and plant-like. A poetic explanation, miraculous and still poetically logical, such as the Old Testament motif of the root of Jesse could never have yielded!

We may pause a moment at this point to consider the question whether such allegorical and didactic art is truly poetic. Have we not since our schooldays been imbued with the notion that didaxis is the death of poetry? Have we not learned more recently: "A poem should not mean, but be"? But it is obvious that the didactic explanation of the Nativity given by our poet is not one based on the laws of our rational world; indeed it reveals a world beyond our senses even more irrational and problematic than the dogma of theology, a world where plant-life, humanity, and deity are fused—and a miracle still more incredible than the miracle narrated in the Gospel. And the manner, too, in which the poet explains the miracle is poetic, in that it evokes a poetic personality, that of the naïve, child-like, but thoughtful believer whose voice we hear as he explains, full of awe and elation, the religious mystery. As we see him who proceeds methodically from "Of a rose . . . to the rose is Mary," who didactically repeats his own words as if to suggest the innate poverty of vocabulary of popular speakers ("a rose began to sprynge"—"the flour sprong"—"the blosme sprong"), who is able to describe the divine flower only in so simple a verse as "that is bothe bryht and schen"—we come to love this naïve, but deep Christian soul who reminds us of the shepherds who, untouched by the learning of the Pharisees and Scribes, were the first in the simplicity of their hearts to understand the New Dispensation. An explanation offered by a poetic explanator is poetic.[21]

We may here turn to a parallel German anonymous Christmas carol about the birth of Christ, written probably in the 15th century (although preserved only in a version of 1599) : "Es ist ein' Ros' entsprungen," which is similarly based on the simile of the rose-bush.

> Es ist ein' Ros' entsprungen
> Aus einer Wurzel zart,
> Als uns die Alten sungen;
> Aus Jesse kam die Art,
> Und hat ein Blümlein bracht

---

[21] Sophisticated romantic poets who endeavoured to revive ancient folk-poetry have used the naïve didaxis of medieval poetry—but their poetic restoration lacks convincingness because they themselves lack the medieval belief. In a masterpiece of this genre, the "Lorelei" of Heine, the medieval didaxis (for example, in the final lines: "*Und das* hat mit ihrem Singen / die Lorelei getan") is practically destroyed when the poet who from the beginning has interposed his own modern personality between the old legend and us ("ein Märchen aus alten Zeiten / das kommt mir nicht aus dem Sinn") intervenes a few lines before the end with a skeptical: "*Ich glaube*, die Wellen verschlingen / am Ende Schiffer und Kahn." We should expect to find the mysterious attraction of the boatman by the demoniac Lorelei to be presented either as a fact ("und das hat . . .") or as hearsay ("ich glaube")—both attitudes at once are impossible.

Mitten im kalten Winter
Wohl zu der halben Nacht.

Das Röslein, das ich meine,
Davon Esaias sagt,
Hat uns gebracht alleine
Marie die reine Magd:
Aus Gottes ew'gem Rat'
Hat sie ein Kind geboren
Wohl zu der halben Nacht.

We see here the same allegorical procedure which begins with
"a rose [-bush],"[22] to tell us later that this bush produced
("bracht") a flower ("Blümlein") at midnight in the midst
of winter. The Biblical miracle is described by the German poet
as a miracle of nature, for to him, so familiar with the harshness
of the German winter, the flowering of a rose—"mitten im kalten
Winter" (in the well-known melody composed for the poem by
Praetorius, the emphasis in the sentence is on the adjective
kalten)—is in itself miraculous. The imagination of the German
is not as bold as that of the English poet who has the rose spring
from Mary's bosom; his individual contribution or modification
consists in localizing the Palestinian story in a northern land.

As the opening lines indicate, the fructifying rose-bush, anachronistically presented as belonging to pious legend of hoary
antiquity ("wie uns die Alten sungen"), and the word "Jesse"
(avoided in our English version) situates the story of the rose
exactly in Biblical history. With this reference to "Jesse" (and
perhaps also with the reference to legendary tradition) we are
warned immediately that our rose-bush can be no plant, but an
allegory—though in the next line ("und hat ein Blümlein
bracht") we return to the simile, to learn in the second stanza
its explicit allegorical meaning: the lines: "Das Röslein, das ich
meine, / Davon Esaias sagt, / Hat uns gebracht alleine / Marie

[22] In view of the Middle English parallel I cannot accept the opinion
of many German commentators that *Ros'* is an alteration of *Reis*=Middle
English *ris*=Latin *virga*. *Ros'*="rose-bush" (as opposed to *Blümlein*=
flour and *Röslein*) must be the original version in the first line.

die reine Magd" are exactly parallel to the English line: "The rose is Mary." In the German poem, however, once the doctrinal definition has been offered and the identity of the rose-bush established, the simile disappears. Here, too, we hear the voice of the naïve believer who "explains" the miracle with fervent awe, unrhetorical simplicity, and brevity (in only two well-balanced stanzas). When listening to the poetically cogent words, we are likely to forget that the poem is a sermon and contains a doctrine. The poem surely "means" ("das Röslein, das ich *meine*"), but the meaning itself is a problematic and irrational one.

The comparison of our English with the German carol must, incidentally, suggest that the two poems go back to one, probably Latin, original and that the second part of the English carol in which the three branches of Christ are mentioned must be a posterior addition to the original first three stanzas, concerned with the Nativity, whose protagonist is more Mary than Christ (the German poem leaves us with the final impression: "Marie, die reine Magd"). What must have prompted the addition of the second part is the intention of the English poet, quite unlike the German, who in transplanting the scene from Palestine to Germany succeeds in imposing spatial limits on the event, to describe this as a miracle not only in time (the fulfilment of Isaiah's prophecy), but also in space; Christ's birth (and it is Christ who now moves to the foreground) has impact on the whole universe: Heaven, Earth, and Hell are henceforth bound together by Him —that is, lines of communication are established by the three branches.[23] This idea, already foreshadowed in stanza 2, is, as we have seen, the basic idea of the poem.

The treatment of the three branches is surely inspired by the literary device found in Latin with Hugh of Saint-Victor or in the Provençal *Breviari d'Amor* (cf. my article no. 2 in *Essays in Historical Semantics*, New York, 1945), of presenting the

[23] Of the three branches, only the second and third are described in terms of spatial extension, the first is presented only as symbolizing the powerful ("ful of myght") effect of Christ's birth—a reference to this earth, however (in contrast to Hell, 2nd st., and Heaven, 3rd st.), is surely intended, given the mention of the star that shone over Bethlehem, attracting, as we know, the shepherds and the Magi, men of good will.

logical relationships between abstract concepts as so many rami-
fications of a tree, "a tree of moral genealogy," ultimately derived
from the Tree of Knowledge of Good and Evil. According to
this device (often represented by elaborate designs of stem-
mata), from the root of Charity are shown to spring enormous
trees with many branches and twigs, every ramification signify-
ing a logical implication of the basic virtue or force embodied in
the tree. In this manner medieval man was allowed to indulge
in his bent for classification and logical order which he introduced into the moral and historical world, and at the same time
to represent sensuously moral or abstract values—by a luxuriant
vegetation which has all the organic richness of plant-life. Indeed, the moral genealogies of the Middle Ages present an intellectual order superimposed on the universe, in the form of
natural, organic growth.

The three branches of our poem, then, are allegorical actualizations of the power exerted by Christ, that tender scion sprung
from the breast of the Virgin: the first seems to reveal (cf. note
below) the powerful effect of His birth on this world; the second
is His conquest of Hell and of Satan's "power" (a reference to
the Harrowing of Hell), and the third His resurrection and ascent to Heaven (which means also the potential participation of
regenerate man in heavenly bliss). To the spatial extension of
the power of Christ a temporal element is added: *now*, in our
Christian era, no longer is Hell the eternal dwelling-place for
all souls; henceforth Paradise is accessible to man (therefore
"Blyssed be *the time* the rose sprong!"), even on earth "every
day" man has access to Heaven in the communion. With line
24 we are abruptly transported from heaven to earth, to the interior of a Christian church where we see a priest at his minis-
tration. No classical poet would have been able to effectuate
such an abrupt transition which roots in the Christian belief that
indeed heaven and earth are in constant communication. Christ
has thus abolished the limits of both time and space. His believers "dwell" in the era, not of the prefiguration of Christ (the
root of Jesse), but of *imitatio Christi* (of the conquest of Hell,

ll. 17-18). Our poem, beginning with a rose-bush, ends with the vision of a gigantic world-tree.

But what of the tree from which the three branches spring? Can we visualize this organism? That from the root of Jesse a *virga-virgo* springs in the form of a rose-bush—this we can easily conceive, but what is the connection between this growth and "the three branches" of whose source nothing is said? Do they represent a separate growth? Surely in the absence of any such suggestion this possibility must be rejected. "The" first branch of line 13 must somehow be a branch of the rose-bush which was described in the three previous stanzas. But if this is so, at which point do the three offshoots branch off? Moreover, once it is clear that they represent three manifestations of Christ Himself, they cannot branch off directly from the rose-bush-that-is-Mary—perhaps we are meant to conceive them as springing from the flower-that-is-Christ (to be only indirectly the product of the rose-bush).[24] And to visualize this (branches springing from a flower) is to visualize a monstrosity of Nature:

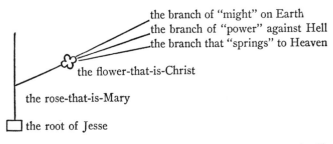

the branch of "might" on Earth
the branch of "power" against Hell
the branch that "springs" to Heaven
the flower-that-is-Christ
the rose-that-is-Mary
the root of Jesse

Thus an object in nature has been first chosen to signify a doctrinal mystery which, since this truth alone is important to the poet, must in the end destroy the context of nature—once it has served its purpose[25] (allegorical art in general is apt to

24 That the connection between bush and branches must not be broken is shown by stanza 5 beginning "The secunde braunche sprong to helle" and ending "Blyssid be the time the rose (= the rose-bush) sprong!"

25 Does the poet not even detach the third branch from its source to endow it with a root of its own (it springs to heaven "crop *and rote*"— Christ resurrected cannot be but a separate, independent plant)? This

be overloaded on the side of meaning: the poet who may have set out to establish the equation A = B, may, at the end, find himself to have proved the proposition B>A). But perhaps we can find a more positive approach to our passage: with the rose-bush springing from the root of Jesse to produce the flower Christ, we have obviously a traditional genealogical tree: but the treatment of the three branches, as we have already pointed out, is inspired by the medieval concept of the tree of "moral genealogy." To the medieval mind these two types of "trees" were basically of the same nature (and equally visualizable); our own poet has taken the bold step (bold to us, perhaps not to him) of juxtaposing the two trees into an "unnatural" but dogmatically satisfying unit. Moving on the plane of dogmatic speculation, he has simply juxtaposed two "systems" (physical and moral genealogy), of which the second is, indeed, only a natural consequence of the first.

Up to this moment, we have purposely disregarded a variant version of our poem (published by Ewald Flügel, *Anglia*, XXVI, 232, from the 16th century Balliol manuscript and henceforth to be called "version B"), because our intention was to base our "direct observations" exclusively on the one poetic organism under study (henceforth to be called "version A"); indeed, I may assure the reader that I myself had recourse to B only after having completed the study of A. But now we must bring B into the picture, in order to verify whether B will, or will not, confirm our assumptions about the texture of A—and, perhaps, will allow us to see more clearly the genesis of the poem (or its prototype X):

> Off a rose, a louely rose
> And of a rose I syng a song!

1. Herkyn to me both olde & yonge,
   how a rose began to sprynge,

---

procedure is somehow comparable to that of the German poet who gave to the rose-bush of Mary a "Wurzel zart," a root of her own in a sense, appropriate to her graceful nature—although we must believe her "root" to be the multisecular "root of Jesse."

A fayerer rose to my lykyng
    sprong yer neuer in kynges londe.

2. VI braunches ar on yat rose beme,
They be both bryght & shene.
The rose ys called mary hevyn quene,
    Of her bosum a blossum spronge.

3. The fyrst branch was of gret myght,
That spronge on crystmas nyght!
The sterne shon over bedlem bryght,
    yat men myght se both brode & longe.

4. The ijde braunch was of gret honowr,
yat was sent from hevyn towr!
blessyd be yat fayer flowr,
    breke it shall the fendes bondes!

5. The thyrd braunch wyde sprede,
ther mary lay in her bede,
The bryght strem iij kynges lede
    to bedlem yer yat branch yei fond.

6. The iiijth braunch sprong in to hell,
the fendes bost for to fell,
ther myght no sowle yer in dwell,
    blessid be yat tyme yat branch gan spryng!

7. The Vth braunch was fayer in fote,
yat sprong to hevyn tope & rote,
yer to dwell & be owr bote
    & yet ys sene in priestes hondes.

8. The VIth braunch by & by,
yt ys the V Ioyes of mylde mary!
Now cryst saue all this cumpany,
    & send vs gud lyff & long!

It is clear that certain assumptions made before are indeed confirmed by version B: the "rose" is a rose-bush (cf. *rose beme* in B, stanza 2) and our interpretation (note 20, page 220) of *began to sprynge* (A, l. 2) is borne out by another example of the verb with ingressive meaning (B, stanza 6: "yat branch *gan* spryng"). And, what is most important, we see that the motif of the branches, the central motif in B (cf. the announcement of the six branches in stanza 2), is independent of the motif of the flower Christ sprung from the Virgin's breast to which we have only an incidental allusion in stanza 2 of B. According to Flügel, B is later than A, as may be inferred from such detail as the alteration of the rhyme (in A) *yinge—sprynge* to *yonge— sprynge* (in B). But this may be a scribal error in the particular manuscript which does not prove the priority of the *version* underlying A. For if we compare the wording in B, stanza 3: "the sterne shon over bedlem bryght, / yat *men myght se* both brode & longe" with that of A: "the sterre . . . that *is* bothe brod & long," it is surely more natural to assume that A is based on B rather than the reverse. Similarly the wording of stanza 7: "The Vth branch was fayer in fote, / yat sprong to hevyn tope & rote" seems to me closer to the original than A's (l. 21): "the thredde braunch is good and swote, / It sprang to hevene, crop and rote": if I am correct in taking "fayer" to mean "promising success, likely to succeed, advantageous, propitious" (*New English Dictionary*, s.v. *fair*, no. 14) and "fote" as "the action of walking, wandering, etc.," the poet prepares the reader for the enormous leap of this root (to Heaven) whereas the wording "god and swote" of A, if more in line with the *fascinans* character of the description of Christ, introduces the detail of "springing to heaven" rather abruptly. That A cannot claim priority is also seen from the fact that here two systems (involving two protagonists: Mary—Christ) have been juxtaposed (and we may remember the difficulty we have had to face in explaining this juxtaposition), whereas in B we are offered really only one system (and one protagonist: Mary), the experiences, the "joys of Mary." Thus B, with its greater simplicity of composition, must have preceded A—but must have been preceded by a purer version (X) which we must postulate, if only because of the even number of branches (six) that are mentioned: it is well known that according to the traditional theme of the "joys of

Mary" (as opposed to the "sorrows of Mary"), these joys (like their foils, the sorrows) are always presented in the number of five (this is the favorite number), seven, nine. Thus we must imagine that in the version on which B is based, the familiar theme of the "five joys of Mary" (chosen by the Church Fathers for mnemonic reasons in their teaching of Biblical history) was presented in the form of so many branches[26] stemming from the rose-bush. This is exactly what we find in stanzas 3-7 of B (stanza 3—the first joy of Mary: the birth of Christ; stanza 4—the second: the "honour" of the Annunciation; stanza 5: the Adoration of the Magi; stanza 6: Christ's conquest of Hell; stanza 7: Christ's Ascent to Heaven),[27] only that the author of this version has incongruously added a sixth branch (which should not, however, represent a true sixth joy, but the ensemble of the five previously enumerated).[28] As for A, whose priority we rejected because of its greater complication, we now see that it deviates from the original also in the substitution of three branches for five—which, moreover, are the branches not of Mary, but of Christ. The poet of A has selected branches 1, 4, 5 from the five of his model and in so doing has been able to depict the "world tree" of Christ which embraces Earth, Hell and Heaven. By thus reducing the number of branches (which are no longer the "joys of Mary"), he has achieved an intensified representation of the power of Christ, and, having eliminated branch (joy) No. 2, the Annunciation, he chose to use details of this scene, for example, the messenger who came from "hevyn towr" to greet Mary with "gret honowr" (stanza 4 of B), for his first part (stanza 2 of A). This feature of presenting the Annunciation as an independent scene, not merely as one of

[26] The branches offer us, so to speak, a systematic, supra-temporal classification of the historical facts. In such a system, the historical succession of events is of secondary importance: the Annunciation appears in B *after* Christ's birth, which for the poet of B was the all-important event "of gret myght."

[27] Cf. the Middle English *Prayer of the Five Joys* in Brown, no. 18.

[28] This is a "disorder" typical of allegorical poetry in which any abstraction, *qua* abstraction, reaches an equal degree of independence: the "five joys of Mary" become thus an abstract concept which can be presented on one level with any one particular "joy of Mary."

five "joys," is, of course, in line with A's attribution of the (three) branches to Christ: in both we sense the poet's intention to make of Christ also a protagonist—the ultimate protagonist. And this intention is visible again in the handling of the line from B (stanza 2): "Of her bosum a blossum spronge": whereas in B this statement is offered incidentally and without prelude or conclusion, in A the textually identical line 12 ("out of here bosum the blosme sprong") is the culmination of the unit, beginning with stanza 2, in which the angel of the Annunciation himself prophesies the birth of a flower ("and seyde sche xuld bere the flour . . ."—the angel in Luke had said: "Ecce concipies *in utero* et paries *filium*"). In every step of his adaptation the poet is acting "in maiorem gloriam Jesu Christi."

That the author of A was inspired by the single line of B "Of her bosum a blossum spronge" is obvious; but how to explain the presence of this line in B? We have presented this version as deviating from the original pattern only in the introduction of a sixth branch: that is, continuing in the same vein of abstract enumeration. The same cannot be said, however, of the line (stanza 2) "Of her bosum a blossum spronge" in which the detail of the birth of Christ is added: for here there is a hint of that quite different "system" developed more fully in A (the system of physical genealogy)—and which we cannot imagine to have been alluded to in the original X, as will be clear from the following hypothetical delineation of thematic development.

That Mary is seen first of all as the mother of Christ and that the familiar medieval theme of her five joys is only one consequence of this motherhood is obvious; for the moment, however, let us consider as two separate themes (1) that of Mary as a link in the genealogical chain leading to Christ, and (2) Mary of the Five Joys. We must also remember that, in the various poems in praise of Mary, the rose was the favorite symbol, as we have said. Connecting these two apparently disparate observations, we may imagine two different poets, one intending to treat the genealogical theme, the other the five joys, but both alike haunted by the symbol of Mary the rose[-bush] and desiring to present their particular theme by means of that symbol.

Surely the first can present Mary only as a rose-bush bearing the flower Christ, the other will see her as a rose-bush with five branches (joys). It is the latter version that we have already postulated as X; we must, similarly, postulate another quite separate original Y for the former—and indeed, it is precisely the theme and the image of this Y (the rose-bush bearing the flower Christ) that we have already seen in the German poem. B, in turn, while mainly reflecting X, must have been influenced by some derivation of Y, if only in the line "Of her bosum a blossum spronge." For while the poet who first transferred the theme of the joys to the vegetal realm must have focussed exclusively on the picture of the branches springing from the rose-bush, his imitator B, who could only add trimmings to a symbolical representation already achieved, decides (with as little artistic motivation as in the addition of the sixth branch) to add a sudden, unprepared allusion to the quite different theme (and image) of Y. Finally (although the manuscript in which the version B is preserved is more recent than that of A), we must assume that the poet of A has used B, the representative of the prototype X, but has more fully developed the version of the prototype Y, at the expense of X, subordinating both to a plan in which the true protagonist is Christos Pantokrator, the conqueror of Earth, Hell, and Heaven, who appears as the *numinosum fascinans* which sprang from a lovely rose-bush. Thus, while both versions reflect a blend of different medieval poetic *topoi*, themselves tributary to the poetic exegesis of the Fathers, A is the greater poem in that it offers an original and artistic organization which succeeds in making the paradox of the Christian deity graphic and poetically convincing.

III

The last poem to be treated here will be a carol of the beginning of the 15th century, printed in *The Oxford Book of English Verse* (second edition, No. 26):

> 1. I sing of a maiden
>   That is makeles;

> King of all kings
> To her son she ches.
>
> 2. He came al so still
>   There his mother was,
>   As dew in April
>   That falleth on the grass.
>
> 3. He came al so still
>   To his mother's bour,
>   As dew in April
>   That falleth on the flour.
>
> 4. He came al so still
>   There his mother lay,
>   As dew in April
>   That falleth on the spray.
>
> 5. Mother and maiden
>   Was never none but she;
>   Well may such a lady
>   Goddes mother be.

The "immediate observation" with which we shall start is the introduction, into the traditional story of Christ's birth from a virgin, of the element of "poetic time," by which term I mean the relative time allotted by the poet to the enunciation of his themes in correspondence with their weight or nature, "time" used as a poetic device, as a means of expression. Within the framework offered by the first and the last stanza of our poem, the three central stanzas, with their parallelistic structure and their repetitions, have an inherent solemnity, a *rallentando* quality which forces us to linger on their content: on the poet's simple assertion that Christ came to earth as a *natural* phenomenon comparable to the dew in April.

The first and the last stanza, the *exordium* and the *conclusio*, as it were, are conceived in rigorous parallelism as befits the framework of the poem: in each the first two lines predicate the perfection of Mary, in each the third line offers a proud,

triumphantly ringing title, first of Christ ("King of all Kings,"
the phrase generally used of the Old Testament God, appears
here without article—as a title), then of Mary ("such a lady"
—I take the word in the meaning of "sovereign," "ruler,"
"queen," parallel to that of "ledy of lealte" in our first poem);
in each the last line establishes the relationship: the son-hood of
Christ, the motherhood of Mary.[29] Whereas the title of Christ
is announced (like a trumpet blast) at the beginning of the
poem immediately following the statement of Mary's perfection, the poet withholds Mary's title until the end—until the
great, miraculous event has taken place, which justifies, as it
were, the title of "lady." At the same time, however, this title
is offered as justifying the event: it is because she is "such a
lady" that she may be "God's mother." To the modern reader,
the circularity of such reasoning is startling: he is tempted to
smile at the naïve tautology which indeed is perhaps always involved in any proof of religious beliefs—even though he must
concede that this naïve intellectualism (the *Q.E.D.* quality of
"*well may* such a lady") is poetic.

We have just spoken of circularity of reasoning—but, perhaps, we should rather think in terms of spiral movement:
"spiral," for with the last stanza, we are on a higher plane,
and "movement," since in the three central stanzas we are offered not static explanation, but the re-enactment of an event
which is the result of a fact announced in the first stanza: there
we are informed of Mary's choice; in the stanzas that follow,

---

[29] Along with the parallelism just pointed out one may note a different,
a chiastic parallelism of the tenses used in stanzas I and 5:

| present: | stanza I: *is* | stanza 5: *was* |
| preterite: | *ches* | *may . . . be* |

The poem opens and closes with a statement in the present tense, presenting Mary as a timeless being. With the preterite of stanza I (*ches*)
we begin to proceed in time (a choice has been made at a given moment)
and are thereby prepared for the unfolding of the event in time, described
in the *narratio* of the three central stanzas. And the preterite opening
in the final stanza ("was") offers a similar fusion with the preceding
narrative (throughout presented in the preterite), but is itself not narrative in character and rather represents a judgment which must lead
immediately to the timelessness of the final prediction ("never *was* none
but she" must become "she alone *is*").

we *experience* the event which is Christ's response to that choice. She chose—He came. All that Mary did was to choose: "Ecce ancilla tua." And thus she elicited the divine response, the miracle. Her passive act made possible the manifestation of divine power. How great then must be the implicit primary power of the gentle maiden—how great a "lady" must Mary be![30] "Well may such a lady Goddes mother be," the poet tells us in the quietly elated tone of one concluding a demonstration. Now that we have *experienced* the miracle, the factual concluding statement has become incontrovertible and the theorem-like proposition of the first stanza is vindicated.

What of the miracle itself as described in the *narratio* of the three central stanzas? "He came al so still—as dew in April," that is, the miracle is immediately described in terms of a regular phenomenon in nature which works quietly, with unassuming consistency. A miracle is generally defined as the extraordinary suspension (for the benefit of a human being) of the laws of nature (cf., for example, the "winter rose" of the German carol mentioned above)—but has not Augustine said that the greatest miracles are those which seem natural to us, the daily rising and setting of the sun, etc.? The regular functioning of the laws of nature is indeed the greatest of miracles. In our poem, by a somewhat reverse procedure, the greatest miracle of Christianity and the most dramatic event in the Augustinian picture of the history of mankind, the descent of the deity to earth, is portrayed with the stillness and undramatic sweetness of a phenomenon in nature which can be expected to happen according to general laws, but when it happens is always wondrous as on the first day of creation. Christ comes with the *fascinans* quality of the Christian *numinosum*, gentle but all-pervasive. Suddenly the spring dew is here, one April morning, after the winter of our discontent (the winter of mankind's

---

[30] The quiescent nature of the Lady Mary, whose inner being elicits outward response, is, of course, also in harmony with the picture of the lady, as seen in courtly poetry, according to which the beloved lady must be self-contained and passive, her power being that of eliciting powerful reaction. As Ortega has pointed out, in the culminating periods of civilization, woman has the prerogative of *being*, action remaining the province of man.

unredeemed age) has gone. The scene in our poem is indeed not that of Christmas, as in the previous carol, but of spring, the Easter setting of Resurrection. "Still" as the miracle of resurrection comes about in nature, it is all-pervasive in its quiet power: once dew is on the grass, it is also on the flower, it is also on the bush. The three stanzas which move in slow gracefulness make us sense this divine ubiquity—in terms of nature (and nature, as is well known, is never brought into art in the Middle Ages for nature's sake, but for the purpose of the demonstration of the divine). The cool freshness of the morning dew is allowed to convey to us the idea of the moral *refrigerium*, or the rejuvenation, brought to humanity by the Redeemer. There may be sensed a climax in the extension of the dew from the grass to the flower to the bush, and parallel to this development runs another concerned with the presentation of the Virgin: the line "there his mother was" (the demonstrative "there" being equal to the relative "where") indicates a minimum of locality, merely the fact that there was a place where Mary was; the line "to his mother's bower" provides an environment that befits a noblewoman (a "lady"); and finally the line "there his mother lay" delicately[31] suggests the bed of child-birth. Just as in the treatment of the dew, we feel the movement of extension in space (symbolizing the ubiquity of divine grace), here the development goes from the abstract to the concrete: a point postulated in space becomes a lady's chamber, and from the abstract predication of her presence ("where his mother was") we come to a slight indication of the physical attitude of a recumbent woman receiving her newborn son—who comes, we must believe, not from within her, but from without, from above, like the gentle dew that falls softly from the heavens.[32] The two parallel series ("on the grass—on the flour—on the spray" and "there his mother was—to his mother's bour—there his mother lay") suggest two different movements: extension and contraction: while the vista of dew-covered nature expands, our gaze is attracted more

[31] Compare the outspokenness of our previous poem, version B: "ther mary lay in her bede."

[32] Cf. *New English Dictionary*, s.v. *dew*: "Formerly supposed to fall softly from the heavens."

and more insistently toward the focal point of divine grace. Or rather, divine grace at the same time that it is unstintedly expended and everywhere visible, manifests itself in creative concentration. She-who-chose and He-who-came are only two aspects of the same divine act. And the solemnity of the three slow-cadenced stanzas that tell us thrice of the same event, holding our attention by the two devices of extending and contracting movement (which fall into one), has been achieved in order to give us that feeling of participation in an event for which the consciousness of the passage of time is necessary. For any inner event is characterized by the feeling of *durée réelle*, as Bergson has called it: conversely, in order to give us the feeling for the reality of the event, the impression of the passage of time was created—by a poet possessed, like Dante, of the sense for "poetic time."

Up to this point we have treated the comparison of Christ with the dew as an original invention of our poet which allowed him to depict the coming of the Saviour in terms of a natural miracle. The question whether there exists a dogmatic basis for this comparison, so poetically convincing, has purposely not been raised because of my (tacit) pledge to the reader to "stay within the poem." I confess that only by chance did I indeed discover a general dogmatic basis for the comparison in question: by looking up (in connection with a problem quite different from our poem) the article *manna* in the *Thesaurus linguae latinae*. As is well known, the story of the manna appears in Exodus 16, after the mention (l. 13) that "dew lay in the morning round about the host" of the Israelites wandering in the desert: "after the dew that lay was gone up" they saw the manna which is defined (l. 14) as "a small round thing, as small as the hoarfrost on the ground." The patristic writers seem to have identified the *manna* = "hoar-frost" with the "dew" that preceded it, cf. *Itineraria Antonini*: "*ros* de caelo quem manna appellant" (obviously a blend of ll. 13 and 14). Later the equation "manna" = "dew" must have been followed by the other equation, of the well-known prefigurative type, "manna

= Christ" and this we find in Pelagius: "manna figura corporis Christi fuit" and Augustine: "manna Christus tamquam panis vivus": the manna which in the Old Testament served as bread to the Jews wandering in the desert foreshadows (is a prefiguration of) the spiritual food given to the Christian who may derive sustenance in the form of the sacrament in which Christ's living body is present (in the words of the previous poem: "Every day it schewit in prystes hond").[33] Given the two equations:

[33] These patristic conceptions have left their imprint in Romance literature: Trénel, *L'Ancien Testament et la langue française*, 79, quotes from Gautier de Coincy (12th century): "Ave, Virge florie, qui aportas la manne" (manna = Christ), Charles d'Orléans (15th century): "Noble enfant [= Christ] de bonne heure né / à toute douleur destiné, / manna du ciel, céleste don"; Littré quotes the lines of Bossuet: "La manne cachée [= *manna absconditum* of the Apocalypse] sont les consolations spirituelles; la manne cachée c'est la vérité; la manne cachée c'est *le sacré corps de Jésus.*"
In the 14th-century Italian poem *Intelligenza*, devoted to the praise of Love, seen as an emanation of God, we find the identification of earthly love with manna and dew (ll. 28 seq.):

> Discese nel meo cor *sicome manna*
> Amor soave come *in fior ruggiada*,
> Che m'è più dolce assai che mel di canna.

Here, earthly love is conceived as a secularized version of divine love (charity). The third line quoted is derived from Ex. 16:31, "gustusque eius [mannae] quasi similae cum melle."
In a Peruvian 17th century mystery play, *A la natividad del Señor*, by Sor Juana María, there is found an exhortation of an angel to the Shepherds in which the whole of Nature is shown to take part in that "gran *milagro* de la naturaleza" of the birth of Christ (a feature to be found also in medieval poems, e.g. in the 13th/17th century Franco-Italian *Ystoire de la Passion*, ed. E. A. Wright): one of the "natural miracles" that take place here *after* the birth of Christ is the fall of the dew: "Ya en la casa del pan / brotó la espiga tierna; / ya *descendió el rocío* / sobre la verde hierba" (cf. the review *Mar del Sur*, VIII, 80).
A student of the English department of my university, Mr. Watson, drew my attention to the two poems of Andrew Marvell: *Ros* and *On a Drop of Dew*, in both of which the drop of dew, considered, it is true, from the point of view of its microscopic-macroscopic qualities, and of its origin from and return to Heaven, is exemplified by the Manna (in the English version we find "the Manna's sacred Dew," in the Latin, dew is defined as "Mensis exundans Manna beatis"). The return of the manna to Heaven whence it came is obviously an allusion to Christ's resurrection, here fused with a Platonic theme.

$$manna = dew$$
$$manna = Christ,$$

it must follow (according to the principle: if two things are equal to a third, they must be equal to each other) that a third equation is possible:

$$dew = Christ.$$

This is the one we find expressed in our poem, with the intermediary concept "manna" eliminated—a condensation (similar to the omission of Jesse in our second poem) highly poetic in which is presented the direct identification of natural phenomenon and deity, without the burden of Biblical lore.

Now that the basic conceit of our poem has been found to be based on a traditional idea, should we feel disappointed and tempted to blame indiscreet philology for the disenchantment it may produce to the reader? But, granted the traditional character of the idea that manna is dew and Christ is manna (and consequently dew), we should not lose sight of the fact that our poet has proceeded as if unaware of such tradition. Not only is there no mention of manna as such: there is actually no direct identification, the "third equation" is presented as a simile ("He came al so still *as* dew in April"), as a simile that suggests poetically the mysterious comparability of divine action with natural development. We may conclude then that the simile of the dew, even though inspired by dogmatic literature, has been relived by this extraordinary poet who was able to give the pristine beauty of nature to a venerable scriptural concept.

And our admiration for the poet must increase still more when we learn that our 15th century carol is a reworking of a quite mediocre longer 13th century version (published by W. Greg, *Mod. Phil.*, VII, 166-7, also printed in Carleton Brown's anthology, No. 31):

Nu þis fules singet hand maket hure blisse
and þat gres up þringet and leued þe ris;
of on ic wille singen þat is makeles,
þe king of halle kinges to moder he hire ches.

4

Heo his wit-uten sunne and wit-uten hore,
I-cumen of kinges cunne of gesses more;
þe louerd of monkinne of hire was yboren
to bringen us hut of Sunne, elles wue weren for-lore.　　8

Gabriel hire grette and saide hire, "aue!
Marie ful of grace, vre louer be uit þe,
þe frut of þire wombe ibleset mot id be.
bu sal go wit chide, for sout ic suget þe."　　12

and þare gretinke þat angle hauede ibrout,
he gon to bi-þenchen and meinde hire þout;
he saide to þen angle, "hu may tiden þis?
of monnes y-mone nout y nout iuis."　　16

Mayden heo was uid childe & Maiden her biforen,
& maiden ar sot-hent hire chid was iboren;
Maiden and moder nas neuer non wimon boten he—
wel mitte he berigge of godes sune be.　　20

I-blessed beo þat suete chid & þe moder ec,
& þe suete broste þat hir son sec;
I-hered ibe þe time þat such chid uas iboren,
þat lesed al of pine þat arre was for-lore.　　24

As the editors mentioned above have pointed out, it is obvious
that lines 3-4 and 19-20 of this older lyric form the opening and
concluding lines of our poem while the repetitional part (the part
dealing with Christ as Dew) is an addition of our poet. The
"not very remarkable" 13th century version is a quite traditional
poem about the Annunciation, including a mention of the tree of
Jesse, a transcription of the *Ave Maria*, and a prayer at the end.
Both commentators remark on the uniqueness of a verbatim ap-
propriation of 13th century poetic material by a 15th century
poet. Professor Greg adds a quotation from Gummere's book on
the "Popular Ballads" (p. 116) to the effect that "incremental
repetition," as known in the ballads, occurs exceptionally in our
15th century lyric "as if 'dancing for joy.'" The latter remark
must be taken together with Gummere's derivation of the ballad

from a dance-song (as the term "ballad" implies). I may offer a typical instance of incremental repetition from the ballad "Sir Patrick Spence":[34]

> And mony was the feather bed
> That flatter'd on the faem;
> And mony was the gude lord's son
> That never mair cam hame.

[34] The international character of this ballad style which respects the "epic law" of Three may be shown by a passage from the Rumanian *Miorita* in which the shepherd doomed to die gives to his faithful lamb the following indications about the burial of his body near the fold:

Iar la cap să-mi pui	And close by me lay
Flueraș de fag	My little pipe of beech,
Mult zice cu drag!	Silver of speech!
Flueraș de os,	My little pipe of bone,
Mult zice duios!	With melting moan!
Flueraș de soc,	My pipe of elder-tree,
Mult zice cu foc!	Fiery and free!

(Translated by N. W. Newcombe in Gr. Nandriș, *Colloquial Rumanian*, p. 264.)

This lyrical interlude (one of several inserted into the narrative) concerned with the theme of idyllic rest in Nature consists of three "dance-like" couplets in which Death is represented as overcome by the beauty of music in Nature. It remains to be seen whether such repetitions in lyrical poems originate in the elementary tendency to help the singer-dancers by imposing a lesser strain on their memory. We may also consider the *parallelismus membrorum* of the *Psalms* and the *Song of Songs* as a source—and also the epic technique of the *laisses similaires* (*répétitives*): for instance, in *Aliscans* (cf. Bartsch-Wiese, *Chrestomathie de l'ancien français*, no. 19), in the lament spoken by Guillaume d'Orange over the corpse of his nephew Vivien, we find, in repetitive tirades, such repetitions as

> l. 90 or vos ont mort Sarrasin et Persant (in an -*ant* laisse)
> l. 181 or vos ont mort Sarrasin et Escler (in a -*e*- laisse)

or:

> l. 52 parmi le cors ot .XV. plaies tés,
>   de la menor *morust uns amirés*
> l. 109 parmi le cors ot .XV. plaies grans,
>   de la menor *morust uns amirans*

But in my opinion, these epic variations which occur generally in episodes tense with lyrical emotion, in lines separated from each other, must rather go back to an original (lyrical?) scheme in which the varied lines were contiguous. Incremental repetition, then, originates in lyrical poetry —a circumstance which does not, however, exclude that our 15th century carol may have borrowed that feature from 15th century ballads (which in turn imitate earlier carols with repetitive devices).

O lang, lang may the ladies sit,
  Wi' their fans into their hand,
Before they see Sir Patrick Spens
  Come sailing to the strand!

And lang, lang may the maidens sit
  Wi' their gowd kames in their hair,
A-waiting for their ain dear loves!
  For them they'll see nae mair.

Gummere and Greg evidently assume that from the ballad, originally a dance-song, the incremental repetition was extended to our carol, where it should express the "dancing for joy" of the believer. But the genre of the carol originates in a dance-song too (cf. Margot Sahlin, *Étude sur la carole médiévale*, Uppsala, 1940). Moreover, parallelistic structure with word variation is characteristic of English religious poetry, cf. the first poem contained in Brown's anthology:[35]

Nou goth sonne vnder wod,—
me reweth, marie, þi faire Rode.
Nou goth sonne vnder tre—
me reweþ, marie, þi sone and þe.

A student in Romance will immediately be reminded of Old Portuguese popular dance-songs, the *cantares de amigo* sung (and danced) by women, parallelistic in style:

Levad' amigo que dormides as manhanas frias,
  toda' las aves do mundo d'amor diziam.
Levad' amigo que dormide las frias manhanas,
  toda' las aves do mundo d'amor cantavam.

Even though we must assume for the incremental repetition in our 15th century carol the source of a dance-song (whether derived directly from popular dance-songs or ballads retraceable thereto), the fact is undeniable that this dance-element was secondarily introduced into a carol which showed no repetitions or parallelisms. That this happened as late as the 15th century (a period when incremental repetition occurs also in

[35] I am indebted to Mr. Karl Denner for this parallel.

the ballads), this fact must testify to a changed *Zeitgefühl*, a change in sensibility by which the inner evidence of a feeling is rendered dramatically in terms of the passage of time (as opposed to the indifference to poetic time of the high Middle Ages as evidenced in the 13th century version of our carol) : the "dancing for joy" occurs precisely in that section of the 15th century carol in which the miracle of the Nativity is re-enacted. Moreover, the introduction of the incremental repetition, so essential for "poetic timing," must be seen in connection with another alteration which our commentators have failed to notice: line 4 of the older version reads: "Þe king of hall kinges to moder he hire ches" (notice *to moder*, not "to His mother"), lines 3-4 of the more recent version: "King of all kings / To her son she ches." If we take the former rendering together with line 20 of the same version: "well mitte he berigge of godes sune be," we must infer that in this version it was God the Father who chose Mary to be the mother of his son, whereas in the new version it is the Virgin who chooses her divine son (thereby deserving the title of a Lady). It was this all-important change that brought an inner dramatic movement (which was then explicited in the incremental repetition) into the poem. Mary is here not a purely passive instrument of the will of God, but active-passive: by her "choice" she unleashes the divine, or natural, forces which will bring about the miracle of His coming. The poet has cut off two significant couplets from the older version, those dealing with the beginning and the end of the development[36]—to fill the gap not only by what our too technical-minded commentators call "incremental repetition" (a ballad-esque device), but precisely by the re-enactment of the miracle. There is a threefold activity to be observed on the part of our poet: his changing of Mary's inaction into dramatic action, his selection, from a banal sequence of lines, of two climactic couplets producing a *rondo* effect and his addition of a new *adagio* part which renders, by a musicality all its own, an inner experience transcending all experience.

[36] It is also clear that A has taken the motif of the spring ("April dew") from the *Natureingang* of the longer, older version whose *décor* is definitely spring.

The achievement represented by our poem whose author has made artistic what was banal may be compared, in one respect at least, to the artistic improvement wrought by the anonymous Spanish 15th century poet to whom we owe the reduced version of the *Romance del Conde Arnaldos* (which Americans may know from the—somewhat sentimentalized—paraphrase offered by Longfellow in his poem "The Secret of the Sea"). The original complete story (which Menéndez Pidal, *Revista de filología española*, III, 281, has reconstructed from a Judeo-Spanish source originating in Tangiers) begins by showing us the Count in the midst of hunting; he suddenly notes a galley approaching the shore and hears a strangely sweet melody that the boatman is singing. Entranced by the song, which he implores the boatman to teach him, he boards the ship, to become involved in a series of adventures: he is captured by corsairs, rescued by a fleet sent by his kinsmen, and, in the end, marries happily. This trite story of adventure was, by a poet of genius, cut short at the point when the Count's request is answered by the words of the boatman: "Yo no digo esta canción / sino a quien conmigo va" —making of this sententious reply a startlingly abrupt conclusion that forces us to peer beyond the horizon of the poem in search of the mysterious link between the lure of the sea and the power of music. Obviously the simple act of cutting a poem in the middle and leaving the lines of this fragment untouched is totally different from the creation of a second poem containing only a few lines salvaged from the first. Nevertheless, the act of elimination which has given us the famous *romance* with its new poetic emphasis, was motivated by the same concern with "poetic time" which has inspired our 15th century carol. Obviously, a new *Zeitgefühl*, evidenced in the (15th century) ballads of several European nations (cf. also the shorter version of *Sir Patrick Spence*), has given the poets of this time the possibility of dramatic concentration by means of a fragmentary or epigrammatic presentation of a longer sequence, itself inarticulate and amorphous.

It is astonishing how at closer inspection so many inner and outward relationships can be discovered in a poem as short and apparently as simple as our 15th century carol. The "clear profundity" of this popular poem can rival that of lyrical master-pieces written by learned poets such as *En una noche escura*[37] and *Selige Sehnsucht*.

In treating the three poems in question, the analysis of each of them was determined by a single, central observation: in the first, emphasis was laid on the totality of the phenomenon of love there encompassed by means of a rich synthesis of all the extant motifs of medieval love poetry; in the second, on the fusion of historical periods and spatial realms into one universe permeated by Christ, who is close to man; in the third, on the inner lyric-dramatic cohesion achieved by an appeal to the reality-giving force of time. These observations I believe to be objectively verifiable and capable of gaining the *consensus omnium*. In any case, I have made every effort to avoid the dangers inherent in all *explication de texte*: impressionistic overinterpretation, entailing a secondary lyricism of the critic's own making.

[37] With this Spanish poem of the Golden Age our carol shares also the feature that its language, in spite of the date of composition, is practically the language of today (only *makeles* and *ches* are archaic words).

Post-script to the poem Blow, northerne wynd:

[1] Mr. Paul Trost, *Neuphil. Mitt.*, LII (1951), 10-13, has shown, by examples drawn from French popular poetry ("Au clair de la lune"), a Portuguese *trova*, a German *Schnadahüpfl*, and the medieval Latin *Stabat mater*, the existence of a general law in poetry according to which femi-nine rhymes produce an effect of suspense while masculine rhymes strike a conclusive note and will consequently find their preferred place at the end of stanzas (the first stanza of the *Stabat mater*, for example, shows the rhymes *dolorosa—lacrimosa—*FILIUS*—dolentem—gementem—* [*per-transivit*] GLADIUS*—*with *gladius* the action appears finally consummated). This law is corroborated by our poem *Blow northerne wynd* in certain of the stanzas: in 6 when the picture of the perfection of the beloved is offered (*godnesse—ryhtfulnesse—clannesse—*BEALTE*—largesse—prouesse —suetnesse—*LEALTE), and especially in the last stanza which depicts the endless suffering of the lover (*care—dare—bare—*WON*—slake—wake— make—*MON).

2. G. L. Brook in his edition of "The Harley Lyrics," Manchester, 1948, has commented upon our poem in a manner not quite satisfactory to me: he proposes to remove the possessive pronoun *hire* in line 21

because "it interferes with the allegorical interpretation" (cf. however above, p. 208) ; he finds in the images of our poem a "closeness to common life," a "vivid and homely" or "picturesque" quality ("a lover disdained by his mistress falls like mud dropping away from a lifted foot . . . a lady's complexion is like a lantern at night")—their function of express-ing perfection or lack of perfection is not recognized; and he presents as "the faults" of the Harley lyrics the "excessive use of conventional phrases and the lack of a sense of balance and proportion" (as evidenced, for example, by *Annot and Johon*, which is "unfortunately reminiscent of 'I love my love with an A' ")—a statement itself unfortunately reminis-cent of the aesthetic conventions of an age which had no sympathy for the medieval aesthetic canons.

APPENDIX

....

American Advertising Explained
as Popular Art*

....

THE PHILOLOGICAL METHOD of *explication de texte* is usually applied to works of art and works of great art. But, at all times, there has existed, side by side with great art, that everyday art which the Germans have called *Gebrauchskunst* ("applied practical art") : that art which has become a part of the daily routine and which adorns the practical and the utilitarian with beauty. At no time has this type of art played so compensatory a role as is the case today, in the age of machinism, of rationalization, and of the subjection of man to the impersonal necessities of social, economic, and political life. An emphasis on the beautiful has penetrated all levels of fabrication, down to mucilage bottles and matchbooks, and to the packaging of goods; it has also penetrated to the forms of propaganda used to advertise these goods. And the success of such attempts at aesthetic appeal achieved by modern advertising is borne out by the many exhibits of original commercial designs which have attracted a large public. It is also true that particularly novel and clever devices of advertising find an appreciative echo among sophisticated journalists, and there exists today a whole literature devoted to the requirements of effective advertisements.[1] In such treatments, however, the emphasis is generally placed on the psychological element and on the utilitarian efficacy of the propa-

---

* From *A Method of Interpreting Literature* (Smith College, 1949), pp. 102-49.

[1] I have read in this connection, H. F. Adams, *Advertising and Its Laws* (New York, 1916), Brewster and Palmer, *Introduction to Advertising* (Chicago, New York, 1925), and H. E. Burtt, *Psychology of Advertising* (Cambridge, 1939).

ganda, while little or no attention is paid to the aesthetic as such,[2] to the artistic tradition in which the particular advertisement has its place, to the satisfaction which advertising may offer of contemporary extra-commercial needs, or, finally, to the historical explanation of the phenomenon of advertising, which must, somehow, be related to the American national character and cultural history.[3] Can the linguistically minded literary historian, who harbors no snobbish feelings toward this genre of applied art, give an *explication de texte* of a good sample of modern advertising, in which he would proceed from the exterior features to the "spirit of the text" (and to the spirit of the genre),

[2] The psychologists of advertising recognize the influence of advertising on the aesthetic taste of their public only insofar as they admit that public taste may be educated by the display of artistic objects (Burtt, p. 8); they acknowledge also (p. 50) that it is sometimes possible for the advertisement to provide for the beholder "a vicarious fulfillment of desires." I would say that it is possible to see these two facts together, and to state that advertising as such may offer a fulfillment of the *aesthetic* desires of modern humanity.

[3] Such a study presupposes that type of "symbolizing" thinking which has been advocated in the introduction to my book, *Linguistics and Literary History* (Princeton University Press, 1948); to see the relationship between an everyday detail which is, all too often, simply taken for granted, and a spiritual entity in itself not unknown, but only vaguely and separately conceived—this is, I believe, to take a step toward the understanding of the well-motivated, coherent, and consistent organism which our civilization is. It is not enough, in the case of American advertising, to admire or savor a new coinage, psychological trick, or strategy, as this may develop in the technique in question: one must try to see the manifold cross-relationships between the detail (the advertisement) and the whole (our civilization) in order that our capacity for feeling at home in this civilization and of enjoying it will be increased. I may say that, in the matter of understanding one's civilization, the French (incidentally, the inventors of the *explication de texte*) have a great advantage over Americans, who, as it seems to me, are less given to probing into the motivation behind the products of their civilization; the French are past masters in establishing (sometimes to excess) relationships between specific aspects of their civilization (French literature or French cuisine) and this civilization itself; they are able to recognize even in the most trivial detail the expression of an implicit national profession of faith. The present writer must confess that it was by applying *explication de texte* to American advertising that he was given the first avenue (a "philological" avenue) leading toward the understanding of the unwritten text of the American way of life.

just as he is accustomed to do with literary texts? Let us try the experiment.

In undertaking this study, I shall be attempting to apply my method to things American, with which my listeners will be much more familiar than I—a circumstance which, in itself, can only provide a better test of the method. It is needless to state that, in line with this method, I shall here carefully avoid the biographical or pragmatically historical approach: I know nothing about the genesis of the particular advertisement to be discussed, about the persons involved in the choice of the name of the particular product, or about the history of the business firm in question. I shall seek to analyze a given advertisement in the same unbiased manner as I have attempted to do in the case of a poem of St. John of the Cross or of a letter of Voltaire, believing, as I do, that this kind of art, if not comparable in greatness to the texts usually analyzed by the scholar, offers nevertheless a "text" in which we can read, as well in its words as in its literary and pictorial devices, the spirit of our time and of our nation—which are, surely, in their way, "unmittelbar zu Gott." To adopt a resentful or patronizing attitude toward our time is, obviously, the worst way to understand it.[4] Meditation

---

[4] My distinguished friend and colleague, the Spanish poet Pedro Salinas, has said (in an address to the University of Puerto Rico, entitled "Aprecio y defensa del lenguaje," printed in Puerto Rico, 1944) in regard to the language of advertising: "La sociedad capitalista ha producido en este siglo un nuevo tipo de retórica, la retórica del anuncio. Recortes lingüísticos eficaces, matices delicados, que han hecho sus pruebas en la lengua literaria, y que se empleaban para provocar la emoción pura y desinteresada, se combinan para formar una habilísima maquinária verbal, que suscite en el lector pasiones menores, violentos deseos posesivos, relativamente fáciles de apagar sin tragedia, por tal o cual precio, en tal o cual establecimiento. En este caso el utilitarismo ha llegado a atreverse a asaltar el lenguaje, no ya en sus obras exteriores, el idioma hablado y corriente, sino en su misma ciudadela, en la lengua literaria, servidora exclusiva hasta hoy de los sentimientos puros."

I must protest against the sentiments expressed in this paragraph: it is surely not true that the literary language has always served "exclusively" the expression of pure, disinterested feelings; I would say that the prose of Cicero, the attorney, which has influenced European writing (and not oratory alone) for 1800 years, was "utilitarian," that is, was used for definite practical purposes. Thus, the use of refined literary de-is needed in the face of things modern as of things ancient. Finally, since the following study is intended as an *explication de texte*, it is hardly necessary to warn the reader that the discussion will be mainly limited to one "text," to one example of one particular type of advertising; there is no intention on my part of offering a general survey of advertising trends.

In the drugstores throughout our country, the brand of oranges known as *Sunkist* was advertised some years ago by the following picture-with-text:[5] on a high mountain range, covered with snow that glistens in the bright sunshine, furrowed by vertical gullies, towering over a white village with its neat, straight rows of orange trees, there rests a huge orange-colored sun, inscribed with the word "Sunkist." In front of this vista, set squarely in the midst of the groves, is a glass of orange-juice which rises

---

vices in the "rhetoric of advertisement" is not necessarily reprehensible on the grounds of its purely utilitarian nature. It is precisely the purpose of this article to show that art can arise within the realm of the utilitarian.

A view somewhat similar to that of Salinas' is expressed by S. I. Hayakawa in *Etc.: A Review of General Semantics*, III (1946), 116 seq. According to the aim of this journal, which is to teach us how to distinguish words from facts and how to learn what the words "really" mean, Hayakawa would see in advertising (which he defines as "venal poetry"), the enemy of true poetry (which he calls "disinterested poetry"); according to him, one of the main reasons why poets in our time have become esoteric, obscure, pessimistic, "unpoetic" is that any genuine and hearty expression of common feeling is suspected of being salesman's poetry, i.e., advertising. Of course, he is forced to admit that venal poetry is as old as the world; and I would add, for my part, that the esotericism of poets did not start as a counteraction to advertising; Maurice Scève and Góngora were esoteric poets, and esotericism has only become more conspicuous in the democratic age: the *sottisier* of Voltaire, the *dictionnaire des idées reçues* of Flaubert testify to the existence of the misuse of word symbols by the masses, long before advertising, as we know it, was invented. I think it only fair to replace the pejorative label "venal poetry" applied to advertising by my term *Gebrauchspoesie*, which takes into account the unquestionable fact that the masses have come to absorb the standard poetry of the ads. Great poets find probably no more difficulty in writing today than they have at any other time: the pre-emption of words for common utilitarian purposes has to be undone at all times by any great poet, who must always react against trivial poetry.

[5] The genre of picture-with-text is, obviously, a development of the "cartoon"—which, itself, can be traced back to the emblem literature of the 16th and 17th centuries.

to the exact height of the mountain range and whose color exactly matches that of the sun ball. Next to this gigantic glass of juice is a smaller one of the same color, and next to that, a fruit-squeezer on which lies the orange to be squeezed. In the left corner of the advertisement we read, as the only inscription:

From the sunkist groves of California
Fresh for you

The first feature we will observe is that in advertising its *Sunkist* oranges, the firm did not expatiate on the goodness, juiciness, flavor, *etc.*, of this particular "ready-made" type of product, but chose to trace the origin of the product back to the groves which yielded it, so that we may concentrate our attention on the natural beauty of California. From the fruit, our glance is allowed to pass to the countryside, to the soil, to Nature that grows the fruit—and only to Nature, not to the orange-growers or those who pick the fruit, not the packers who prepare its distribution, not to any human factor. It is Nature that, as by a miracle, brings forth these "sunkist" oranges, brings them "fresh for you," from California. The commercial product (those millions of oranges packed methodically in thousands of cases and transported by the railroads) is shown against the background of its natural environment—indeed, the glass of orange-juice, as we have seen, is set down right in the midst of Nature. In the inscription, there is not even the verbal form "brought" which would suggest human activity: the oranges kissed by the sun are there as an accomplished fact; their transportation over miles and miles of territory is passed over in silence. The elimination of man from this pictorial representation, the concentration on productive Nature and on the miracle of the final appearance of the juice, as we have it before us in our drugstores, represents a highly poetic procedure, since, thereby, our everyday causality (the laws of supply and demand, of mass production and lowered prices) is replaced by other laws (the laws of Nature—and of the miracle); and on our routine reality there is superimposed another, dream-like, reality: the consumer may have the illusion, for a moment, of drinking nectar at the source.[6] And the public accepts willingly the hypocrisy of the artist. It is as though this manifestation of commercial self-expression were denying its essential purpose, that of selling and of profit-making; as though the business world were engrossed only in harvesting what Nature gives and in bringing her gifts to the individual enjoyer —in an Arcadian life harmonious with Nature. In the city drug-store, over whose counter this sunny picture shines, the wall opens up before us like a window on Nature.[7] Business becomes poetic because it recognizes the great grip which poetry has on this modern unpoetic world. It is true that the subtle device of eliminating man is calculated only to bring man back again into the picture; for what, the spectator must ask himself upon re-flection, has made possible the miracle of transportation and of transformation, if not the skill, indeed, the magic, of modern industry? And the modest way in which the business firm hides its own tremendous activity behind anonymous Nature will impress us favorably.[8]

[6] In radio advertising, the transposition of the utilitarian into art must necessarily tend toward the acoustic; when, in the advertisement of "Rinso," the notes of the bird bob-white are introduced as an accompani-ment to a lyric boasting of the accomplishments of the soap in question, this is intended to provide the housewife with an ingratiating domestic song ("happy little wash-day song"), so that the drudgery of her house-hold tasks may be lightened by an association of her work with bird life, with outdoor life, and Nature. The creators of this tune have taken into account the nostalgia for Nature which is a part of our urban civilization.

[7] Unwittingly (?), the advertisers of *Sunkist* oranges have acted in agreement with the associational psychology of G. Th. Fechner, who in his *Vorschule der Aesthetik* (1876) gives as an example of such associa-tions precisely an orange—which would suggest to him the whole of Italy: whoever finds an orange beautiful "sieht sozusagen ganz Italien mit in ihr, das Land, wohin uns von jeher eine romantische Sehnsucht zog." The advertisers have caused "the whole of California" (the "ro-mantic" equivalent, for Americans, of Italy) to be associated with the orange.

[8] It may occasionally be true that the industrial process would be pain-ful to visualize; in such a case the procedure of advertising will consist in evoking the beauty of the natural origin without insisting on the neces-sary subsequent stages. I remember seeing a pictorial advertisement of "Jones' Country Sausage," in which there is shown only the diptych of the beginnings in Nature and of the final industrial product: above, there is pictured the deep green of mountain pastures in which cattle graze

Now, when business becomes poetic, for whatever reasons, it must subject itself to the ancient laws of poetry, which remain unshaken by the technical developments of the modern world. We can, then, expect to find in this business art the old, time-honored poetic devices. And, indeed, is the poetically achieved evocation of the natural state of the product of human industry anything but the repetition of a device known to the ancient and the Renaissance poets? We may remember the anonymous inscription (listed in Bartlett's *Familiar Quotations* (11th ed., p. 1092) discovered on an old violin: *Arbor viva, tacui; mortua, cano.* Or again—why not?—we might think of the lines in Góngora's *Soledades* in which the drowning protagonist rescues himself by means of a floating spar—which is described in terms of the original living pine tree, that once resisted the blasts of the north wind and now resists the floods:

> Del siempre en la montaña puesto pino
>   al enemigo Noto
> piadoso miembro roto
> —breve tabla. . . .

Similarly, the poet who devised the *Sunkist* advertisement reminds us, when we put a dime down on the counter for a glass of orange-juice, of all the sunshine that went into this refreshing drink: as if we should be able to buy for so small a sum the inexhaustible source of warmth and fecundity, the Sun. We came to the counter for reasons of practical necessity; we walk away, having seen the picture and enjoyed the juice, with an insight into the generosity of Nature and the persistence of its goodness in its smallest yields.

Recourse was had to another ancient poetic and pictorial device when our poet chose to point out a continuous line between the orange-juice and California Nature: he wished to

---

idyllically among the trees and flowers; below, we see the small cones of the processed meat. Hypocrisy? Yes, but the hypocrisy inherent in any poetizing of our animal instincts. After all, we wish to enjoy the meat we eat, and this enjoyment is not furthered by a realization that we are carnivorous animals.

trace a consistent link between the *Sunkist* orange and the orange-juice by use of a motif which shows how Nature plans and man carries out her will: this fusion of man's and Nature's activities manifests itself in the repetition of one motif which has a central part in these activities—the motif of the orange, pictorially represented by means of the unifying orange color. In all, we have the one orange-color motif repeated four times:[9] a natural orange, two glasses of orange-juice, and the "sun" itself (which bears the inscription "Sunkist") ; in this representation is offered the symbol of the unity, of the harmony of Nature's and man's concern with the fruit. And, here, modern advertising is returning to a medieval form. On the 11th century portal of the Hildesheim cathedral, in a bas-relief representing the scene of the Fall of Man, we may see four apples which traverse the sculpture in one horizontal line: one is in the mouth of the dragon in the tree, one in Eve's hand, one is figured as the apple of her breast, and one is in the hand of Adam.[10] The central motif in the medieval work of art, the apple, is, of course, the symbol of the forbidden fruit, whereas the central motif in our modern work of *Gebrauchskunst* serves the praise of the natural fruit accessible to all; again, the momentous event of Man's Fall is presented in slow motion, broken up into stages, whereas man's progress in the exploitation of Nature comes to us with an acceleration provided by the technique of the "accomplished fact." Nevertheless, the basic technique, that of the didactically repeated central motif, is the same; modern pantheism

[9] We have here the principle of "repetition," so basic to all forms of propaganda, except that here it is no word, no slogan, which is repeated, but a single feature abstracted from the objects pictured; namely, their orange color.

[10] There'll always be an ad-man: this very biblical scene in its medieval presentation has been adapted to an advertisement of Countess Mara's ties: the 4 apples are replaced by 4 ties, and Eve, acting as always under the command of the serpent, is luring the reluctant Adam, who has already taken one tie, into acceptance of a second, and perhaps a third (a fourth being also visible in the background, guarded by the serpent in the tree). While, in the medieval sculpture, the forbidden fruit was multiplied only for didactic reasons, in the modern advertisement the device of multiplication is exploited as an excuse to display a variety of wares, presented as forbidden fruit.

has espoused forms of art devised in the religious climate of the Middle Ages.

There may be discerned in this device a subsidiary feature which might appear incongruous with the realism supposedly required in a genre devoted to such practical ends: the "sun-orange" which figures in our picture and which borrows the *exact* shade of coloring from the fruit on which it shines, is a quite violent, surrealistic misrepresentation of reality, apparently symbolical of the powerful attraction exerted by business, which draws all things into its orbit—which puts even the sun to work. Or, perhaps, may we not have to do with the myth of an orange-sun (figured by a sun-orange), which would have the particular function of nurturing orange groves—just as there were ancient *Sondergötter*, particular gods devoted to the growing of wine, of cereals, etc.; just as there are Catholic saints devoted to particular industries and particular natural processes? (A black Madonna caring especially for Negro worshippers is no more startling than is the orange sun which takes its color from the thing it grows.)

As for the gross misrepresentation of size which appears in the gigantic glass of orange-juice in the foreground, which is equal in height to the California mountain range and, despising all laws of proportion, completely overshadows the orange-squeezer, this focuses our attention on the protagonist of the scene, on that glass of juice you will order at the counter—with the same "naïve" technique of the medieval paintings, in which Christ is presented taller than his disciples and these taller than common folk (and which is reflected also in the Nuremberg tin soldiers, whose captain is twice as tall as the common soldier); the significance of a figure is translated into material size. One could, perhaps, think that the huge size of the glass in the foreground is due to a naïve application of the law of the perspective—if it were not for the presence, also in the foreground, of the smaller glass and the fruit-squeezer of normal proportions.

But why does the glass appear twice, as giant and as dwarf, when there is no difference of technical stages between them?

Is the glass of normal size a concession to the realism of the beholder, an apology for the colossal glass which had to be honored and magnified as the protagonist? According to this, we should have, along with the fantastic, the criticism thereof—as in the *Don Quijote*, with its double perspective. Thus the element of naïveté would be far from absolute: the naïve and the critical attitudes being justaposed. And this twin presentation serves also the more practical aim of attracting "consumer interest": we see first the sun, then the groves of California, then the picked fruit, then the finished product (the glass of orange-juice)—and, finally, in the glass of normal size (the size of the glass to be had at the drugstore counter) we are shown the customer's own personal glass of *Sunkist* orange-juice: by this reduplication in small, the line beginning at the sun is prolonged out from the picture, in the direction of the customer—who, in taking up the glass of orange-juice, puts himself into direct contact with the California sun.[11] In the glass-that-is-the-customer's-glass there is the suggestion to the prospective customer: "*Have* a glass [of this juice]." The imperative which was carefully avoided in the text is insinuated by the picture.[12]

[11] It may be noted that the invitation to drink offered by our advertisement stops short of guaranteeing either the virtue of the product or the happiness in store for the consumer.

If Philip Wylie, in his diatribe, *Generation of Vipers* (1943), 220, is right in indicting "90%" of commercial advertising on the grounds that it promotes a general feeling in the public that material goods can add to their personal happiness and social worth ("cars are, after all, mechanical objects, and nothing else. The rest of the qualities that are attributed to them in the ads . . . belong to *people*. Purchase and possession does not, in itself, do anything to an individual"), then our *Sunkist* advertisement, which promises no transformation of character, would belong to the unimpeached 10%.

[12] This technique of extension, by which you, the consumer, are drawn into the orbit of the picture, is the main feature of a certain advertisement of Campbell's soups (highly praised by critics of advertising), in which we see, seated at an elegant table, partaking of a certain Campbell's soup, three persons: a couple and a single lady—the suggestion being that you, the (masculine) prospective customer, should join the group and retrieve the single lady from her loneliness (and also, enjoy with her some soup of the brand in question).

It is not blasphemous, in this regard, to call to mind the magic intention

If we now analyze our own analysis, we see that the first general impression was that of a tribute to the fertility of Nature; after reflection, we are made aware of the necessary intervention of man himself (not only the enterprise of the business firm but also the participation of the consumer). We are left, then with the realization that the advertiser has fooled neither us nor himself as to the real purpose of his propaganda. That glass of orange-juice as tall as the mountains of California is a clear testimonial to the businessman's subjective estimation of the comparative importance of business interests. Indeed, when we review the violence done to Nature in our picture (displacement of proportions, surrealistic use of a motif, change of the natural color of objects), we see how, in a very artistic manner, this procedure has served to illustrate, in a spirit,

---

underlying many religious paintings and sculptures of late Greek and Christian times, in which the imperious look of a frontally represented deity with "starry" eyes draws the beholder into its orbit (cf. P. Friedländer, *Documents of Dying Paganism*, 1945), or in which the tympana, representing peoples from all corners of the earth obeying the call of Christ, are located above the entrance of Romanic and Gothic churches so as to force the Christian believer to enter the church (cf. Richard Hamann, *Geschichte der Kunst*, 1933). Classical Greek or Renaissance art shuns such drastic devices of stepping out of the frame of the work of art—but then, the art of advertising is not classical.

The imperative implied in the repetition of the "glass motif" has been overstressed in a recent advertisement of "Valliant California Burgundy": at the left we see a couple dining happily and drinking the Burgundy in question, while, at the right, there opens up before us the wide expanse of Burgundian landscape, out of which grows the magnified hand of the lady which holds the (also magnified) glass of Burgundy: the correspondence of the "actual" hand of the lady with the hand coming out of the Burgundian vineyards is surprisingly exact—even to the manicuring. The imperative suggestion seems to be that the hand of a real lady (outside of the picture) should meet the magnified hand of the picture which holds the glass of Burgundy. But the "avis au lecteur" is marred by the quite inorganic and rather ghastly conceit of a hand coming out of a vineyard. Moreover, in the *Sunkist* advertisement, the source of the bliss prepared by Nature for man (*i.e.*, the sun) was at the left, and the "life-sized" glass which appealed to the customer, at the right (closer to the right hand, the active hand, of the customer), while in the Valliant Burgundy advertisement it is Nature which has been presented at the right—so that the appeal to the customer's right hand must be artificially engineered by the weird figure of a lady's manicured hand in the midst of Nature.

ultimately, of candid self-criticism, the very nature of business which, while associating itself with Nature, subordinates her to its purpose—and to ours. Our picture has used all the attractions of living Nature in order to advertise her commercialized form.

Before concluding the analysis of the pictorial elements of our advertisement, we must note the failure to present graphically the metaphor indicated by the trademark: we do not see the oranges being kissed by the sun. No trace of solar activity is suggested—even in the traditional, schematic form of rays. For this sun is no living entity, it is an emblem, an ideogram created by the advertisers to bear their label. Emblematic poetry uses stereotyped symbols; just as in 16th and 17th century imagery, the arrow of Cupid or the scythe of Death represented ready-made ingredients, the modern industrial labels are (or at least anticipate being) permanent: the *Sunkist* business firm is more interested in propagating its label than in re-enacting the original metaphor. (We are far from the atmosphere of the Greek world where personal gods embrace and beget.) On the other hand, we do not find in the caption of our advertisement the label as such, only a reference to *sunkist groves*. In this way, the reader is cleverly led to retrace the origin of the label. Many years ago the label *Sunkist* had been coined and it had become generally accepted, its pristine freshness lost. With the reference to *sunkist groves* (notice that *sunkist* is not capitalized!) it is as though we were presented with the original situation that inspired the name, with the "pre-proper-name state" or etymology of the trademark.

Now, if we consider the phrase "sunkist groves" from a philological point of view, it is to be noted that this was intended as a poetic expression:[13] it is to be doubted whether millions

---

[13] I do not know the exact date of the coinage of the *Sunkist* trademark, but I assume that it preceded the expansion of the "vitamin myth" as we have this today in America (the word *vitamin* itself was first used by Casimir Funk in 1912). Nevertheless, it is possible that the originally "poetic" term *Sunkist* may have become secondarily attracted into the orbit of that "poetry of science" which has developed from the vision of a world in which longevity and undiminished vigor will be the result of a

of Americans have ever read or heard the word "sun-kissed"—except as the denomination of a brand of oranges. At the same time, however, it does not have the flavor of distinguished poetry; the expression "sun-kissed" itself is rather stalely poetic (the only attestation, according to the NED is from a certain E. Brannan: 1873),[14] and the particular form "-kist" is, in addition, a sentimental pastiche of Shakespearian style.[15] It

---

diet of correctly balanced vitamins. Since oranges, like other citrus fruits, contain the (anti-scorbutic) vitamin C, and since the development of the (anti-rachitic) vitamin D is promoted by the sun (particularly by its ultra-violet rays), and since, too, there is a general tendency on the part of the public to associate loosely all the various vitamins, it would be in line with that poetry of science espoused by the salesman to present the oranges as actually containing the vitamins fostered by the sun: in the advertisement of another firm of orange-growers their fruit-juice is presented as "canned liquid sun." Again, we find, in one of Katherine Anne Porter's short stories, the picture of a travelling salesman of cooking utensils who praises a particular vegetable cooker for its vitamin-preserving qualities, and uses the phrase "those precious sun-lit vitamins"—as if assuming that wherever there are vitamins there the sun must be also. I cannot, of course, be sure how much this secondary flow of scientific poetry has colored, for the minds of the average person who sees the *Sunkist* advertisement, the traditional associations of the all-embracing and all-nurturing sun.

[14] For passages of Shakespeare referring to the kiss of the sun cf. the article "Hamlet's 'god kissing carrion'" by John E. Hankins, *PMLA*, LXIV, 514.

[15] It is obvious that "the poetry of advertising" can never be vanguard poetry: in the period of a Frost it can never be "Frostian," but only Emersonian, Tennysonian, Swinburnian, Elizabethan; it must have a familiar ring, must reproduce the stock poetic devices which the average reader of advertising has been taught to accept as poetic—the folklore of poetry, as it were.

Miss Anna Hatcher has shown in *MLN*, LXI (1946), 442-47, "Twilight Splendor, Shoe Colors, Bolero Brilliance," that the style of advertising, in borrowing from stock poetic devices, may succeed so completely in acclimatizing these that they are henceforth ruined for poetry. Shakespeare could coin *maiden blushes*, and Keats, *maiden bloom*, but this type is apt to be eschewed in poetry today, when *Maidenform* is the trademark of a brassière.

Incidentally, advertising may set its mark not only on "poetic" patterns but also on phrases common in everyday use: for example, when I wished to conclude a scholarly article with the statement "The reader must be the judge [in this moot question]," I was warned against using a formula current in advertising ("The consumer must be the judge").

One might also mention, in this connection, the verb "to offend," which has become a euphemism for "to smell of perspiration."

is very interesting to note, however, that this would-be poetic spelling is also reminiscent of the tendency illustrated, for example, by the use of *nite* for *night*, or *u* for *you* (*Uneeda Biscuit*), which is to be found only in arrantly commercial language (and which is due, I have been told, to an economical desire to save space;[16] for myself, however, I am inclined to believe that it is inspired by the more positive desire to create an energetic, streamlined impression of efficiency).[17] We have,

[16] The eccentric spelling of trademarks is, of course, one of the devices intended to facilitate their registration (or the copyrighting of the labels): *Sunkist* can be legally protected as "intellectual property" much more easily than would *Sun-kissed*. The spelling gives to the trademark that exclusive right to which the "generic use" of the words of the language can not pretend.

It could be said in general that the law on trademarks and copyrights is a powerful promoter of linguistic change—and linguistic sham-originality, and, with each registration, forces upon the language a new "proper name" which, as is the function of proper names, presents things as unique, irrespective of their actual status in this regard. Are not *all* oranges "kissed by the Sun"? Is the shampoo called "Tallulah" truly as outstanding among shampoos as Tallulah Bankhead among actresses? The protection given by the law to such *"ad hoc* proper names"—in which the usual process of name-giving (first an emotion concentrated so intensely on an object that it appears unique—then the actual word-coinage) has been reversed (since it is taken for granted by the manufacturer that a proper name *must* be coined)—is the ultimate consequence of the concept of "intellectual property," a concept, unknown to antiquity and to the Middle Ages, which has developed as a result of modern man's decreasing consciousness of a common human heritage and of the increasing insistence on the rights of the individual. The author of that truly unique poem "to which heaven and earth have collaborated" was satisfied with the quite generic name: "Commedia"!

But linguistic standardization, as active in our times as before, sets certain limits to the individualism of the trademarks. Not only is their proper-name character gradually weakened as the product and its name become familiar to the buying public, not only is their phonetic form not respected (*Coca Cola>coke*); it may even happen that the individual trademark, precisely because it has become so familiar to the public, is used in a quite generic sense: in spite of repeated warnings: "A camera is not a Kodak unless it is an Eastman Kodak," that most original coinage *Kodak*, which, because it had no connection with any word of the language, seemed to enjoy the privileges of an *Urwort* (comparable in this respect to *gas*), has acquired in common speech the generic meaning of "small, portable camera"; and similarly *Victrola* has become the synonym of "phonograph."

[17] How the idea of efficiency and easy functioning may influence the syntax of advertising ("This car parks easily," "This paint applies easily")

that is, to do with a hybrid form, suggestive of two mutually exclusive stylistic environments. And something of this same duality obtains with the compound form consisting of "ablative" + participle: unlike so many compounds, this particular type (*God-given, heaven-blest, man-made, wind-tossed, rain-swept, etc.*) was originally highly literary, and even today it is excluded from colloquial speech. When first introduced into advertising, it represented a literary effort on the part of the writer—though this may no longer be true of all advertising writers, just as it is probably not true of most of their readers, who perhaps are acquainted only with the commercial flavor of the type *oven-baked beans, etc.*[18] As for the particular expression *sunkist*, we are probably justified in assuming a "poetic" intention on the part of the creator of the coinage because of the poetic nature of the concept involved ("kissed by the sun"); at the same time, however, he must have been conscious of its commercial by-flavor; he has been able to play on two chessboards, to appeal to two types of consumers: those who admire a brisk, efficient businesslike style, and those who think that "the sun of Homer, it shineth still on us." Thus our hybrid word, which is without roots in normal speech, is doomed to a homeless existence: *sunkist* is possible only in that No Man's Land where the prosaic is shunned—but the poetic is taken not quite seriously.[19]

---

and, subsequently (if ironically), common speech, has been shown in an article by Professor Hatcher in *MLN*, LVIII (1943), 8-17: "Mr. Howard amuses easy."

[18] The psychologists of advertising are agreed as to the pleasant atmosphere created by the trademark *Sunkist*, but they seem to lack the linguistic categories in which to place it: Burtt (p. 373) groups *Sunkist* along with *Holeproof, Wearever*, and *Slipnot* (probably only because of the compound character of all these coinages); Brewster and Palmer (p. 124), with *Sun-Maid* (where a pun is involved—as is also the case with *Slipnot*), and with *Sealdsweet* (where we have a spelling-pronunciation—with none of the connotations of *Sunkist*).

[19] There is also contained in this half-serious poetry of advertising, a consolation of a sort, an assurance for the average reader, to whose self-confidence and vanity advertisements are always addressed: truly perfect form, truly ideal beauty is crushing; it leaves the beholder breathless, humiliated; "there is nothing one can say" when looking upon the Venus of Milo or a painting of Raphael. I would paraphrase Keats: "A thing of

And this last fact explains, perhaps, why it can be that businessmen should be so eager to coin, as a technical, commercial term, such a word as *sunkist*, which appeals to poetic imagination in a manner and to a degree quite at variance with their own and their public's speech, and in utter contradiction to what we are supposed to accept as the essential characteristic of business. Psychologists would answer with the concept of "affective appeal," the tendency by which feelings that are aroused by one stimulus will spread and attach themselves to other stimuli (Burtt, p. 437).[20] But I fear that the psychologists of advertising oversimplify the psychology of the advertiser—who is not only a businessman but a human being: one who is endowed with all the normal potentialities of emotion and who finds expression of these in the exercise of his profession. In his private life, in his social relations, he has been taught to minimize or even to ridicule the poetic apperception of life;

---

beauty is a *grief* forever"; its seriousness and self-contained disregard for all other things of this world allow for nothing but a mystic self-absorption in the thing of beauty. Nothing could be less congenial to the American public, which prefers not to be reminded of self-annihilation and which is more active than contemplative. It is true that many advertisers resort to the reproduction of classical works of art; but by the very fact that they are used in a subordinate function, that they are "only advertisements," which the beholder is free to accept or reject, they can be better enjoyed by the average public than when they are seen in a serious exhibit.

[20] The "affective appeal" envisaged by advertising is not, of course, limited to the (semi-) artistic form given to the advertisement itself: we also find works of pure art put to the service of advertising—as when, for example, symphony programs are sponsored by commercial firms. Thus it is calculated that the pathos and tenderness aroused in us by Rodzinsky's performance of the *Eroica* will inspire us with tender feelings for the "service through science" of the U.S. Rubber Co.

And yet, we should not, I think, be too quick to deny the vein of idealism underlying the artistic programs sponsored by industrial firms. Quite aside from, and above, all their calculating and budgeting, they begin by generous giving (knowing quite well that many who listen to the *Eroica* will not buy one ounce the more of rubber goods). And this giving without immediate returns is capable of awakening a certain loyalty in the listener: I know of one young businessman who reproved his wife for turning off the radio immediately after a concert; to his mind, she should return the courtesy she had received at least to the extent of listening to the advertiser's words.

the idea of whiling away his leisure time by composing sonnet sequences, as is quite common with his counterpart in South America, would be almost unthinkable to him. But his copywriter feels free to indulge in that poetic fancy from which his superior, the business executive, ordinarily shies away (let us not forget that many a copywriter is a thwarted poet whose college dreams have not quite come true). And why does the advertiser, whose mouthpiece is the copywriter, allow himself to be presented before the public as a poet *malgré lui*? Surely it is because he feels himself protected, he feels the fanciful words of the advertisement protected, by invisible "quotation marks" which can ward off the possible ridicule of the public and which exculpate him, in his own eyes, for his daring.

By "quotation marks" I mean to characterize an attitude toward language which is shared by the speaker and his public, and according to which he may use words with the implication: "I have good reasons for saying this—but don't pin me down!" The public, for its part, reacts accordingly: there is on both sides a tacit understanding of the rules of the game (a game which also involves the necessary embellishment by the seller of his products and a corresponding attitude of sales-resistance on the part of the prospect). Thus the word *sunkist* comes to us with its range calculated and delimited, with its impact of reality reduced; this word is noncommittal of reality; it transports the listener into a world of Arcadian beauty, but with no insistence that this world really exists. Of course, the beautiful groves of California which produce excellent oranges do exist, but a world in which they may really be called "sunkist" does not. And everyone knows that, while the advertised goods may be quite first-rate, the better world which the advertiser evokes is a never-never land.[21] Nonetheless, the ideal-

[21] The world of optimism and idealism which advertising unfolds before us is reflected in its predilection for the superlative; each of the goods praised is supposedly the finest of its kind, from the tastiest bread in America to the most perfect low-priced car in America. This superlative which rules supreme, and which is not challenged by any factual comparison (since disparaging statements about goods of competitors is prohibited by law) tends to destroy the difference between the superlative

izations of advertising are not wasted upon the listener: though he cannot take up forthwith his dwelling in the paradisiac world filled with fragrant groves where golden fruit slowly ripen under the caress of the sun,[22] his imagination has made the detour through this *word-paradise* and carries back the poetic flavor which will season the physical enjoyment of the orange-juice he will drink for breakfast the next morning. Here, in an unexpected corner of our technologically organized age,

---

and the elative: "the finest . . ." becomes equal to "a very fine . . . ," somewhat equivalent to the Italian elative *buonissimo* (not *il migliore*). The abolition of true comparison ("good"—"better"—"best") is easily understandable in a world containing only "best" things.

As another variety of the advertising elative, we may mention the use of the comparative, which the *New Yorker* has recently defined as the "agency comparative" or the "comparative without comparison": an item is called "better" without any further qualification: "Better than what?" asks the *New Yorker*. (A parallel case is the absolute use in advertising of "different" [even a laxative medicament is called simply "different"], patterned on the popular usage with its slightly snobbish overtones.) Cf. E. K. Sheldon's article on "The Rise of the Incomplete Comparative" in *American Speech*, XX (1945), 161-67.

Incidentally, it is interesting that in a satirical magazine such as the *New Yorker*, where the stories as well as the illustrations and cartoons are intended as a criticism of the easily beautiful and of conventional standards—the advertisements are allowed to provide, unquestioned, the illusory beauty and the snobbism typical of their genre.

[22] Often, he is portrayed by the advertiser as already dwelling in (a rather bourgeois and mechanized) El Dorado: if a historian of American civilization were to base himself exclusively on the representation of daily life which is offered in advertisements, he would reach the conclusion that this country is now an Arcady of material prosperity and social ease (and of questionable moral worth); but the spectator, we may be sure, is equipped with his own criteria, and subtracts automatically from the pictures of felicity and luxury which smile at him from the billboards. Nevertheless, while making this subtraction, he is able to gaze at the beauty portrayed, with disinterested enjoyment, *in abstracto*.

The tendency toward over-glamorization in advertising must constantly be counterbalanced by the "as-if" attitude, in order to avoid becoming ridiculous and ineffective. When, occasionally, one advertisement oversteps the mark, rival advertisers are quick to exploit this excess by excessively discreet understatement in regard to their own products: the sensational picture of the passionate havoc which perfume may wreak, in an advertisement circulated several years ago to publicize "Tabu," has resulted in such mock-modest claims, by other advertisers, as "We do not guarantee that this perfume will make of you a *femme fatale:* we only say it smells nice."

and in the service of the most highly rationalized interests, poetry has developed its most miraculous quality: that of establishing a realm of pure, gratuitous, disinterested beauty, which has existence only in the imagination. And the poetic achievement is presented to the public with all sincerity—and with all cautiousness: with overtones of irony which preclude any too-serious commitment.

If we ask ourselves with which historical literary climate we should associate this playful language of advertisement, which is satisfied with feigning gratuitously an ideal *word-world* in empty space, the kinship with certain baroque or *précieux* ways of speech becomes evident: "sunkist" for "oranges" belongs to a poetic "as-if" speech, no different essentially from *conseiller des grâces* for *miroir*.

Préciosité and the parallel baroque styles of euphuism, *Schwulst, marinismo*, and *gongorismo* (it was not unadvisedly that we quoted above a passage from Góngora) have their cultural roots in a polar tension between life as it is and life as it should be: reality appears on the one hand with all the attractions of beautiful sensuousness and, on the other, beclouded by our consciousness of the futility of these attractions, by the feeling of *desengaño*—a feeling which prevailed even in France, where only the most "reasonable" variant of the baroque existed. One knows quite well that the mirror cannot always counsel graceful behavior, but one lends it this role in order to create an illusion absolutely unwarranted by reality. The *précieuse* dwells in that borderland of poetry which could "perhaps" be true, but, as she knows, is not true—this is an example of the same mild form of wishful thinking which is at the bottom of American advertising. The American public, exposed at every moment to the impact of advertising propaganda, easily applies its grain of salt; it does not condemn outright the excesses of *préciosité*, as did Molière's Gorgibus; it can afford to let itself be seduced to a certain point, for it is fully aware of the matter-of-fact reality of the product advertised. Thus, an attitude of *desengaño* would seem to be present here, too; does this represent a general disillusionment, due to particular un-

fortunate experiences in American history: to the disenchantment of pioneers who had left the Old World in search of
a better one—or who, already in this country, had turned to
the West in search of gold—and have often seen their hopes
frustrated? In view of the ingrained optimism which still today
enables the American to meet each calamity with his hopes
of a better deal just around the corner,[23] this hypothesis can
hardly endure. Nor can we assume, in the case of the situation
of advertising, any actual distrust of the merits of any particular
product; there is, undoubtedly, in America an attitude of confidence (supported, it is true, by a whole framework of super-
visory regulations) in the factual truthfulness of the claims
made by manufacturers.[24] I should say that, in the skeptical, or

[23] It could be said that the American's optimism is also reflected in the
abundance of neologisms in advertising: by coining new words one suggests a picture of new and therefore better things to come. This tendency
also reveals a special attitude toward language itself as something con-
tinuously in flux (as Mencken has repeatedly emphasized)—an attitude
which shares with the first a basic "future-mindedness."
  Any neologism, however, in the course of time, tends to lose its freshness once it has been accepted by the community—in which case the linguists must speak of "lexicological petrification." The advertisers themselves eventually recognize that the inevitable stage of lexicalization has
set in, and are careful thereafter not to stir the ashes of the dead—for
any insistence on the symbolic value once possessed by the label would be
tedious to the public.
  And our *Sunkist* had, obviously, to go the way of all linguistic creations:
at a certain moment it stopped being a living expression to become a label
used glibly and matter-of-factly by the community. That this has been
recognized by the advertisers is indicated by the fact that the *Sunkist*
advertisement we have been describing, and which I had seen for four
summers in the same drugstore, was replaced, in 1945, by one of a quite
different type, and one which did not go to the length of "explaining"
(verbally or pictorially) the choice of the label. The new advertisement
was of a schematic or ideographic character: it showed a frieze with
an ornamental arrangement of bunches of flowers and fruits (oranges
and lemons), underneath which were seen two glasses (of orange-juice
and lemonade, respectively) forming a cross-bar and bearing the label
Sunkist. Sun and Nature had disappeared, except for the slight and
stereotyped reminder of the latter offered by the fruits.
[24] The confidence of the public in the honesty of advertisers is an established fact in this country; there seems to be little or no suspicion that
the advertiser is advancing false claims. In a country where moral in-
tegrity in business life is not taken for granted by principle, advertising

AMERICAN ADVERTISING

half-skeptical attitude of the American public[25] in regard to advertising, we may see that basic mistrust of language itself which is one of the most genuine features of the Anglo-Saxon character,[26] as opposed to the trust in words by which the

---

can develop no gratuitous poetry; such an attempt would invite the question, fatal to poetry: "Are your words true or false?"

[25] In no language, so far as I know, are there so many prefixes which tend to unmask false values: *pseudo-*, *sham-*, *make-believe-*, *makeshift-*, *mock-*, *would-be-*, *fake-*, *phony-*, *semi-*, *near-*[beer], *baloney-*[dollars], *synthetic- etc.*; it is as though the Anglo-Saxon attitude of distrust of the pretentious would find for itself a grammatically fixed pattern of expression in the language. Americans delight in their impermeability to "bunk" (as is shown by the fertility of the "buncombe" word-family).

[26] It would seem that there is a difference in this regard between the two Anglo-Saxon nations themselves, if we are to believe D. W. Brogan (*The American Character*, New York, 1944), who has been struck by the American love for oratory (p. 131): "In Chambers of Commerce, at Rotary Club meetings, at college commencements, in legislatures, in Congress, speech is treated seriously, according to the skill and taste of the user. There is no fear of boss words or of eloquence, no fear of clichés, no fear of bathos. . . . The British listener, above all the English listener, is surprised and embarrassed by being asked to applaud statements whose truth he has no reason to doubt, but whose expression seems to him remarkably abstract and adorned with flowers of old-fashioned rhetoric." Mr. Brogan gives himself the explanation that Americans "like slogans, like words. They like absolutes in ethics." And the English critic might have brought up the contrast between the American Constitution and the unwritten British Constitution.

On the other hand, I would suggest that there is an English brand of oratory which is slightly alien to the American—for example, the prose of Churchill, which, with its archaisms and periphrastic turns of speech, weaves poetry round the casual concrete happenings of history; by the Americans the "word" is considered less as an artistic than as a moral tool, as abstractly purposeful as the flag. But, even in the realm of absolute morals, the distrust of language is not entirely lacking with Americans; Mr. Brogan himself cannot overlook the fact that many slogans are greeted by Americans with an ironical "Oh, yeah?" or "However you slice it, it's still baloney." How else save by mistrust of the word could one explain the fact that after the exchange of wild abuse indulged in on both sides during an election campaign, Americans, once the election is over, are able to go quietly to work the next day, no attempt being made by the defeated party to start a revolution. The word in itself is not "sacred" and final to the Americans. The difference between the American and the German concepts of the word can be seen in the absence of free speech in Germany: freedom of speech involves a concept of non-finality of speech. In America the human word is thought of only as having a provisionary value. One word can be undone, and outdone, by another.

Romance peoples are animated—those *Wortmenschen,* as Schuchardt has called them, whose esthetics Benedetto Croce has formulated in the postulate: "Quello che non è espresso non esiste!" For the Anglo-Saxon, on the contrary, reality remains ultimately inexpressible. Such a people will, obviously, have a mistrust of poetry because of its too easy, too felicitous finds which cannot be made to square with the complexity of reality. Now since, in the game continually going on between the advertiser and the public, the customer is expected to take the role of skeptic, it is possible for poetry to be given full play; the advertiser does not ask that his words be taken completely at face value, and he must not be held to literal account for the truth of every syllable. Thus the poetry of advertisement can be truly enjoyed because it makes none of the solemn claims of literary poetry. It is precisely because Americans know reality so well, because they ask to face it, and do not like to be hoodwinked, because they are not easily made victims of metaphysical word-clouds as are the Germans, or of word-fulgurations, as are the French, that they can indulge in the *acte gratuit* of the human word in its poetical nowhereness. So fully aware is the advertiser of this discounting attitude on the part of his public that, not infrequently, he anticipates the forthcoming skepticism by the feint of self-indictment—as when Macy's apologizes prettily for its many entrances, but insists, for the reassurance of harassed husbands shopping for their wives, that not *all* subway exits lead to their store. And, in a more pedantic, statistical vein, the well-known claim of "$99\frac{44}{100}\%$" of purity uses a screen of scrupulous precision and self-criticism to advance the claim of what is, after all, an extraordinary degree of near-perfection.

Every work of art is addressed to a public, whether outspokenly or implicitly. A painting on the wall, for example, is an invitation to the beholder to engage in a relationship with it; there are always involved in the painting $n + 1$ elements, with n elements included from the beginning in the work of art itself; and $n + 1$ remains the formula even when there are several beholders. In the case of three persons, for example, the relationships between them and the picture of n elements would be $n + 1^a$, $n + 1^b$, $n + 1^c$ respectively—and in the case of x persons $n + 1^x$. Now, we have seen how, in the case of our advertising picture, there has been established, by means of that second glass of normal proportions, a relationship between the groves of California and the ultimate individual consumer. At the same time, this personal relationship is underscored (in a manner unknown to other works of art) by the phrase "fresh *for you*," which every customer must understand as a personal address to himself (incidentally these three words of personal address are printed in script). In this *you* we have, obviously, a device which is not peculiar to the picture in question but is highly representative of the genre itself, and is a quite common feature to be found in every page of the daily newspaper.[27] If we would ask ourselves what is involved in the use of this advertising "you," we must first inquire, superfluous and far-fetched as the procedure may seem, into the meaning of this second personal pronoun, according to the philosophy of grammar. "You" is a startling word: it calls up the dormant ego in every human being:[28] "you" is in fact

[27] This "for you" is not limited, of course, to advertising, but is a generally characteristic feature of the language of the tradesman when addressing his customer: "Shall I wrap it *for you*?" "I'll fix it *for you* by tomorrow." We may see here the influence of the idea of service to one's fellow man, which has permeated so many of the formulae of commercial life: "May I help you?" "What can I do for you?" said by clerks in shops and offices; or "Have you been taken care of?" a question of waiters—which may be contrasted with Fr. "Madame désire?" Ital. "commandi?" Germ. "Sie wünschen?"

[28] This personal susceptibility of the individual to any address which is intended generally, has been, perhaps, nowhere more effectively exploited than in the famous cartoon of James Montgomery Flagg which was used as an enlistment poster in the first World War (and was revived in the second): "Uncle Sam Needs YOU For the United States Army" is written beneath a picture of the stern-eyed old gentleman who fixes with his gaze, and singles out with an accusing finger, whoever steps within the range of the picture. (Needless to say, such a drastic method of attracting the attention of the individual is not recommended for advertising.) The constant "you see" of the radio announcers is a characteristic insertion in an otherwise impersonal broadcast—motivated only by an initial vocative such as "Men," "Ladies." It simulates a conversation with a "you," instead of a one-sided harangue; "you see" (which is equal

nothing but the ego seen by another; it addresses itself to our feeling that we are a unified person recognizable from the outside; it also suggests someone outside of us who is able to say "you" and who feels akin to "us" as a fellow man.[29] Now, in English, the pronoun "you" enjoys an ambiguity to a degree unknown in the main European languages, which are characterized by greater inflection; it is equally applicable to a singular or a plural audience, and, in advertising, this double reference is fully exploited: the advertiser, while preparing his copy for the general public, thinks the "you" as an "all of you"—but intends it to be interpreted as a "you personally," applicable to the individual A, B, or C. In the case of our advertisement A translates the algebraic X of the "you" as "fresh for *me* has the orange been brought here from California"; and B and C do the same. Though he is only one of millions, every single individual is individually addressed and flattered.[30]

---

to a "let me explain it to you") seems intended to counteract an observation or a resistance on the part of the partner in the conversation. The *New Yorker* once remarked that this device is coming to be used as a means of introducing the most startling contentions of the advertiser, in order to make them appear as something quite evident on closer investigation.

[29] Coming from an anonymous being, as does the "fresh for you" of our advertising picture, the effect is perhaps more startling than when a radio announcer (who has a human voice and may be known to us by name and voice) addresses "you." Nor, as often is the case in written advertisement, has the firm in question presented itself first as "we": suddenly, an appeal is made by an undefined agency to "me personally." By the elimination of the human element at work, by the retreat behind things, by the assumption of a miracle to which is due, for example, the arrival of the oranges from California—it is as if we were told: "*Nature* has brought fresh for you . . . ," "*God* has brought fresh for you . . ."; the identity of the fruit-packing firm disappears within the greater connection of a helpful universe, mindful of each man and woman dwelling therein.

[30] Compare also "I have arranged this sale with you in mind. You, Mrs. America, are the best buyer and the best-dressed woman in the world" (from an advertisement of furs) ; "For you, Madame, I have done the utmost to bring you more valuable things than ever. For you, Madame, I have traveled to Europe. Your taste is to us all we do, think, plan." (It is obvious that the "for you" pattern, while appealing to the vanity of the buyer, also implies self-praise of the services rendered by the merchant.)

It is also true that he has come to accept this flattery as no more than his due. Of all the peoples among whom I have lived, the Americans seem to me most jealously insistent on the right of being addressed as individuals. It is an interesting paradox that the same civilization that has perfected standardization to such a degree is also characterized by this intense need for the recognition of one's personal existence. And this need, which is most acutely in evidence when individuals deal with each other (the relationship between teacher and pupil in America, for example, must impress any European) can, evidently, not be ignored even when both parties are anonymous. The concern shown in American advertising for the individual psychology, in spite of the impersonal relationship which is given with such a setup, must have deep roots in the American soul. And with this, we reach out for a historical explanation of the genesis of American advertising itself (for, so far as chronological priority and degree of development and intensity are concerned, advertising must be considered as an Americanism).

And here I would take into account what Max Weber and Tröltsch have called "Religionssoziologie": the discipline which sees in economic and social developments ultimately the workings of the "only powerful lever of all civilization, religion" (as the Romantic philosopher Bachofen has expressed it). Thus it was possible for these scholars[31] to explain modern capitalism from the religious background of Calvinism: this religion, which preaches a God far removed from man and his earthly doings, and, in spite of the inscrutability of Providence, still insists on the sanctity of work, with the implication of its possible influence on the decisions of Providence: this has encouraged a program of work for work's sake (and of capital for capital's sake), according to which the individual must work as if God had selected his soul for salvation—in the hope

[31] Among the later exponents of this doctrine may be mentioned Herbert Schöffler, who has explained certain typical features of Anglo-Saxon civilization (such as sports, freedom of parliamentary debate, *etc.*) from the "religious-sociological" basis of English life.

that, perhaps, the resultant increase in worldly goods may be a sign of this selection. Thus the most transcendent of religions has, paradoxically enough, served to encourage the pursuit of the most secular of interests. Now, in America, as is well known, the Calvinism of the early English immigrants was overlaid by deistic teachings, which proved more congenial to the Americans than did the Genevan doctrines, because of an even greater emphasis on human values at the expense of concern with the divine, and an even more optimistic picture of the universe.

As far as the field of advertising itself is concerned, I would say (and I do not know whether or not this point has been made before) that the "Reklame-Gesinnung," as the Germans would call it, the "advertising mentality," is not alone due to the Calvinistic-deistic business-mindedness which encourages the increase of goods for the sake of increase. In order to explain the tremendous development of advertising, which today is an industry in itself, we must take into account a second factor, itself related to religious Protestant impulses: this is the "preaching mentality" which has impressed so many observers of American life (one thinks immediately of certain observations of André Siegfried), and which is based on the conviction that every man, possessed as he is of the divine spark of reason (in this connection we may remember the words of De Tocqueville, who observed that the Americans are the most Cartesian of peoples), has only to be taught what is the good in order to accept it and to pursue it to the ever-increasing perfection of his nature. There is no doubt that, to a great extent, present-day advertising has taken over the role of the teacher of morals who, by an appeal to their reason, points out the good to his pupils, confident, like Socrates, that man needs only to be shown the good in order to do it—though, given the weakness of human nature, he must constantly be reminded of his real advantage, lest he slip back into apathy; the advertiser, like the preacher, must "create the demand" for the better. This belief in the teachability of man and in his readiness, if duly and regularly aroused, to improve his condition (here, of course, his material condition) is everywhere evident in advertising: "You can have what you want if you save for it"[32] and "Do not look back. Past is past. You are over the dam. Look forward!" are exhortations appearing in banking advertisements; "I can resist no temptation!" are the opening words of an advertisement for a digestion aid. Not always, of course, is the didactic note so strongly in evidence, but it would not, perhaps, be wrong to see a sermon in all advertising:[33] the advertiser is one who preaches the material good with confidence in the ever-possible increase of material welfare and in the ever-possible self-perfectibility of man in his rational pursuit thereof. And, true to Protestant sectarian tradition, every advertiser preaches a gospel of his own. Voltaire has said: "Tout protestant est un pape, une bible à la main." Similarly, every advertiser points you to his product as the only way to salvation.

And, in his preaching, the advertiser must always envisage the individual listener, just as the Protestant pastor seeks to press his truths home to each individual member of his congregation. Indeed, in our "for you," we have a phrase which can, perhaps, be traced back directly to statements of dogma made from the pulpit. When the pastor declares that "Christ has suffered death for *you*, for the liberation of *your* soul from sin," he is presenting this divine intervention as working for each individual separately, and his "you" is interpreted by each of his listeners as "for me personally."[34] Here we have

[32] It is to be noted that, in this example, we have to do with the "gnomic *you*." Here, then, is still one more possibility of the English pronoun, which is equivalent, not only to French *tu* and *vous*, but also to *on*—though, even in its gnomic use, the personal overtones are not entirely lacking.

[33] A particularly interesting example of the directly moralizing note is offered by a series of advertisements for Seagram's whiskies which preach the virtues of moderate drinking! It was, perhaps, shrewdly calculated by the firm that such admonitions would do nothing to decrease the sales of their products; the result might, indeed, be to increase them, because of the tacit flattering assumption that consumers of this particular brand are persons of decorum (if not of distinction).

[34] The reader may recall having heard in his youth the evangelical hymn "Whosoever will may come" with the final line: "*Whosoever* meaneth *me*."

not so much an exhortation as a promise. And a comparable note of promise is present in our advertisement—which, obviously, does not belong to the didactic type noted above; here, the command to buy is present only in the sublimated form of the "second glass" inviting to drink; the emphasis is on the riches of the earth waiting to be enjoyed by man. In a secularized, laicized civilization, where human activity in pursuit of material welfare is not shunned but accepted as a blessing from God, it was easily possible for the mysticism of the pastor's "for you" to become diluted: material welfare, too, could be seen as something willed by God "for you," "for me," personally; there is only a small step from the optimistic preaching of the boundless, the paradisiac possibilities of divine goodness which man must only be ready to accept, to the optimistic preaching of the boundless, the paradisiac possibilities of earthly well-being which, likewise, man must simply allow himself to enjoy.[35]

With its insistence on the *you*, advertising is closer to deism than to Calvinism: whereas (Calvinistic) capitalism, with its sternness and austerity, tends to ignore the consumer, bent as it is toward what Weber has called an "innerweltliche Askese," that is, toward production for production's sake, for the sake of the morality of the producer and for the glory of God ("Work in order to acquire riches for God!" as Richard Baxter said), advertising, the byproduct of capitalism, takes into account the consumer's rights: his rights to happiness; it is "for him," for his enjoyment of earthly pleasure, that the effort of production has been made. Advertising appeals to the eudaemonism of the consumer.[36]

[35] It may be noted that the first advertisements to appear regularly in American newspapers (in the middle of the 19th century) were those of patent medicines, with their claims of miraculous efficacy. It is highly significant that the industry of advertising had its inception in an appeal to the age-old craving to be saved by magic from the ills and shortcomings of the flesh.

[36] The two tendencies, Calvinistic austerity and eudaemonistic deism, are often met side by side within the individual American—who can be at one moment the "Pflicht- und Arbeitsmensch" and at another the pagan enjoyer of earthly goods. In the features of the American man and woman there is often revealed a sternness of purpose—which is given a

Professor Alexander Rüstow, in a witty article on "Der moderne Pflicht- und Arbeitsmensch" (*Revue de la faculté des sciences économiques*, Istanbul, v, 1) characterizes the mentality of the modern capitalist by ascribing to him the implicit attitude: "To produce and to sell belong to the elect, to buy and to consume, to the damned" (he also brings out the fact that the capitalist is unable to enjoy the fruits of his own labor, and compares him to the cormorant which is used by the Chinese fishermen to catch fish, the bird being prevented from swallowing them by means of an iron band around its throat). Advertising, on the other hand, seems to scream from all the billboards and posters: "To the buyer and consumer belongs the paradise!" This eudaemonistic deism with which advertising is informed is the same philosophy underlying the faith of Adam Smith, who believed that, by the "invisible hand" of Providence, the private egotisms of all human individuals are welded together into the common good. While, in the offices and factories, the "Pflicht- und Arbeitsmensch" may fulfill his relentlessly austere duties, in the shops and on the streets, advertising proclaims the rights of man to the "pursuit of happiness." It is this basic right of the American which is pictorially emblazoned in the many pictures, lining the highways and byways, of man enjoying the goods of life. American advertising thus becomes one of the greatest forces working to perpetuate a national ideal: in their own way the pictures of happy family life or of private enjoyment have a conservative function comparable to that of the statues in the old Greek Polis; though the American images are not embodiments of gods and heroes, they preach an exemplary well-being as an ideal accessible to every man in the American community.

While I do not claim that, in "From the sunkist groves of California Fresh for you," which contains the impersonal-personal "you" of the preacher, the religious implications are still present to the mind of the public (or were present to that of

---

lie by their (Arcadian) happy smile. Historical conditions have made of the American a somewhat "relaxed pioneer": a pioneer who manages also to "take it easy."

the advertiser), there is nevertheless to be found in the sentence, it seems to me, the deistic, optimistic confidence in a world-order in which Nature works for the good of the individual man and in which helpful, busy mankind joins with Nature in creating, without stint and with the modesty that comes from acting in harmony with the universal laws of Nature, all possibilities of relaxation for the fellow individual who is asked only to follow the precepts of reason by taking unto himself the gifts of Nature. We have, it is true, shown also that the utopian hopes for mankind which are suggested are somewhat toned down by a feeling of *desengaño*; but, in the interstices between paradisiac dreams and harsh reality, the gracious and gratuitous flowers of poetry, aware of their own unreality, spring up here and there, offering glimpses of an oasis in the aridity of a modern mechanized and pragmatic world. Thus our advertisement designed to promote the retail sale of oranges, offers a colorful image of quiet Nature to refresh the city dwellers in their environment of hustle and drabness.

SELECTED BIBLIOGRAPHY

I. WORKS IN ENGLISH

A. Books

Essays in Historical Semantics. Testimonial Volume in Honor of Leo Spitzer on the Occasion of His Sixtieth Birthday. New York, 1948.

Linguistics and Literary History: Essays in Stylistics, Princeton, 1948.

A Method of Interpreting Literature. Northampton, Mass., 1949.

B. Articles

"History of Ideas versus Reading of Poetry," *SR* VI (1941), 584-609.

"A Linguistic and Literary Interpretation of Claudel's *Ballade,*" *French Review* XVI (1942), 134-142.

"Why Does Language Change?" *MLQ* IV (1943), 413-431.

"Geistesgeschichte vs. History of Ideas Applied to Hitlerism," *Journal of the History of Ideas* V (1944), 191-203.

"Classical and Christian Ideas of World Harmony (Prolegomena to an Interpretation of the Word 'Stimmung')," *Traditio* II (1944), 409-64, and III (1945), 307-364.

"Answer to Mr. Bloomfield (*Language* XX, 45)," *Language* XX (1944), 245-251.

Correspondence on Robert Hall, "State of Linguistics: Crisis or Reaction?" *Modern Language Notes* LXI (1946), 497-502.

"The Style of Don Quixote," in *Cervantes Across the Centuries,* ed. Angel Flores and M. J. Benardete, New York, 1947, pp. 94-100.

"German Words, German Personality and Protestantism Again," *Psychiatry* XII (1949), 185-187. With Arno Schirokauer.

"The Formation of the American Humanist," *PMLA* XLVI (1951), 39-48.

"Ronsard's 'Sur la mort de Marie,' " *The Explicator* X (1951), 1-4.

"The Mozarabic Lyric and Theodor Fring's Theories," *CL* IV (1952), 351-362.

"Language—the Basis of Science, Philosophy and Poetry," in *Studies in Intellectual History*, ed. G. Boas (Baltimore, 1953), pp. 67-93.

"Balzac and Flaubert Again," *MLN* LXVIII (1953), 583-590.

"The Works of Rabelais," in *Literary Masterpieces of the Western World*, ed. Francis H. Horn (Baltimore, 1953), pp. 126-147.

"The Ideal Typology in Dante's *De Vulgari Eloquentia*," *Italica* XXXII (1955), 75-94.

"The Individual Factor in Linguistic Innovations," *Cultura Neolatina* XVI (1956), 71-89.

Review of Herbert Seidler, *Allgemeine Stilistik*, in *CL* VIII (1956), 146-149.

"*Situation* as a Term in Literary Criticism Again," *MLN* LXXII (1957), 224-228.

"A New Book on the Art of the *Celestina*," *Hispanic Review* XXV (1957), 1-25.

"A New Synthetic Treatment of Contemporary Western Lyricism," *MLN* LXXII (1957), 523-537.

Review of Stephen Ullmann, *Style in the French Novel*, in *CL* X (1958), 368-371.

"The Artistic Unity of Gil Vicente's *Auto da Sibila Casandra*," *Hispanic Review* XXVII (1959), 56-77.

Review of Ludwig Schrader, *Panurge und Hermes, zum Ursprung eines Charakters bei Rabelais*, in *CL* XII (1960), 263-265.

"The Influence of Hebrew and Vernacular Poetry on the Judeo-Italian Elegy," in *Twelfth-Century Europe and the Foundations of Modern Society*, ed. Clagett, Post, and Reynolds (1961), pp. 115-130.

"On the Significance of *Don Quijote*," *MLN* LXXVII (1962), 113-129.

II. WORKS IN OTHER LANGUAGES

A. BOOKS AND MONOGRAPHS

Die Wortbildung als stilistisches Mittel exemplifiziert an Rabelais. Nebst einem Anhang über die Wortbildung bei Balzac in seinen "Contes drolatiques." Halle, 1910. (Beihefte zur Zeitschrift für romanische Philologie, no. 19.)

Über einige Wörter der Liebessprache. 4 Aufsätze. Leipzig, 1918.

Aufsätze zur romanischen Syntax und Stilistik. Halle, 1918.

Motiv und Wort. Studien zur Literatur- und Sprachpsychologie. Hans Sperber, *Motiv und Wort bei Gustav Meyrink.* Leo Spitzer, *Die groteske Gestaltungs- und Sprachkunst Christian Morgensterns.* Leipzig, 1918.

Betrachtungen eines Linguisten über Houston Stewart Chamberlains Kriegsaufsätze und die Sprachbewertung im allgemeinen. Leipzig, 1918.

Fremdwörterhatz und Fremdvölkerhass. Eine Streitschrift gegen Sprachreinigung. Vienna, 1918.

Studien zu Henri Barbusse. Bonn, 1920.

Die Umschreibungen des Begriffes "Hunger" im Italienischen. Halle, 1921. (Beihefte zur Zeitschrift für romanische Philologie, no. 68.)

Lexikalisches aus dem Katalanischen und den übrigen iberoromanischen Sprachen. Geneva, 1921. (Biblioteca dell' *Archivum Romanicum,* Series II, no. 1.)

Beiträge zur romanischen Wortbildungslehre. (With E. Gamillscheg.) Geneva, 1921. (Biblioteca dell' *Archivum Romanicum,* Series II, no. 2.)

Italienische Kriegsgefangenbriefe. Bonn, 1921.

Italienische Umgangssprache. Bonn and Leipzig, 1922.

Hugo Schuchardt-Brevier. Ein Vademecum der allgemeinen Sprachwissenschaft. Zusammengestellt und eingeleitet von Leo Spitzer. Halle, 1922.

Puxi, eine kleine Studie zur Sprache einer Mutter. Munich, 1927.

Stilstudien. 2 vols. Munich, 1928. (Reissue announced for 1961.)

Meisterwerke der romanischen Sprachwissenschaft. 2 vols. Munich, 1929-1930.

Romanische Stil- und Literaturstudien. 2 vols. Marburg, 1931.

Die Literarisierung des Lebens in Lopes "Dorotea." Bonn and Cologne, 1932.

Critica stilistica e storia del linguaggio. Saggi raccolti a cura e con presentazione di Alfredo Schiaffini. Bari, 1954.

Lingüística e historia literaria. Madrid, 1955.

Romanische Literaturstudien, 1936-1956. Tübingen, 1959.

Marcel Proust e altri saggi di letteratura francese moderna. Con un saggio introduttivo di Pietro Citati. Turin, 1959.

Interpretationen zur Geschichte der französischen Lyrik. Herausgegeben von Dr. Helga Jauss-Meyer & Dr. Peter Schunck. Heidelberg, 1961.

B. Articles

"Stilistisch-Syntaktisches aus den spanisch-portugiesischen Romanzen," *Zeitschrift für romanische Philologie* xxxv (1911), 192-230, 257-308.

"Matilde Serao (Eine Charakteristik)," *Germanisch-romanische Monatsschrift* vi (1914), 573-584.

"Zur stilistischen Bedeutung des Imperfekts der Rede," *Germanisch-romanische Monatsschrift* ix (1921), 58-60.

Review of E. Winkler, *Die neuen Wege und Aufgaben der Stilistik,* in *Literaturblatt für germ. und rom. Philologie* xlvii (1926), 89-95.

"Der Romanist an der deutschen Hochschule," *Die Neueren Sprachen* xxxv (1927), 241-260.

"Zu den Gebeten im 'Couronnement Louis' und im 'Cantar de mio Cid,'" *Zeitschrift für französische Sprache und Literatur* lvi (1932), 196-209.

"Erhellung des 'Polyeucte' durch das Alexiuslied," *Archivum Romanicum* xvi (1932), 473-500.

"Zur Nachwirkung von Burchiellos Priameldichtung," *Zeitschrift für romanische Philologie* lii (1932), 484-489.

"Racine et Goethe," *Revue d'histoire de la philosophie et d'histoire générale de la civilisation* I (1933), 58-75.

"Zur Auffassung der Kunst des Arcipreste de Hita," *Zeitschrift für romanische Philologie* LIV (1934), 533-588.

"Zur 'Passion' und zur syntaktischen Interpretation," *Zeitschrift für französische Sprache und Literatur* LVIII (1934), 437-447.

"Die 'Estrella de Sevilla' und Claramente," *Zeitschrifte für romanische Philologie* LIV (1934), 533-588.

"En lisant le *Burlador de Sevilla*," *Neuphilologische Mitteilungen* XXXVI (1935), 282-289.

"Une habitude de style—le rappel—chez Céline," *Le français moderne* III (1935), 193-208.

"Notas sobre romances españoles," *Revista de filología española* XXII (1935), 153-174. See also *Adiciones, ibid.*, pp. 290-291.

"Explication linguistique et littéraire de deux textes français," *Le français moderne* III (1935), 315-323, and IV (1936), 37-48.

"Zum Text und Kommentar der *Flamenca*," *Neuphilologische Mitteilungen* XXXVII (1936), 85-98.

"Kenning und Calderóns Begriffspielerei," *Zeitschrift für romanische Philologie* LVI (1936), 100-102.

"Remarque sur la différence entre 'poesía popular' et 'poesía de arte,'" *Revista de filología española* XXIII (1936), 68-71.

"Die Frage der Heuchelei des Cervantes," *Zeitschrift für romanische Philologie* LVI (1936), 138-178.

"A mis soledades voy," *Revista de filología española* XXIII (1936), 397-400.

"Au sujet de la répétition distinctive," *Le français moderne* IV (1936), 129-135.

"Bemerkungen zu Dantes *Vita Nova*," *Travaux du Seminaire de Philologie romane* (Istanbul) I, 162-208.

"Pour le commentaire de Villon (*Testament* v.447)," *Romania* LXIV (1938), 522-523.

"Le lion arbitre moral de l'homme," *Romania* LXIX (1938), 525-530.

"Eine Stelle in Calderóns Traktat über die Malerei," *Neuphilologische Mitteilungen* XXXIX (1938), 361-370.

"Mes souvenirs de Meyer-Lübke," *Le français moderne* VI (1938), 213-224.

"Verlebendigte direkte Rede als Mittel der Charakterisierung," *Vox romanica* IV (1939), 65-89.

"Le prénom possessif devant un hypocoristique," *Revue des Études indoeuropéenes* I (1939), 2-4, 5-17.

"Reseñas" [Review of Félix Lecoy's *Recherches sur le Libro de Buen Amor de Juan Ruiz*, archiprêtre de Hita, Paris, 1938], *Revista de filología hispanica* I (1939), 266-274.

"La *Soledad primera* de Góngora, notas críticas y explicativas a la neuva edición de Dámaso Alonso," *Revista de filología hispanica* II (1940), 151-181.

"Le prétendu réalisme de Rabelais," *Modern Philology* XXXVII (1940), 139-150.

"Le *Bel aubépin* de Ronsard, nouvel essai d'explication," *Le français moderne* VIII (1940), 223-236.

"El conceptismo interior de Pedro Salinas," *Revista hispanica moderna* VII (1941), 33-69.

"Notas sintáctico-estilísticas a propósito del español *que*," *Revista de filología hispanica* IV (1942), 105-126, 253-265.

"Le vers 830 du *Roland*," *Romania* LXVIII (1944-45), 471-477.

"Sobre las ideas de Américo Castro a próposito de *El villano del Danubio* de Antonio de Guevara," *Boletín del Instituto Caro y Cuervo* VI (1950), 1-14.

"Dos observaciones sintáctico-estilísticas a las coplas de Manrique," *Nueva revista de filología hispánica* IV (1950), 1-24.

"Analyse d'une chanson de Noël anglaise du 14ème siècle, 'I sing of a maiden,'" *Archivum linguisticum* II (1950), 74-76.

"Wiederum Mörikes Gedicht 'Auf eine Lampe,'" *Trivium* IX (1951), 133-147.

"La danse macabre," *Mélanges de linguistique offerts a Albert Dauzat* (Paris, 1951), pp. 307-321.

"Les théories de la stylistique," *Le français moderne* XX (1952), 160-168.

Review of Dámaso Alonso, *Poesía española*, in *Romanische Forschungen* LXIV (1952), 213-240.

"La mia stilistica," *La cultura moderna* (Bari), no. 17, Dec. 1954, pp. 17-19.

"Stylistique et critique littéraire," *Critique* XI (1955), 597-609.

"Le due stilistiche di Giacomo Devoto," *Lo spettatore italiano* VIII (1955), 356-363.

"Risposta a una critica," *Convivium*, n.s. V (1957), 597-603.

"Una questione di punteggiatura in un sonetto di Giacomo da Lentino," *Cultura Neolatina* XVIII (1958), 61-70.

Review of Wolfgang Kayser, *Das Groteske*, in *Göttinger Gelehrte Anzeigen* CCXII (1958), 95-100.

Review of M. Riffaterre, *Le style des Pléiades de Gobineau*, in *MLN* LXXIII (1958), 68-74.

"Zu einer Landschaft Eichendorffs," *Euphorion* LII (1958), 142-152.

"La bellezza artistica dell' antichissima elegia giudeo-italiana," *Studi in onore di Angelo Monteverdi*, Modena, 1959, pp. 788-806.

"Die Figur der Fénix in Calderóns Standhaftem Prinzen," *Romanistisches Jahrbuch* X (1959), 305-335.

"La particella *si* davanti all' aggettivo nel romanzo stendhaliano *Armance*," *Studi francesi* VIII (1959), 199-213.

Review of Ludwig Schrader, *Panurge und Hermes, zum Ursprung eines Charakters bei Rabelais*, in *CL* XII (1960), 263-265.

"Lo sviluppo di un metodo," *Ulisse* XIII (1960), 26-33. A fuller version in *Cultura neolatina* XX, 109-128.

"Rabelais et les *rabelaisants*," *Studi francesi* IV (1960), 401-423.

"For de la bella cayba," *Lettere italiane* XII (1960), 133-140. Not identical with piece of same title in *Romanische Literaturstudien*.

"Natthias Claudius' *Abenlied*," *Euphorion* LIV (1960), 70-82.

"Adiciones a 'Camino del poema (*Confianza* de Pedro Salinas),'" *Nueva revista de filología hispánica* XIV, 333-340.

"Quelques aspects de la technique des romans de Michel Butor," *Archivum linguisticum* XIII, 171-195.

"Les études de style et les différents pays" in *Langue et littérature* (Actes du VIIIe Congrès de la Fédération Internationale des Langues et Littératures Modernes) XXI, 23-38.

INDEX